MR. GEORGE JEAN ⌊NATHAN PRESENTS

PN
2266
N3
1971

NEW. YORK   ALFRED A. KNOPF   MCMXVII

Republished 1971
Scholarly Press Inc., 22929 Industrial Drive East
St. Clair Shores, Michigan 48080

MR. GEORGE JEAN NATHAN
PRESENTS

An After-Piece of More or Less Critical Confidences and Memoirs Touching Lightly Upon the Various Somethings Which Go to Constitute What is Called the American Theatre

CONTENTS

Contents

"*The ideal critic is pictured by the crowd, now as a milestone 'standing upon the antique ways,' now as a finger-post on the 'high priori' road. I have taken the less stately view of him as a vagabond, who accepts his impressions as they come, and changes his moods with his horizons. Hence, like other vagrom men, I have had an instinctive repugnance for the methods of the Bench.*"

—ARTHUR BINGHAM WALKLEY, MDCCCXCII

MR. GEORGE JEAN NATHAN PRESENTS

THE PHILOSOPHY OF PHILISTIA

(Salutatory)

NOTHING is so essentially undramatic as clear thinking. Various attempts to devise serious drama out of the thoughtful figures of history — out, even, of reflective figures of the playwright's fancy — have for the most part rolled the stone of Sisyphus. A play with John Stuart Mill, Herbert Spencer or Renan for its central rôle would last out probably one evening in the theatre. The meditative man, when employed for purposes of the playhouse, must, if he would be used at all, be made the figure of farce *in nubibus,* as with Napoleon in " Sans Gêne " and " The Man of Destiny," or the figure of cheap gilt-furniture comedy, as with Disraeli in the play of Louis N. Parker. For the needs of the stage, the thinker must be operated upon, his heart placed in his head, his mind placed in his bosom. It is, indeed, the first rule of the acting stage that the hero must not think out the drama to its conclusion but that, *per contra*, the drama must think out the hero to *his* conclusion.

In plainer phrase, the central figure of a play must be influenced not from within, but from without. If, for example, one were to write a play with Friedrich Wilhelm Nietzsche as the hero, the drama would needs be generated and carried on to its climacteric consummation not by that gentleman's energetic mind and philosophies, but rather by the objection to that energetic mind and philosophies on the part of the leading lady. There can be no substantial thought in the drama of the stage. Such drama is created rather out of a contradiction and negation of thought: by proving either that the thought in point, while sound up to eleven o'clock, is then and finally impracticable if not, indeed, ridiculous (as in the instance of Mr. Shaw's Tanner) or that, while the thought may have been quite rational around quarter after ten o'clock in Act II, it had not yet at that time realized that its wife was in a family way or that its loved one was dying of tuberculosis, and so witnessed its own intrinsic vacuity.

Drama in its entirety consists in the surrender of accurate and judicious thinking to emotionalism: either to the emotions of its central figure or to the emotions of its second figure (symbolic of the mob emotion) operating upon that central figure and forcing him, breathless and beaten, to the wall. For the partial victory of an Undershaft or a Trigorin,

there are the thousand routs of the Johannes Vocke-
rats and Gabriel Schillings. The clock strikes
eleven and the Jules Lemaîtres of " Révoltée " and
" L'Age Difficile," the Brieuxs of " La Foi," the
Sudermanns of " Der Sturmgeselle Sokrates," an-
æsthetize their minds and deck their hearts with
daisies. But, here I wander probably somewhat
afield — afield from the popular stage.

The logic of the popular stage is a logic " not of
facts, but of sensations and sentiments." When
Hamlet and Iago, when Brand and Orgon spake
truth or made to think, such thoughts were kept
apart from the direct action of the drama and from
the ears of such other characters as might interpose
objection to them, in soliloquies and asides. The
thoughts so spoken were mere *pourboires* tossed by
dramatist to audience, mere refractory golden pen-
nies — the literary man triumphing momentarily
over the stage merchant. The imperturbable *rai-
sonneurs* of such drama as Georg Hirschfeld's "At
Home," Hartleben's " Education for Marriage,"
Andreyev's " Savva," Wedekind's " Pandora's Box "
— even such drama as Galsworthy's " Eldest Son "
or the Howard-Mizner " Only Law " (a play
greatly underrated) — are not for the popular
stalls.

The heart must do the thinking in the mob drama.
The mind of the stage protagonist must never be
more alert, more deeply informed, more practised,
than the mind of the average man who pays his two

dollars for a chair in the auditorium. And I beg
of my dear reader that he remember this when,
upon concluding these remarks, he will feel himself
moved to dispatch me a saucy letter on the dubiety
of my designation of certain stage heroes as thinkers. I use the word, of course, but comparatively:
I am charitable, for argument's sake, to the paradox.

Marivaux observed that he did not believe the
playwright should be prohibited from thinking.
The playwright, true enough, may not be prohibited
from thinking — up to his last act; but woe to him,
popularly speaking, if he keep his reason cool and
clear to final falling curtain. I here allude, of
course, to the maker of what the public knows as
serious drama, that is to say drama, good or bad,
purged of humour. This is why present day playwrights possessed of even half-way valid ideas seek
to protect their box office revenues by giving their
ideas a farcical garb — and even so, as witness the
instance of Brieux and " Les Hannetons " (the idea
of which is a haul from Flaubert), frequently in the
Anglo-Saxon theatre fail. Such playwrights appreciate that it is essential, if they would play with
ideas in the theatre, first to impress the audience
(by pretending the play is farce) with the notion
that the ideas are ridiculous, thus gaining the audience's willingness to listen to opinions which the audience has not heard before, and thus also flattering
the audience's ignorance by assuring it that the ideas

are mere nonsense and with no foundation in philosophy or fact. This, as well known, is the method of Shaw. George Birmingham, in his excellent "John Regan," was less successful than his Irish colleague in captivating the yokelry for the reason that he permitted his farce to be slightly too logical and so raised the yokelry's suspicions that, after all, there might be a grain of truth in his central idea. The same idea was used, several years before Birmingham employed it, in a farce manner more susceptible of box-office hospitality by a Spanish dramatist. In order to avoid all danger of failure — even in more practised Berlin — Schmidt, having a good idea, wrote two entirely different endings to one of his farces and experimented publicly with both in order to determine which was the less in accord with dispassionate logic and hence more likely to charm trans-Channel and trans-Atlantic auditoriums were his play to be produced at a distance.

When the thoughtful man is lifted onto the illuminated platform, the cautious playmaker exercises a care sedulously to eliminate from the character all suspicion of the mind that has identified him in history. For the cautious playmaking fellow appreciates that " the conception of theatrical art as the exploitation of popular superstition and ignorance, as the thrilling of poor bumpkins with ghosts and blood, exciting them with blows and stabs, duping them with tawdry affectations of rank and rhetoric, thriving parasitically on their moral diseases instead of purging their souls and refining their senses: this is the tradition that the theatre finds it hard to get away from." And so, the playmaker presents Cromwell (Charles Cartwright's " Colonel Cromwell ") in terms of an ancestral Chauncey Olcott, Dante (Sardou's) in terms of a paleo-Laurence Hope, and Jesus Christ (" Ben Hur ") as a spotlight.

The sober, serious figures of history, when dramatized for the stalls, are box-officed into so many Mascarilles of " Les Précieuses," Crispins of " Le Légataire " and Scapins of " Les Fourberies," with right hands inserted into the bosoms of their Prince Alberts and brows a-wrinkle with the weighty problems imparted by a brown lining-pencil and a touch of mascaro.

In the drama of yesterday, it was requisite that the heroine's body be compromised; in the drama of to-day, it is requisite that the hero's mind be compromised. However substantial the thought which the playmaker causes to motivate his hero, the playmaker must bear in mind this established Anglo-Saxon formula: Act I, the hero has a sound idea; Act II, he becomes doubtful as to the soundness of his idea; Act III, he is convinced that his sound idea is absurd. Whether the hero is of the J. Rufus Wallingford order or of the rarer order of the central personage of Galsworthy's " The Mob " (though it must be confessed that Galsworthy is in general one of the exceptions), the thing holds true.

And if to this there come interposed the contention
that, after all, it is only nature that one's philosophy,
whatever its strength and vitality, be riddled in the
many ambuscades on the great highway of life, one
may but answer with Sir Leslie Stephen that he
never saw the word " nature " without instinctively
putting himself on his guard against some bit of
slipshod criticism or sham philosophy, and that he
heartily wished the word could be turned out of the
language. The truth of the matter, of course, is
that for the most part these last act changes of
philosophy and viewpoint are brought about not by
God's nature, but by the Shuberts'. The hero's philosophy is influenced, in the contemporaneous Anglo-Saxon drama, less by the bearing upon his own
brain of the force of other brains than by the scent
of a woman's hair, Christmas bells, and the spectacle of a small blonde child creeping down the
stairs in a nightgown. For this drama, in the line
of the Major Barbara that was, declines to regard
that there are larger loves and diviner dreams than
the fireside ones.

But —

To blame this condition of affairs, as our cur-
rent-drifting playmakers are forever so affectionate
in blaming it, entirely upon the audience, seems a
trifle short-sighted even to one, like myself, who appreciates only too well from long and intimate contact the vulgarity and opalescence of the listless
groups of bedizened pot-wallopers who smell out

of court by their very patronage all that may be beautiful and worth-while in drama. Why should sound thinking, thought that sparkles and crackles like burning diamond dust, ideas that, like so many rings of smoke, dissolve into wistful smiles and musings — why should these be believed irrevocably to be not the food of which theatrical amusement and stimulation are made? The notion that the emotions of a group of persons gathered into a theatre auditorium to witness drama will respond only — or at least chiefly — to a like set of emotions displayed upon the platform before them is pretty poor psychology. The notion that such an audience may be made to cry only by showing it an actress sniffling or be made to feel joyful only by exhibiting to it an ingénue sticking her nose gleefully into a bouquet of sweet peas and meanwhile hopping on one foot, seems a sorry conceit. And by audience, in this connection and by way of reassurance, is meant not what Dryden, in another direction, described as souls of the highest rank and truest understanding, but that mob something which is ever given less to caviar than to sausage.

There are certainly more audience tears, speaking practically from the standpoint of the popular theatre, in such a reflective, hard and unsentimental philosophy as is contained in Shaw's Cæsar's reply to Shaw's Cleopatra, " Shall it be Mark Antony? " than there are in a round dozen such artificial quasi-throat-lumps as Mr. Broadhurst's Henry Maple-

son's quavering " You shall have diamonds and
pearls, my dear, diamonds and pearls." There is
a louder commercial laughter in a philosophic line
like Schnitzler's on the sentimentality of a lady's
stomach than in fifty allusions on the part of a fat
man in a green waistcoat to Peoria, Ill., or even to
Gatti Casazza. Which, let me ask in the vernacular of the theatre, makes you " feel sadder ":
the sight of an emotional John Mason bellowing
and salting upon the bosom of emotional Jane Cowl
in a " Common Clay " or the ring of such a bit of
worldly philosophy as concludes Lennox Robinson's
" Patriots " when the fiery zealot, come to inflame
and impassion his fellow countrymen, is informed
by the janitor of the hall which he finds empty that
" They've all gone t' the movin' pictures,"— or the
ring of such an observation as comes from Fer-
rand's lips in " The Pigeon "? Which makes you
laugh louder: such a passage as Mr. Harry B.
Smith's " What is that you are playing, Mr. Dusenberry? "; Mr. Dusenberry: " The piano," bandied
by a grotesquely clad spinster and a comedian in a
sailor suit — or such a passage as that between Il-
lingworth and the lady in the first act of " A Woman
of No Importance "? . . . The plays of Wilde will
live on the stage long after the plays of Mr. George
V. Hobart are forgotten. The plays of Shakespeare and Molière will probably survive even the
plays of Alfred Sutro and Jules Eckert Goodman.

The theory that a dramatic audience's emotions

will inevitably respond largely, if not only, to a lit-
eral picturization upon the stage of those same emotions is akin to the theory that an impressionable
art lover will, upon entering the Glyptothek in
Munich and beholding the statue of Mercury, forthwith feel like undressing himself — or, somewhat
more pertinently, that the lusty laughter of Feste
and Falstaff will bring out an equally lusty laughter
on the part of their spectators. The opposite is,
of course, true. The laughter of the Merry Wives
depresses one, as the tyranny of the tears of Haddon Chambers' heroine exhilarates one.

The stage, true enough, is intrinsically not the
place for thought, but one may therefore no more
fairly say that thought cannot, and successfully, be
placed there than one may say that James Huneker
should not contribute to the pages of *Puck*. It is
much like Huneker's own retort to the solemn sa-
vant of the *Evening Post* who lamented that the
critic should be writing serious articles in a funny
paper. "It doesn't strike me as any more incon-
gruous," replied our James, "than your writing
funny articles in a serious paper." Freud would be
Freud in the pages of *Fliegende Blätter;* Bourget
would be Bourget in the pages of *Le Rire;* Havelock Ellis would be Havelock Ellis in the pages of
the *Pink 'Un;* a smart intelligence would still, despite the distractions of gamesome lights and enam-
eled cheesecloths, be intelligible and remunerative
in the theatre. I have said, in my first sentence.

that nothing is so essentially undramatic as clear thinking. Had I not better have said that nothing is so essentially undramatic as the theatre which believes this to be true and practises, so rigorously, its faith?

L'Envoi

Such a piece, however, as Shaw's fantastic " Getting Married," presented for the first time in America in the Booth under the auspices of Mr. Faversham — a piece that comes more or less under the head of a play of ideas — misses of effect in the theatre for the simple reason that it was never meant seriously by the author for the theatre. " Getting Married " is no more a theatre play than "Shenandoah " is a book play. The notion that any piece of writing is suited to the theatre merely because the names of its characters are indented and their physical movements italicized is, despite Mr. Shaw's cunning and not altogether unconvincing cajolery of the notion, a little like believing drama to be only a matter of typography. The truth is that this manuscript of Shaw's is pretty uncomfortable going in the playhouse. In the library, it is amusing enough — for the simple reason that there but the eye, as the viaduct to the mind, is called upon to engage it. In the theatre, it misses for the equally simple reason that not only the eye, but the ear as well — to say nothing, recalling vividly the hardness of the chair in J 14, of the nether physiology —

are called upon to attend and receive it. Where, therefore, in the library the manuscript gives ample return for the exercise of a single organ, in the theatre it seems somehow to be overcharging the physical effort of its reception two-and-threefold. For in this manuscript there is no call, as there is call in other manuscripts of Shaw, for a pinchable wench to charm the vision as Cleopatra, for a Drury Lane lion to antic its way with physical jinks into one's surface humours, for the ear-tickling furies and cussings of a giant to the Russian court, for the haze of a Joseph Harker moonlit Nile nor the fisticuffs of an athletic young mummer. And so there is small call here to dim the reading lamp and raise the footlights.

" Getting Married " is Shaw at his weakest: the great ballyhoo hard at work before the tent when all the freaks are off, for the time being, having their lunch. There is, of course, wit to the piece — here and there a liberal sprinkling — but the resident impression is of the character in " The Fortune Teller " who had a good joke and wanted to get some one to write a musical comedy around it. The manuscript reminds one of a Wilde epigram rewritten by Dostoievski.

THE HAWKSHAVIAN DRAMA

THE melodrama of our youthhood was based largely upon the theory that the most momentous crises in life occurred always in the vicinity of railroad tracks or at the foot of Pier 30, North River. The melodrama of present-day geniture is based to a similar degree upon the theory that the most important eventualities in life come off always in the vicinity of long writing tables standing in the centre of libraries in private houses and having on them a push button.

Melodrama, in short, has been moved indoors. And with this removal has departed, alas, the bulk of its erstwhile gaudy bounce, its sometime lively witcheries, its quondam naïve charm. For melodrama, surely, belongs indoors no more than a Barnum's circus belongs in Madison Square Garden or upon the stage of the Hippodrome. Melodrama, above every other mould of drama, is essentially a thing of " exteriors." Move it under a roof and into " interiors " and it becomes effeminate, maidenly — a thing to curve the spine and benumb the pulse. The current importing of an air, of a saucy politeness, into the melodrama of the days of ten and twenty and thirty, has rendered soul-

less that antic and favourite prank of other times,
aye, has caused it for the most part to die as a dis-
tinctive, if forsooth peculiar, art form from the
earth.   And what has taken its place?   Melodrama
in name only — a species of harlequinade neither
good melodrama (in the old and truest theatric
sense) nor good drama.   A cheap and posturing
synthesis, rather, of the least gay and stimulating
portions of the two plasms.

Whereas melodrama falls without the frontiers
of critical appraisal, whereas it is, very frankly, designed merely to toy in innocent manner with the
blood pressure of the youngster that is a part still
and ever of all of us, it follows that the only equit-
able estimate of melodrama is in terms of what the
theatrical jargon knows as " getting over," to wit,
the measure of success with which the show regis-
ters upon the audience its component parts, sepa-
rately and collectively.   And it is by such standard
alone that comparisons are to be brought about.
And it is by such standard, therefore, that we must
persuade ourselves that with the possible exception
of the interior melodramas of Mr. William Gillette,
the two interior melodramas of Mr. Bayard Veiller
and the last act interior of " Mr. Wu " (as
it was done in London), there has been not a single
so-called interior melodrama unfeignedly promulgated under the designation in our more modern
epoch that has bounced our little omegas off the orchestra chairs with one-hundredth the resilience im-

parted by the infinitely cruder exterior thrill confections of the era of " The Soudan " and " Across the Pacific," " The Span of Life " and " Burmah," " The Queen of the White Slaves " and the illustrious " Opium Ring " cycle, " The Bowery After Dark " and " Wedded and Parted," " Tracked Round the World " and the Lincoln J. Carter *opera,* the " Edna " and " Nellie " and " Bertha " dramaturgy of cloak models, typewriters and sewing machine girls, " The Chinatown Trunk Mystery " and " The Cherry Pickers " and " One of the Finest." . . .

In that era, too, were there of course successful exceptions to the exterior rule — pieces in which, like " Blue Jeans " and " Nobody's Claim," the extremest perturbation was of an interior gender — but in nine cases out of ten the batteries of such papas of the period as Hal Reid, Owen Davis, Theodore Kremer and Isaac Swift were trained upon the stall vertebræ from outdoor sets. And in the instance even of several of the exceptions, the really grand jounce of the occasion was derived from sources intrinsically somewhat exotic to an interior — the driving, for example, of a horse through a pine frame and plate-glass window, as in " Nobody's Claim."

A tear for these noble old rough-houses that are gone. No pricely Jane Cowl delivering an Harvard oration on the poor working-girl's virtue from the witness box of a " Common Clay " can ever bring half so much *l'allegro* as the twenty-five-dollar-a-week hamfatter who in " Chinatown Charlie " climbed up the backs of half a dozen other hams standing on each other's shoulders and rescued the lovely one who was being held prisoner by some malefic fellow on the top floor of an obscene *pension*. No glossy Courtenay as an Irish soldier who enlists, for purpose of espionage, as an officer in the German army in an " Under Fire " can bring to blush the proud moment in " The Ninety and Nine " when the brave chiclet ran the express locomotive through the raging forest fire in order to save the life of the producer.   And no dinner-jacketed Barrymore puncturing an officer of the law into somnolence with a hypodermic needle in a " Kick In " can ever compare with the human bridge across the yawning abyss in " The Span of Life," or the big race between the automobile and the express train to beat the villain to Denver in " Bedford's Hope," or the tunnel rescue in " After Dark," or the deep-sea divers' feat in " At the Bottom of the Sea," or the race of the locomotive to get to the switch in " The Fast Mail," or the horse race in " The Sporting Duchess " . . .

Boys will be boys — and so will men be boys. And no Roi Megrue literature will ever satisfy them as did Tom Taylor's

BRIERLY [*rapidly closing trap-door on the villains and standing on it*]. Now's the time! [*Seizes pen and writes, reading as he does so.*] " To Mr. Gibson, Peckham. The office will be entered to-night; I'm in it to save the property and secure the robbers.". . . But who will take this letter?

HAWKSHAW [*having come up unnoticed behind him*]. I will!

BRIERLY. And who are you?

HAWKSHAW [*pulling off his whiskers*]. Hawkshaw, the detective!

Those, gentlemen, were the days of true sport in the theatre, the days when no heroine ever knew at the beginning who her parents were . . .

She was one o' thet party what the Injuns massacreed some fifteen years ago, jes' outside o' Deadwood. Jim happened to be along o' the boys that drived the critters off, an' he found her thar in one o' the wagons asleep.

Asleep!

Yes. Yah see, she was only a babby then an' all the racket in the world couldn't disturb her slumber.

But what become o' her folks?

Jim never could find any trace o' them. As she happened to be the only survivor, why the old man kinder took a fancy to her and decided to take her home with him, and she's been right h'yar ever since.

In the last act discovering that she was not, after all, the daughter of the rascally Dalton. . . .

DALTON. It means that this locket belonged to your mother. And there, on the inside, is her picture! [*Passes heroine the locket.*]

HEROINE. My — mother! [*Looks at picture.*] And you say — she was your wife?

DALTON. Yes — she was my wife!

HEROINE. Then I — I am — [*Looks pleadingly from kind old gentleman who has been acting as a father to her to Dalton.*]

DALTON. My daughter!

HEROINE [*firmly*]. I don't believe it! [*To kind old gentleman.*] Daddy! You who have been a daddy to me so long! Say it ain't true! Say it ain't true!

. . . but none other than Miss Laura Courtlandt, heiress to the Courtlandt millions, in whose cradle a spurious child had been placed when she was abducted at the age of three months by old Eleanor, the blackmailing nurse.

Those, as I say, my friends, were high days in the playhouse. Where now in the moment's more modish melo-piece the paradise of such a thrill as churned our fifteen-year-old hæmoglobin when the proud Lady Audley, forefinger to brow, pondered so: "Once was I fool enough to wed for love. Now I have married for wealth. What a change from the wife of George Talboys to the wife of Sir Michael Audley! My fool of a first husband thinks me dead. Oh excellent scheme, oh cunning device, how well you have served me! Where can he be now? Still in India, no doubt! Ha, ha, ha! Why, I have only just begun to live — to taste the sweets of wealth and power. If I am dead to George Talboys, he is dead to me. Yes, I am well rid of him, and on this earth we meet no more!" And when, in the midst of the haughty jade's meditations, we beheld George himself stealing noiselessly up from the rear, at the "meet no more" flicking the Lady upon the shoulder with a triumphant "Yes, my proud beauty, we do!"

There was a moment for you! There was no missing of it. Nor that other moment in the Western blood-and-thunder libretto of name forgotten, where noble old Uncle Dave and the detestable Earl of Ramsey bantered thuswise:

THE EARL. You Americans are a sanguine lot of people.

UNCLE DAVE. Oh, I see! You're an Englishman, ain't you? *They* never kin believe how fast we grow in this country. They won't believe that George Washington ever made 'em get out of it either, but he did!

THE EARL. Ah, my dear fellow, *our* country has grown up! You get emigrants to help build up *your* country — but what are they?

UNCLE DAVE. That's so; they don't amount to nothing until they come here and inhale the free and fresh air of liberty. Then they become American citizens and they amount to a great deal. Fer we build up the West and feed the world.

THE EARL. Feed the world! Oh, no! Certainly not England.

UNCLE DAVE. Oh, yes, we do! We've fed England. We gave you a warm breakfast in 1776, a boiling dinner in 1812, and we got a red-hot supper waitin' for you any time you want it!

Nor still that other moment at the end where Uncle Dave, facing the Earl, shouted: "These papers were stole from me and the estates were secured — by *you!*" With the Earl's snicker "Ha, and who is an idiot enough to believe such a story." With Pietro Spaghetti, the erstwhile dago comedian, stepping forward and exclaiming, "*I* am! I am a

fool enough to believe it! I am also a fool enough
to believe that one Jack Mayburn, alias the Earl of
Ramsey, is wanted in Michigan for killing a keeper
to escape from jail. I am fool enough to believe
Ramsey is wanted for murder, robbery, train wreck-
ing, arson, kidnapping, embezzling, counterfeiting,
burglary and safe-breaking!" With the Earl's
" You Italian dog, what do you mean? Curses on
you — who are you? " And with Pietro's removal
of his moustache and imperial, and exclamation:
" *Bob Brenham, United States detective, at your
service!* "

But was this all? Was the littérateur of that
happy day content, as now, at this juncture to rest
his typewriter? Not on your life. " Here's my
warrant," continued the United States detective,
" and here (*producing a revolver*) is my per-
suader! "

Imagine the picture, all you who still have a soul!
Then recall the heroine's " Oh, Bob! Bob, is it you?
(*embracing him*). And to think I didn't know
you! " And recall how the villainous Earl, taking
advantage of the United States detective's temporary
abstraction, with the words, " one dash now for liberty! " sought to escape R. U. E. and found himself
confronted at that point of egress by Otto Snitz-
poonerkooker, the erstwhile Dutch comique, with a
gun. " No you doan'dt! " (we remember Otto's
words as if they were spoken, ah, but yesterday),
" no you doan'dt. I'm a Cherman detective in der

employ of Bob Brenham — ha, ha, ha!" And recall how now the evil Earl turned and dashed for the
left upper entrance where he was stopped, also at
the nozzle of a gun, by Gee Ho, the erstwhile Chinese pantaloon, with the grinned " Not muchee, you
vellie bad man. This pistol, he will hurta like hellie.
(*Dropping dialect*) I am a Norwegian detective also
in the employ of Bob Brenham!' "

One grows warm yet at the mere recollection.
What, indeed, if certain flaws appeared in the logic
or certain discrepancies with a bland conspicuity in
the coincidences? The old, strict and authentic
definition of melodrama (from the Greek meaning
song plus action) has ebbed long since. The word
has taken on, these years gone, another and less
exact theatrical translation.

Melodrama is to drama as musical comedy is to
grand opera. And melodrama and musical comedy
have much in common. Each holds the back of the
mirror up to nature. In its bottom sense, in good
sooth, what is melodrama but musical comedy played
with a straight face? Substitute Willard Mack for
Frank Daniels in " The Idol's Eye " and you have a
Wilkie Collins thriller. Substitute Douglas Fairbanks for Raymond Hitchcock in " The Red
Widow " and you have back your basic tale of Russian intrigue and adventure. Or, on the other hand,
to test the rule, substitute Mr. Hitchcock for Mr.
Fairbanks in " Hawthorne of the U. S. A.," and you
have musical comedy. The dividing line 'twixt the

two forms is of a hair's breadth. Henry Blossom
might make a serviceable libretto out of " Under
Fire " without altering more than a line or two.
And Augustus Thomas might without much more
difficulty make a serviceable melodrama out of
" Eva " or " Royalty Dances Waltzes " or " The
Waltz Dream " or " The Purple Road " or " Little
Johnny Jones " . . . George Cohan's musical comedies, indeed, are already but Harry Clay Blaney
melodramas embellished with Harrigan and Hart
melodies.

The old melodramas, much like a country girl, in-
trigued even the wearied and sophisticated by virtue
of their frank crudeness, their charming lack of literary lip rouge and nose powder. Yet, just so,
were their banalities at which now the superior sniff,
quite so cheap and so raw as some profess to believe? If it was always Christmas Eve in prison
scenes in the old ten-twenty-thirty, is it not Christmas Eve, too, in the prison of John Galsworthy's
" Justice "? If we snicker at Lady Audley's " Let
me pass! ", at Robert Audley's " Never! The law
shall have its own! ", at the Lady's " And who is to
be my accuser? ", and at the brazenly opportune entrance at this juncture of Luke Marks (who was
supposed to be dead) with his " I am! "— if we lift
a nostril at such nick-of-time materializations in left
upper entrances, let us remind ourselves, too, that
they are not entirely foreign to the drama of such
as Tolstoi and Hauptmann. Where the great dif-

ference between the cross-examination of C. H. Ha-
zlewood's woman with a past and the cross-examination of Henry Arthur Jones's Mrs. Dane? Where
the diminution of the obvious in the gay gallant
spraying himself with eau-de-cologne in the third act
of " The Great Lover " and with Green Jones spraying himself with the eau-de-cologne in the third act
of " The Ticket-of-Leave Man " ? Compare
" The Lion and the Mouse " with " The Power of
Money." Compare " The Earth" with " The
Power of the Press." Compare " The Lure " with
" The Queen of the White Slaves " or " The Queen
of the Highbinders."

I miss them, the old " You are my son "—" So
you are the man who wrecked my mother's life "
miracle plays. Like the little girls in pigtails and
the heart-shaped white peppermint candies with red
cinnamon mottoes and the telephones fashioned out
of an old baking-powder can and a piece of resined
string and the baseballs made by wrapping twine
around an ink eraser, they are gone but not forgotten. And nothing like them, no fancy imitations,
however improved, have seemed or probably ever
will seem quite the same. Theodore Kremer died
with Santa Claus.

And so, on behalf of the eternal youngster the
nation over, I make a plea for the return to us of
our old beloved gun and gore plays. We want
again to see the Brooklyn Bridge by moonlight.
We want back the railroad station on the Northern

Pacific and the old sawmill (first the exterior, then
the interior) and the Tombs Police Court, and Joe
Morgan shouting, " Villain, your career of landlord
shall be short; for here I swear, by the side of my
murdered child, you shall die the death of a dog!"
— with the professor at the piano manufacturing
quiver *musik*.   We want again to see the villain
stealthily scull his boat up to the end of the dock
at midnight with the sotto voce warning to his foul
partner in crime, " I pulled down the river for a
spell to throw any spies off the track.   It was necessary after what you told me about the girl's threat
to blab about the Boston pier."   And to give ear
to Villain II's " We must get her out of the city!"
and Villain I's " Do you think she'll go easy, or shall
we drug her?" and Villain II's " Just tell her it's
to meet her beau, or give her some such reason and
she'll be as mild as a lamb," and then Villain I's
" Ha!   Just let me get hold of her and I'll answer
she goes, reason or *no* reason!"

We want, just once more before we shuffle off, to
see the hero fastened by the villain to the railroad
tracks —" And now, my fine fellow, I'm going to
put you to bed.   You won't toss much, either.   In
less than ten minutes you'll be sound asleep.   There,
how do you like it?   You'll get down to the Junc-
tion before me, will you, Ralph Beaumont?   You
dog me and play the eavesdropper, eh?   Now do it
if you can!   When you hear the thunder of the
fast mail under your head and see the engine lights

dancing in your eyes and feel the iron wheels a foot from your neck, remember *me*, Clifford Romaine!"
Then we want just once more to hear the express train whistling in the distance and coming nearer, nearer, with the heroine battering at the door of the shed in which the villain has locked her —" God help me! And I cannot aid you!"— and the hero, though gagged, yet shouting the noble sentiments, " Never mind me, sweetheart mine. I might as well die now as any other time. I'm not afraid. I've seen death in almost every shape and none of them scares me. Remember me, sweetheart; treasure my memory, beloved, and I die happy." And, if we seem not too greedy, we would beseech then one last view of the heroine banging down the door with an axe and rescuing our Ralph just as the train of pasteboard cars, amid loud bell-ringing and tooting and off-stage pounding on wash-pans, is pulled across the stage by a plainly visible rope in the hands of an equally visible Hibernian stagehand standing half way out of the first entrance.

We want to see the hero " plied with drink " and to hear some one talk about tarnishing proud es-cutcheons and to hear the villain denounced as a consarned skunk and to hear one character say " Look at me, Clayborne — scan my features closely and tell me have you ever seen me before? " and to see the other fellow start back with a " What! You — Henry Mayfield? Not dead!" No costly mummer, Prince Alberted and gardenia'd like an ex-

pensive barber and gravely grunting specimens endorsed by Professor George Pierce Baker, can tickle
us as we used in the old shirt-sleeve days be tickled
when the rich villain breathed in the poor heroine's
ear, " You can be a lady!   Don't go, but listen to
me for a moment!   I can make a lady of you — a
fine lady — you shall be dressed like a queen and
move in society, loved, honoured, and famous.   This
— all this — I offer you if you will but become my
wife," and when then the spunky colleen turned upon
the presumptuous fellow with a " Your wife!   Not
if all the gold of the world were in your hands, and
you gave it to me.   Your wife!   Never — *never*
— not even to become a lady!   Before I'd be your
wife I'd live in rags and be *proud* of my poverty! "
    But the day of designating villains as varmints
and of " unfolding " plots, of " I have only one
answer for such curs as you — *this!* " (bingo) and
of " At last I have you within me power " is gone,
alas — and maybe forever.   Harvard College and
the actor, between them, have done the trick.   Harvard has spoiled the old melo-pieces by squirting into
them pseudo economic and social problems, by affect-
edly unsplitting their infinitives and by treating them,
in general, to a dosage of sophomore fine writing.
And the actor has done his share by spouting the
result with the gravity of an Ibsen elocutionist.
    The humour of the old plays, their passion and
their sauce — the créme-de-la-Krémer, if the tawdry
jest be overlooked — have vanished.   And with the

humour and the passion and the sauce there have trickled away, too, the old plays' chic scenic juices and beamy properties.

Twenty years ago, the scene plot for any upright, respectable four-act melodrama looked like this:

ACT I

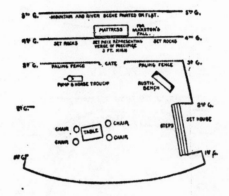

ACT II

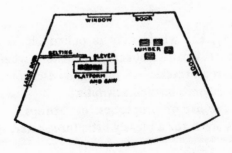

ACT III

ACT IV

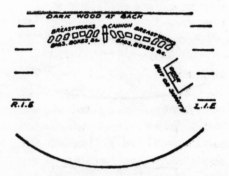

To-day, the whole play is pulled off in a tame interior or two! Bookcases are now where once were railroad tracks. A mahogany escritoire stands now where once buzzed sawmills.

And the list of properties, or "props." In the old days, even for a measly little three-acter, in small part:

ACT I

Small rifle for soubrette lead. Revolvers and carbines for juvenile lead and leading heavy. Dagger for character heavy. Rifle for character lead. Wire across stage to be dropped when telephone wires are cut down. Small telegraph instrument. Bludgeon for leading heavy. Blackjack for Irish comedy. Slug-shot for negro comedy. Bag of nuggets and money-belt for juvenile lead. Brass knuckles for second heavy. Red fire and flash-torch for fire effect. Key to lock door. Axe. Thin boards to make door to be battered in by axe. Half pail of water behind water-tank to come through piping at climax. Brace of pistols and rope for female juvenile lead. . . .

ACT II

Ropes, boat-hook and axe for juvenile lead and second juvenile. Bolt to attach to door. Poniard for third heavy. Revolver for utility and " billy " for soubrette lead. Smoke pots. Gong bell. Life-preserver and large crab. Firenet. Imitation of crying baby and nursing bottle with milk for eccentric character woman. Package of documents. Wallet. Six packages of stage money. Circular saw. Machinery connected with saw. Revolver for juvenile lead. Two sticks nailed together to make a loud noise when used to strike with: one for Jew comedy, one for Chinese comedy. A chicken and an egg negro comedy. Skyrocket. Two stuffed clubs. Bottle marked " chloroform." Kerosene lamp made so it can be upset and smashed. Keg marked " dynamite " and fuse. Wind machine and storm effects. Italian disguise for juvenile lead. Chair with legs sawed half-way through so they will break readily when crashed on leading heavy's back. Hook-and-ladder truck. Steam fire-engine.

ACT III

Brace of pistols for juvenile lead. Revolver and quirt for
leading heavy. Musket for female juvenile lead. Mining
implements. Wine and beer glasses, cigars. Peddler's disguise for juvenile lead. Dice and dice-box. Pack of playing cards containing five aces. Searchlight. Two blood-
hounds. Stiletto for female heavy. Trick bottle to break.
Clasp-knife and gag for second heavy. Window panes covered with isinglass; a box of glass to make noise when window is broken. Two imitation bricks for Irish comedy.
Long rope with noose. Ambulance gong. Warrant and revolvers for juvenile lead. Coloured fire. Gun and hand-
cuffs for second juvenile. American flag. . . .

To-day, a solitary revolver (unloaded) and a writ-
ing-desk set from Brentano's!

Mincing equivoque has spread its pall over the
boards where once Harold Tremaine, the bare-
bosomed, brawny-armed magnifico, struck an attitude
and, covering the low hound of the theme with a
gun, boomed thus the curtain down: " Stand whar
yah are, Jake Dalton, or I'll shove daylight clean
through yah! "   And the love scenes aren't as they
used to be.   For no more, alas, does the little Rocky
Mountain flower implore the manly hero in the pros-
pector's outfit (in reality, the Earl of Sutherland,
incog.) to " tell me 'bout that thar big city whar yah
come from "; and no more, alas, does the hero retort, " I much prefer to speak of the glorious West
— and of you "; and no more, after the little one's
surprised " Gee whiz! What yar see 'bout me to

talk 'bout?'" do we hear the "Little girl, you are the brightest gem in the whole range of these mountains. When I came out here eight months ago to bury myself in the wilds of nature — and forget — little did I dream that amid these canyons and primeval forests I should discover so fair a bud growing wild within the confines of the rugged peaks! Of what interest is the crowded, stifled city to you? To you, a mountain maid, whose home is the finest garden in nature's paradise?"

And no longer does the persecuted heroine, in response to the "Then, what will you do?" retort with, "What thousands of other heartbroken and despairing women have done — seek for peace in the silence of the grave!"

And no longer, as we have lamented, are the poor heroines doubtful of their origins —"You ask who my parents were? I don't know. The furthest back that I can recollect is when I was seven years old I was with an old one-eyed woman who was nicknamed 'The Owl'— she made me sell flowers at the corner of the streets and sometimes I had to beg, for if I did not bring home ten sous at least, she used to beat me instead of giving me my supper. One day, I fled from the house. I have earned a wretched livelihood by singing ballads in the great streets — I have associated with characters the worst and most depraved. Still I have never stolen and have never forgotten that there is a Heaven above (*kneels*) ever watching over our acts and ever ready to administer comfort and happiness to the afflicted and deserving." . . .

No more are these, our old friends, the boon comrades of our nonage, with us. And a sadder, albeit a more knowing world it is, believe me, for their going.

THE AMERICAN MUSIC SHOW

WERE one asked to point to the man whose name, above every other, stands for the typical native music show libretto, the finger quite patently would steer for Mr. Harry B. Smith. Aside from the physiological extravaganzas of Mr. Ziegfeld and the umbilicular exposés purveyed at the Winter Garden, soothing forms of diversion both of them by virtue of the circumstance that libretto is almost entirely omitted in their fabrication, the garnished brain children of Mr. Smith may be accepted by the student as a fair gauge of the American tune stage.

In an effort, therefore, to plumb the mien of the average local libretto, with its physical embellishments and salads, I took my person not long ago to a Smith fruit called by the name of " Molly O " and deposited it in attendance upon the work. A perusal of the playbill revealed the tidings that, in the geniture of this particular libretto, Mr. Harry B. Smith had enjoyed the assistance of Mr. Robert B. Smith, a gentleman also an obese figure in the fashioning of the native gag-book. But let us not delay; let us hoist the curtain and measure the Smith labours as, from curtain rise to curtain fall, they spir-

43

tled into the aural cavity — and with the elements in
the Smith libretto let us consider also, by way of
appreciating the staging of a libretto at the hands
of the probably not untypical Mr. George Marion,
the manner in which such elements are, on the average, boiled into the finished whole designated generally as musical comedy.

At rise, discovered: "The O'Malley Villa,
Newport," with a view of the Bay of Naples on the
back-drop. Enter Freddy Sands, denominated on
the bill of the play as " a little brother of the rich."
A modish Newporter, Freddy. And thus, therefore, he to a lady of fashion standing near: " I'm
the only guy around here, kid, who knows where
(*indicating a beer glass of noble height with his
hands*) to get a tall one." Freddy then pretends
his walking stick is a musical instrument and fingers
it drolly, as if playing a tune upon it. This done,
he steps to the footlights and sings a lyric pertinent
to Newport about a girl named Anna from Savannah
who met a man from Havana.

Enter now a young miss and her young man. The
latter beseeches a kiss. " But kisses," pouts the
young miss, " are intoxicating." Whereupon her
young man, " Then let's get soused." Follows a
duet, " Marry Me and See," in which the young man
urges the young miss to fly away with him and nest
like a turtle dove, true love, skies fair above.

From the left entrance comes now Dan O'Malley, a whole-hearted Irishman, whose wife, Mrs.

Prunella O'Malley, has social aspirations. Mrs. O'Malley, we are informed, is called Prunella because her husband was instrumental in forming a prune trust. Mr. O'Malley has been forced by his spouse to dress up and is in comic distress because his patent leather shoes pinch his corns, to which now and again he dolorously alludes. (Later, Mr. O'Malley sneaks off and reappears in a pair of carpet slippers, thus amusing the audience greatly.) Freddy now again exposes himself to view and there follows a colloquy between him and O'Malley, the three most telling points in which are a query as to how O'Malley keeps the peas from rolling off his knife, a suggestion as to the noiseless eating of soup, and an allusion to Kankakee. Freddy then refers facetiously to Mrs. O'Malley's diamonds as " ice " and — enter the tenor in the uniform of an huzzar and follows a song on the ease with which a man may tell the right little girl when the right little girl comes along.

The huzzar, it develops, is to marry Molly, the niece of the opulent O'Malleys, who, after a quip to the effect that kisses are not round, but eliptical (a-lip-tickle), comes down and sings that love is an art, to warm the heart, oh Cupid's dart. The irresistible Freddy now approaches and, grasping the huzzar by the hand, tearfully congratulates him on his coming marriage to which he (Freddy) killingly alludes as an execution.

This done, Freddy comes down and, walking back

and forth, sings about the girl who wins my heart,
she must not be too stout, I know what I'm about,
she must have a figure, which is *de rigueur*. For
" business," Freddy jumps over a low bench and the
chorus girls, playing follow-the-leader, imitate his
antic.

Re-enter O'Malley and Mrs. O'Malley. " When
you married me," observes Mrs. O'Malley, somewhat ironically, " I thought you were well off."
" When I married you," retorts Mr. O'Malley,
somewhat more ironically, " I was way off! " Then
a *mot* about the marriage knot being a noose, another about Eve and the figleaf and — Molly comes
out again and, in waltz time, sings " When Fortune
Smiles," taking the high notes with her eye-brows.

Freddy, having in some inscrutable manner insinuated himself once again into the surroundings, presently begins a conversation with the huzzar in which
he (Freddy) refers to the forthcoming wedding and
playfully observes that he will be at the ring-side.

" Do you drink anything? " some one asks Freddy.

" Yes, anything," retorts Freddy.

After an interval, the young miss (described on
the bill as Josette, a Viennese artist) reappears with
a bunch of flowers.

" What are those flowers? " questions Freddy.

" They are wild flowers," replies the young miss.
Freddy reaches for them.

" Oh, no, no," says the young miss, shrinking back,
" you must not touch them."

"Ah, I see," retorts Freddy jocularly, "that's what makes 'em wild."

The young miss' young man comes on and the trio execute a ditty styled "One Way of Doing It," in which are described the different ways to woo a woman. Between the verse and the chorus, the trio illustrate the lyric with "business." For instance, Freddy pretends to enter a jewelry shop with the young miss, the latter's young man posing as the clerk.

"That's a nice necklace, dearie," says Freddy to the young miss; "put it on; you can have it." Then, to the clerk, "How much is it?"

"Fourteen," replies the clerk.

Freddy proceeds to count out fourteen dollars.

"Fourteen *thousand*," says the clerk. Whereupon Freddy pretends to faint.

After another verse, the trio put heads close together and burlesque grand opera, during which Freddy, his back turned, suddenly reverses to kiss the girl and, her place meanwhile having been taken by the young man, much to his dismay kisses the latter instead.

The huzzar now discovers that Molly believes he is marrying her for her money and, his pride stung to the quick, the huzzar decides to leave his bride immediately the ceremony has been performed. After a short interval in which the modish Freddy employs the expression "'at a boy; go to it!" in converse with the society leaders of the environs,

the huzzar and his bride come on from the off-stage
church, a messenger boy delivers to the huzzar (the
Count Von Walden) a telegram which the count-
huzzar has caused to be sent to himself and the
count-huzzar, bringing his palm up in salute of the
messenger boy, tears open the envelope.   Farewell,
farewell, sings the huzzar; Molly staggers backward; the company moves forward as if to prevent
her from falling, and the curtain descends.

The second portion of the entertainment finds
us at a " Students' Ball, Vienna."   The care-free
velvetine students are grouped around dressed up
like planked steaks, singing merrily.   The opening
chorus done and the world being a small place after
all, guess who should appear in this out-of-the-way
place?   Right.   Freddy.   And who else?   Right.
Mr. O'Malley.

" Why, where have you bean? " ejaculates Freddy.

" Bean? " retorts Mr. O'Malley.   " I've bean in
Boston."

The conversation turns now to art.

" Do you know Michelangelo? " inquires our little
scalawag.

" Mike," rejoins Mr. O'Malley, " old Mike
Angelo?   Sure I know Mike.   Me and him used
to work on the railroad together."

Mrs. Kean, a Newport society matron whom we
have met briefly in the first act, happens in at this
juncture and interrupts the proceedings to sing an
appropriate song entitled " Æsop Was a Very

Moral Man," the chorus girls hopping around meanwhile in imitation of dogs, wolves, rabbits, et cetera. Mrs. O'Malley then comes out wearing a small black mask and Mr. O'Malley, utterly deceived, mistakes her for a beauteous Spanish señorita, so he informs us in an aside, and inaugurates a flirtation.

" Sacramento fandango ? " begins Mr. O'Malley archly.

" Chianti spaghetti," returns Mrs. O'Malley demurely.

And when subsequently Mrs. O'Malley unmasks and roundly berates her amorous mate for flirting with a strange woman, Mr. O'Malley blandly assures her that he knew who it was all the time. Mrs. O'Malley exits in a huff and there enters again our favourite, Freddy.

Freddy eyes the grotesque costume in which Mr. O'Malley has adorned himself for the ball.

" What do you represent ? " he asks Mr. O'Malley.

" I'm a Spanish humidor," replies the latter.

" Humidor," says Freddy, " you mean toreador ! "

" Well," says Mr. O'Malley, " it's all the same to me. What's a toreador ? "

" A toreador," says Freddy, " is a Spanish bullfighter."

" Well," says Mr. O'Malley, " I feel like a Spanish onion."

Mr. O'Malley then asks Freddy what a toreador does.

" A toreador," says Freddy, "is a man who throws the bull."

"Well," says Mr. O'Malley, " I've thrown a lot of bull myself."

" But a toreador throws the bull in the arena," says Freddy.

"Well," says Mr. O'Malley, " I had some f-arena for breakfast."

Our two friends now — to our great reluctance — take leave of us and the electrician in the gallery throws a flickering light upon the stage while several persons dance, thus giving the dance the semblance of a motion picture (a novel device used in " The Billionaire " in 1902).

Molly is also at the ball, dressed in boy's clothes. So, too, at the ball — will surprises never cease? — is our hero, the huzzar. The latter espies Molly.

" And what, pray, might your name be? " inquires the huzzar of Molly.

" It might be Smith, but it isn't," retorts Molly.

Molly then pretends to be her own brother and chides the huzzar for the latter's treatment of his bride. The huzzar informs his companion that Molly is the only girl he has ever loved — and Molly, her back turned to the huzzar, indicates to the audience her joy at learning that her husband still loves her. After the joke about having been married but it didn't take, the stage is cleared for a specialty dance in which a man dressed like Percy Mackaye grabs hold of a lady in pink tights and swings round a dozen times on his heel, meanwhile holding the lady in pink tights on his shoulder.

After this divertissement, Freddy comes on again and tells Josette, who is indulging in egregious meditations, to " roll over; you're on your back." Mr. O'Malley starts to sneak off the stage on tiptoes, and, as he gets near the wings, suddenly bends in his bustle as if some imaginary person had kicked him. Then Mr. O'Malley turns and comes back and, together with the huzzar, Freddy and Hal Rutherford (the programme name of the young miss' young man), executes a quartette in imitation of the manner practised in the minstrel shows. After the first chorus, which ends on a prolonged barbershop chord, the four men pick up the stools upon which they have been seated and march off, holding the stools before them. They return and, placing the stools on the floor, wait for the orchestra leader to sound a flourish to seat them. After the second chorus, they arise and, linking arms, do a cross-step dance and exit. Then they return once more, go through the same business with the stools and sing the third chorus —" little women, little women, funny honey little women, you amuse us, you confuse us, but we love you just the same." This done, they march up stage, swing arms 'round in a circle, entwine arms and repeat the chorus pianissimo. As they are singing, a girl crosses the stage and, when opposite the men, lifts up her skirt, inserts a bill in her stocking, and then walks off.

" Do you think that girl had a pretty face? " inquires the huzzar of Mr. O'Malley.

" I don't know; I wasn't looking at her face," responds Mr. O'Malley, making off after the disappearing hussy.

The three other songsters leave the scene. Mr. O'Malley reappears and commences to execute a *pas seul*. As he is dancing, Freddy comes on and pantomimes with his hands that a tall glass of liquid refreshment is awaiting Mr. O'Malley in the wings. Mr. O'Malley abruptly stops dancing and, with a grimace of anticipation, makes after Freddy.

Enters now again the plot. The huzzar has bid $10,000 for a masked model to pose for a picture he is painting. Molly determines to take the masked model's place and so be once more near her husband, whom (she tells us) she finds she still loves with all her heart and soul and every fibre of her being. The huzzar discovers Molly's identity and, with voices lifted in song, all ends happily — for the audience.

And there you are!

What has happened to the Harry B. Smith of a decade and a half ago, the late Harry B. Smith of " Robin Hood " and " The Fortune Teller," " Rob Roy " and " The Highwayman," " The Fencing Master " and " The Serenade " ? And what, synchronously, has happened to the eerie institution known as the American musical comedy libretto? Is it possible that it, too, has succumbed to the prevailing lack of politeness and taste in our theatre stalls?

THE COMMERCIAL THEATRICAL MISMANAGER

THE exhibits displayed in recent seasons upon the illuminated steppes of the Broadway theatres are to the Corinthian profoundly less interesting as specimens of drama than as specimens of the ratiocination and cerebral jigs of the Broadway producer. It is, of course, the mode current to blame the theatrical manager for almost everything, just as it is the mode to trim women's transparent crêpe-chiffon sleeves with fur, to call cinema views of the Italian army war pictures and to indulge in kindred contrary heresies. In point of fact, much of this blame is without reason. The average commercial theatrical manager is, from many points of view, a laudable fellow. Said what there be to the contrary, he generally produces the best plays he can lay hands on; he is lavish in the equipment which he affords his presentations; he builds comfortable museums in which to house his exhibitions. The one thing he may logically be blamed for, this commercial theatrical manager, is that, whatever his artistic aims and artistic accomplishments, whatever his brave and praiseworthy efforts to do the best there is in him, he is usually a perfectly rotten business man.

That, very simply, is the actual trouble with the average amusement caterer. The courts of bankruptcy to this offer up ample testimony. So, by way of prognostication, do the presently frequent Monday *premières* and Saturday *dernières* of plays, which, though otherwise amply boshful, still so clearly miss the necessary flubdubberies for box-office success that one would imagine the deficiencies were apparent even to a blind man. Take, for clinic, a melodrama, " The Ware Case," lodged upon the incandescent prairie of the Maxine Elliott Theatre. Learning that the show, originally produced in London, contained what they were happy to regard as an element of commercial novelty — to wit, a trial scene wherein the audience was enlisted to serve as the jury before which the case was being tried — a posse of native drama-drummers besieged the cable offices and sizzled dumfounding offers overseas, one against the other, for the American rights to the masque. And eventually the glowing victor, trembling with visions of golden reward, set out the piece upon the shelf named and, obviously enough, beheld the article score a shining failure.

If the commercial gentleman who produced and endeavoured to sell " The Ware Case " to an American audience were to gaze into the crystal of an Avenue cigar shop and see a window full of cigars tied individually in pink ribbons with a lithograph of Mr. Bert Williams adorning each, he would doubtless observe to himself that the manager of the tobacco bazaar, if he believed thus to sell his cigars, was by way of being something of a jackass. Yet the cigar fellow, gazing upon the manager's melodrama, would unquestionably be seized with a like reflection. Consider. The manager realized that the melodrama in point, being a usual melodrama in every respect, would have to offer as its selling quality but one thing — and that, the pseudo-novelty already alluded to, the novelty, to wit, of the audience being asked to serve during the trial scene as a jury. Now, as is perfectly well known, it is the chief aim, ambition and dream of nine out of every ten American citizens, whatever their race, colour or previous condition of matrimony, by hook or crook, by fair means or foul, to avoid jury duty. The American who is eager to serve upon a jury — or who even views such a service without dismay and alarm — is as exotic a creature as one might expect to encounter on the day's march. Picture then by what process of mental Twilight Sleep the producer gave birth to the theory that a body of gentlemen, seeking pleasure in a theatre, would welcome such a service, albeit imaginary, as a source of pastime and amusement.

Upon the beamy pampas of the Gaiety Theatre, a like instance of commercial managerial obliquity of computation has been vouchsafed the onlooker. The pampas of this particular playhouse was made the scene of enactment of Mr. Avery Hopwood's farce, " Sadie Love," a dramatization, after a fash-

ion, of the author's novel, " A Full Honeymoon."
To any one with half an eye, it was evident (as I
observed when the novel appeared) that were the
materials of the book transplanted with little altera-
tion to the spotlight pasture and were the cast
selected with reasonable sagacity, the success of the
resulting play would be an eminently safe hazard.
The farce, in a word, seemed in the offing to be
possessed securely not only of genuine intrinsic merit,
humour and smartness, but also of all the qualities,
such for example as naughtiness, a cunning " sympathetic " heroine, a physic of slapstick and the like,
necessary to insure its appeal to the yokels of the
box-office line.   This, then, was the commercial manager's potential property.   But what now?

The commercial manager, one Morosco, being,
like most persons who consecrate their lives to art,
a bad business man, forthwith persuaded himself to
believe that the buying public would be offended if
the virgin flapper of Mr. Hopwood's novel were
made the heroine, as well, of Mr. Hopwood's farce;
that the buyers would question the taste of a young
girl manœuvering the risqué Hopwood situations.
And so the author permitted himself to be tempted
— and the vestal flapper became duly metamorphosed into a widow.   And a success coincidentally
became metamorphosed into a failure.

Every commercial manager in the land, including
Mr. Morosco, has known from boyhood the ancient
theatrical stratagem of making an audience laugh

by placing naughty lines in the mouth of an ingénue
who is supposed to be innocently unaware of their
import. Yet this Morosco, seeking to tone down
the tartness of the Hopwood line and situation, deliberately took a course opposite to that established
from time immemorial by the box-office mariners and
so obtained a result directly the reverse of that which
he sought. With the casting lesson of one farce
success after another literally staring him in the
face and with the correlated knowledge that such
risqué farces as " Baby Mine," " Twin Beds," Mr.
Hopwood's own " Fair and Warmer " and so on are
best to be sold to an audience with a youthful and
guileless-looking little sweetie in the leading rôle,
Mr. Morosco then went a step further and cast the
widow with a one-hundred-and-eighty pounder who,
whatever her other merits, still had ceased to believe
in Santa Claus at least twenty-seven or twenty-eight
years ago. Of course, against these Liverpools,
Mr. Hopwood, however good his farce might otherwise be, could ride but vainly. A playwright's lines
must ever fight against the physical personality of
the actor reciting them. Flapper dialogue coming
from the lips of a grown woman with feet firmly
upon the ground becomes not merely unconvincing
but entirely silly. The laugh so disappears from
the dialogue and its place becomes usurped by unruly
speculations as to whether the lady rolls to reduce.
A big woman cannot be risqué and funny at the same
time. The court of Madame De Staël reflected,

winked, quoted — but it didn't guffaw. Imagine
Bertha Kalish in " Baby Mine," Ethel Barrymore in
" Twin Beds," Sarah Bernhardt in the " The Habit
of a Lackey "— Marjorie Rambeau in " Sadie
Love "!

Thus do our commercial managers lose their
money. Thus do they put on Rostand's " La Prin-
cesse Lointaine," enchant the audience for the entire
first act with dithyramb and lute proclaiming the exquisite and amazing beauty of the leading lady and
then hoist the second act curtain on Madame Simone.
Thus does Mrs. Fiske permit herself to come out
upon the bulb-bordered moor in " The High Road "
as a minx of eighteen summers. Thus are young
leading men called upon to fight duels for Miss
Beulah Pieface. Thus, in plays adapted from
the French, does the heroine beget a baby merely
because the villain has kissed her. Thus is a severe
and sober Englishman cast for the rôle of Max in
" Anatol." Thus do they make a " dress suit " play
out of " The Fable of the Wolf " (" The Phantom
Rival ") and so delete the composition of its two
most profitable ingredients. Thus is Emily Stevens
divulged as a mermaid. Thus does William Gillette
shoot his brother and go to Libby Prison for Miss
Helen Freeman. And thus do they mistake such a
play as " Moloch " to be, like the work of Joseph
Conrad, powerful by virtue of its thematic meaning-
lessness, when in reality it is merely empty.

A rubber-stamp addle argument used by some of

the daily gazetteers to account the successlessness of Mr. Hopwood's play had to do with the circumstance that the playwright had named his product a romantic farce, that it was just that, and that whereas Hopwood had thus mixed his dramatic elements (romance and farce, to wit) he was by the rules of the theatre doomed to frustration. What juicy slices of piffle-pie are such pseudo-critical feats! The notion — it is persistent — that a dramatist cannot succeed in mixing in a single theatrical composition the different dramatic elements is as bovine as it is popular. Shakespeare is full of such mixtures. For example, the romantic farce called " The Two Gentlemen of Verona." For example, the romantic farce called " Love's Labour's Lost." It was of such mixtures, indeed, that Johnson found justification in that in real life the vulgar is found close to the sublime, that the merry and the sad usually accompany and succeed one another. The modern German play — take Hermann Essig or Rittner, for instance — is frequently as mixed of mood as a bachelor with several *Cointreaux* aboard. From the " Orestes " of Euripides, with its catastrophe more suitable to comedy than tragedy, to George Cohan's " Seven Keys to Baldpate," the records of success are adorned with the matrimony of diverse elements. What, at bottom, *par parenthèse,* is Shaw's " Cæsar and Cleopatra " but romantic farce?

The conceit that the theatre-going public is to be

amused only after a strict technique is, in faith, a
sappy comfit. The familiar perfectly human and
highly agreeable impulse to laugh at a funeral
should imply that it is an equally reasonable
and agreeable impulse to be a bit sad, now and again,
at a farce. Why should there not be sentiment in
farce, as there is in Hopwood's? Who passed a
law against it? Probably the same rakish fellow
who censured the late Charles K. Hoyt for playing
with cheap relish on his character's names — Wel-
land Strong, Jack Aspin, Goodrich Mudd, *et al* —
when the same relish is visible in Homer, the Books
of Moses (chock full of it), Petrarch, Cicero, Shakespeare, Farquhar, Sheridan. . . .

The critics, instead of courting progress and in-
fusing new life into the bones of the drama, are
forever yelping " You can't do this," " You can't
do that," and are so constantly doing their little, if
ineffectual best, to keep the theatre in status quo.
The critics said that drama was not a form of literature for the weavings of consistent naturalism, that
" it couldn't be done "— and along came Arno Holz
and Hauptmann and did it. The critics said
a play to succeed had to have heart interest, as they
termed it; that " it couldn't get over without love "—
and along came Shaw. The critics said a play, to interest a modern mixed audience, had to be well-knit
and closely consecutive — and along came the frag-
mentary Arnold Bennett and even scrappier Tristan
Bernard. The critics said you could no longer suc-

cessfully fool your audience — and along toddled Leblanc, Cohan and Megrue in the wake of Baring, Davis, *et al.* The critics said that if you played a joke on your audience at the final curtain, the audience's disappointment at that juncture would not be atoned for by its previous pleasure — and along came Sidney Grundy with his " Arabian Nights " (still running in stock under various titles and still the amateur's favourite) and Thaddäus Rittner with his " Unterwegs " that set shaking the Little Marys of Vienna and Berlin. The critics said a play could not contradict itself and along came Wedekind with " Der Stein der Weisen." The critics said a lot about the unity of time and along came a youngster with his " On Trial." The critics were of the opinion that an operetta must have music and along came Ludwig Bauer with his " The King Trust." They said you couldn't write a successful play without women — and along came Schnitzler with " Professor Bernhardi," which has made money where it has been presented. They said that different characters had to speak as idiomatic individuals and should not be made to serve as a mere grouped mouthpiece for the author — and along came Wilde. And they who are now venerable (and respected) grandpas gave the first spoof-giggle to Ibsen.

The theory that a wooden platform lit up by electricity and hung with strips of painted canvas and cheesecloth may respond only to a fixed and invariable set of rules is akin to the theory that a highly

proficient actress with fat legs may be convincing
in a romantic rôle.   The truth of the matter being
simply that a playwright may successfully do almost
anything he chooses to do, provided only he has
the necessary imagination and inventive skill for the
doing.   The critics confound themselves.   When
they see a new and novel form fail, they imagine it
is the form that has failed when, in reality, it is
merely the playwright.

If the drama is to hold the mirror up to nature,
then let the mirror do some reflecting.   To object
to the presence of a sentimental love scene in a farce,
as has been the objection in the case of " Sadie Love,"
and simultaneously to argue that " Sadie Love's "
weakness lies in its lack of plausibility and remote-
ness from reality, is to argue that life is but one long
and uninterrupted chuckle.   This critical business is
becoming steadily more and more grotesque.   Small
wonder so many of the better critics have given up
their art in disgust and resigned themselves to become playwriters.

The yappishness of the average municipal professional dramatic umpire is no more gayly to be sensed
than in his attitude toward what he calls vulgarity.
To such an important old dear, anything is to be
scowled at as vulgar that might joggle the affectibili-
ties or jounce the suspended animation of the nice
old maids in the Serbian Stomachband Sewing Circle
back in the old home town in Minnesota.   With ear
alert and shooter at his lip trembling to discharge

its devastating pea, he awaits, like cat the mouse, the
first suspicion upon the fair and untarnished American stage of any word, act or line that might possibly
corrupt the morals of little Henrietta Swinkbauer
back in Fishville Springs. And when his eager blue
sniffer detects a vagrant whiff of something that
seems to him not strictly *au fait,* not quite to the
esthetic and ethical taste for which Fishville Springs
or Oswald Falls or whatever it is, is famous, he puts
him on his overcoat and hurries him right down to
the office to write a little piece. And the next morning he reads his little piece and becomes profoundly
impressed with himself as " a champion of clean
plays "— which is to say, the school of Gobbo who
believes that it is better to corrupt the art of drama
with such spotless pish as " Experience " than it is
to corrupt with blushes the jaundiced cheeks of
some spinster numskulls in Finkport with a play like
" The Song of Songs." When one stops to consider
that the young men and women who are admittedly
among the most talented of our younger (or for that
matter, older) essayists for the American illumined
savanna — such writers, for example, as Edward
Sheldon, Knoblauch, Zoe Akins, this same Hopwood,
et cetera — have one and all been denounced for this
vulgarity by these holy sons of slobber, these pure
yokels; when one stops to consider that such in many
respects excellent plays as " Papa," " The Song of
Songs," " The Faun "— to say nothing of " The
Easiest Way," " Baby Mine," and the like — have

suffered in the metropolis the sting of the provincial
bean, one will appreciate the sympathy that is due
the American who wishes to write something other
than Elsie stories for the native stage.

Vulgarity is in itself an art, though it is difficult
so to persuade the average citizen of the Democracy.
Being himself inherently vulgar, the American has
small respect for vulgarity. He has come by it so
naturally, so spontaneously, that he forgets the per-
fected quality of his vulgarity is the result not of
the moment nor yet of the year, but of some one
hundred years of the most assiduous cultivation on
the part of his forebears. Familiarity with vulgarity has bred the American's contempt for it.
And so, being himself something of a genius in vulgarity, he quite naturally fails to appreciate the
quality when it is made brilliantly visible in art forms.
Thus Shaw's creamy study in vulgarity, " Great
Catherine," when locally presented, was certain
to fail of this fellow's approbation. So, too,
would fail Freksa's " The Fat Cæsar." So, too,
Holm's " Mary's Big Heart." So, too, Schnitzler's
" Reigen," the hilarious French farce " The Rubi-
con " and a score of others like it, Wedekind's
" Earth Spirit," " Box of Pandora," " Mine-Haha "
and " In Full Cry," the currently deleted portions of
Shakespeare, Evrinoff's " Theatre of the Soul,"
much of Lothar Schmidt, the Metropol's " Men
from Maxim's " revue, the " Amoureuse " of Porto
Riche, Lavedan's " Goût du Vice," the Renais-

sance's success "L'Aphrodite," Hauptmann's "Before Dawn," nine-tenths of the gay little Guignol
comedies. . . .

The American bumpkin who at home eats ice-
cream with a spoon, has a sepia photograph of the
Colosseum hanging on the wall of what he terms
his "sitting-room," calls the maid familiarly by her
first name, keeps several Coronas around for strictly
company purposes and is fertile in similar vulgari-
ties, immediately he enters a theatre constitutes of
himself an authority on refinement. Once in the
playhouse, he is a beau of precise taste, a howling
swell in finesse. Full of superior bahs and poohs,
he. Does a lady character in the play swig a cock-
tail and say a "hell," shakes he his head on the
malavisé mien of the episode. Does a lady character don a lacy nightie, tightens he his lips in firm
disapproval. He is a soufflé of *au faits, savoir
vivres, comme il fauts, à la modes, bon goûts,* all
compact. This, the fellow the writer for the American stage is called upon to please. This our referee
of vulgarity. Hopwood's "Sadie Love" was a
badly spoiled job, true; but the person who says that
it is unnecessarily and inappropriately vulgar therein
confesses that he is the sort of clown who would
criticize Rabelais after the same standards that he
would criticize "Peg o' My Heart."

LEGEND'S END

TO applaud the practice of Mr. David Belasco in expending infinite care and time in perfecting the production of so empty and bootless a play as " Little Lady in Blue " is akin to an admiration for the sort of adult who triumphantly expends painstaking effort and time in putting together the several hundred little pieces of a jig-saw puzzle. That such veneration is as without foundation as a tent is probably perfectly well appreciated by the folk who participate in it, yet the Belasco tradition dies hard and of that tradition this particular veneration is, one may believe, something in the nature of a death rattle. It is as if they who stand by the bed-side, at a bit of a loss what nice to say, murmur gently, " But anyway — he had a good heart."

It is perhaps now a dozen years since the Belasco legend slid off the well-oiled ways and sailed gaudily forth, with flags flying and guns booming, into the gullibilities of the American public — a public already celebrated for having swallowed in high clover Madame Janauschek as a great artist, Richmond Pearson Hobson as a great naval strategist, Hamlin Garland as a great novelist, Tom Sharkey as a great prize-fighter and May Yohe as a great beauty. Nurtured by the gentleman himself with an even more scrupulous cunning than Barnum exercised in the exploitation of Jenny Lind, the Russian press bureau in preliminary *missa cantata* of the genius of Admiral Rodjestvenski or Mr. Ziegfeld in the glorification of Lillian Lorraine, the tradition fattened with the years and, fattening, established its creator in the American mind as a leading figure in the world's theatre.

To the fattening of this tradition, Mr. Belasco was tireless in contributing albumenoids of various and succulent genres. First, by way of bequeathing to himself an air of aloof austerity and monastic meditation, he discarded the ordinary habiliments of commerce and by the simple device of turning his collar hind end foremost, made of himself a sort of Broadway Rasputin, a creature for awe and pointings and whisperings. Arrayed so, he strode as a messiah among the peasants and, by putting on a show in a barn in El Paso, Texas, brought down the wrath of these esthetes upon the sack-suited infidels of the Syndicate who very probably because his show wasn't so good or so much of a drawing-card in El Paso as the Byrne Brothers' "Eight Bells," denied him their El Paso mosque on the theory that if Mrs. Leslie Carter was a great artist then the whole darned artist business was Greek to them and they would just as lief take their chances on getting simultaneously into the Hall of

Fame and the First National Bank with Nellie McHenry.

But this Belasco, a sapient fellow withal, knew well what he was about. The thing worked like a charm. And the yokelry, egged on by the ever naïve and infatuated St. William Winter and other such credulous emotionals, raised cries of persecution and Belasco became, overnight, the martyred Dreyfus of the American drama. High-salaried press agents who knew how suavely to soule and roget and bartlett were commissioned now to fashion compositions to be signed by Belasco and spread discreetly in the more literary gazettes. And by way of augmenting the aloofness, the mystery, the remote melancholy and the artistic temperament of him, the monsignor sold now his old swivel chair, his old desk light with the green shade and the chromo of Ned Harrigan that hung on the wall and bought to take their places a Ming dais, an altar candle-stick and a copy of the Mona Lisa. Carpets ankle-deep were laid upon the floor, the blinds were drawn and Vantine's entire stock of joss sticks set to smell up the place with a passionate Oriental effluvium. In that corner, a single wax taper, inserted artistically in a Limoges seidel, illumined the chamber with its ecclesiastic glow, and in that was glimpsed a single narcissus in a wistful pot. Upon the inlaid onyx commode that served as a desk rested carelessly a framed photograph of Dante, with the inscription " To my warm friend, Dave,

in token of his services in the cause of art "— and
duly autographed by the poet in that peculiar and
unmistakable flowing hand of his. Outside the
heavy bird's eye maple door studded with big brass
thumb-tacks, two small coloured bellboys impressed
into service from a nearby hostelry and outfitted
with green turbans and yellow togas, were made
to sit cross-legged like twin gods of the mountain.
And atop the door, to be set melodiously ringing at
appropriate moments by a push-button neighbourly
to Mr. Belasco's great toe, was arranged a set of
chimes.

This restful chamber was christened a " studio "
and, so was the news given out, it was here, amid
these classic inspirations, that the Belasco withdrew
from the sordid, work-a-day world to woo the muse.
Among the muses that Belasco wooed in these surroundings was the muse of dramatic criticism, for
here were bidden from time to time, with much
flourish and ado, much subtle greasing and tony
flim-flam, the newspaper theatrical writers. One at
a time, and after much stunning hocus-pocus, were
these gentlemen received. When they entered, Mr.
Belasco was invariably seen to be seated on the
Ming dais, fore-finger to brow, in attitude of profound and impressive meditation. All was still as
the tomb and dim, and but the thin spirals of the
burning joss sticks disturbed the solemn lull. Presently, as from a distance, though in reality hidden
under the dais, a music box began a sweet and mel-

low lay. And as the music died away, a press-
agent, secreted behind a heavy purple Beloochistan
portière at R 1, made sweet sounds on a small
whistle filled with water as of a canary singing.

Suddenly then, as if startled out of deep reverie,
would the surprised Belasco become aware of his
guest's presence. As some kindly and generous
emperor, the Belasco would deign now bid the fellow near his throne and, putting the fellow at his
ease, would express to the fellow his vast admiration for the fellow's critical and literary abilities
and beseech his advice on how best to end the second
act of the play he was even then working on.   Allowing ample time for the grease to sink in good and
deep, the Belasco would then descend in queenly
abandon from the dais and sink wearily into the
tufts of the Louis XIV *chaise* before the Louis XV
table, meanwhile adroitly pressing the button under
the table with his toe and setting the chimes over
the door to dulcet playing. Followed now, *pen-
seroso,* a lament on the crass commercialism of the
theatre, ending up, *allegro,* with a quotation from
Shakespeare and another from a recent article written by the visitor. . . . An hour later, the newspaper writer might be seen on the highway cutting
one of his old friends dead. . . . And the following
Sunday might be seen in his gazette a six column
article attesting to the extraordinary intelligence,
learning, discernment, taste, artistry, and genius gen-

erally of David Belasco, *maitre* and wizard *extra-ordinaire* of the American theatre.

Gradually the legend, nursed and coddled now by an affectionately inscribed card at Yuletide, now it may be by a rarebit *à deux*, now mayhap by an irresistibly polite note of thanks for a favourable bit of written comment, spread its wings in Forty-fourth Street and flew with loud flutter far and wide across the countryside. Did the tradition perchance periodically show signs of drooping, then were *apéritifs* hustled to its reviving in the shape of a couple of recherché lamps hoisted in the aisles during the intermissions or in the shape of one of Gorham's country-house dinner gongs to signal the curtain's rise or in the shape of Reinhardt's old trick of sackcloth hangings for the boxes and proscenium during the presentation of a play of pious countenance or, more recently, in the shape of a series of profound essays on artistic stage illumination and like subjects (signed by Mr. Belasco, but written by Mr. Louis DeFoe) and in the shape of a legend-boosting autobiography written for the Belasco signature by a needy member of the Drama League.

As has been said, this ingenuous bait worked like magic and the yokelry swallowed it hook and sinker. For this Belasco was a clever man — the cleverest, and by all odds, in the native theatre — and, doubtless chuckling up his sleeve, for it is impossible to imagine him deceived by his own tin-pantaloonery, he witnessed the canonization of his simple humbug

and through that simple humbug the canonization
of himself by the absorbent rhapsodists. But this
was yesterday.

Already there is considerable evidence, even in
the newspapers, of a grievous *lèse majesté*. One
observes a profane grinning and head-shaking.
And the Belasco legend shows signs of soon going
to the foot of the class to join its comrades, the
stork and Santa Claus, Friedmann the tuberculosis
curer and Eusapia Palladino, Doctor Cook and
Granville Barker, Augustus Thomas the Dean and
the Mann Act, black hose with white feet and Italian
vermouth, eugenics and neutrality, Rabindranath
Tagore and the Russian Army.

What now is becoming belatedly apparent to the
hoaxed Hazlittry and its proselytes has of course
been familiar these many years to every one else.
The facts, bereft of Ming sofas and perfumed punk
sticks, are these. During his activity as a producer,
Mr. Belasco has produced not one-fifteenth so many
worthy plays as the late Charles Frohman produced
during a precisely corresponding period. Mr.
Belasco has produced " The Easiest Way," " The
Concert " and " The Phantom Rival "— three meritorious plays: so much and no more. As against
these lonely three, he has presented an astounding
procession of show-shop piffle including such things
as " The Governor's Lady," " The Woman,"
" Seven Chances," " The Fighting Hope," " Alias,"
" The Rose of the Rancho," " Adrea," " The War-

rens of Virginia," " A Good Little Devil," " The
Heart of Maryland," " May Blossom," " Peter
Grimm," " The Music Master," " The Case of
Becky," " The Heart of Wetona," " Men and
Women," " The Grand Army Man," " The Wife,"
" The Very Minute," " Little Lady in Blue." . . .
A show-shop peg higher, but certainly of not authentic stature, have been his presentations such as " The
Darling of the Gods," shilling melodrama in
Morocco binding; " The Lily," one of the least interesting specimens of the modern French problem
play; " The Boomerang," a pleasant but unimportant trifle; " The Auctioneer," not to be compared
with the Montague Glass dramaturgy . . . . The
financial success of most of these plays has, of
course, no more relevance to the question of their
artistic status than the financial success of the novels
of A. N. and C. M. Williamson has to theirs.

During a like and parallel period of managerial
activity, Charles Frohman, on the other hand, pro-
duced any number of plays of the order of " Peter
Pan," " Mid-Channel," " The Legend of Leonora,"
" L'Aiglon," " The Silver Box," " Alice-Sit-by-the-
Fire," " Preserving Mr. Panmure," " The Twelve
Pound Look," " The Admirable Crichton," " The
Mollusc," " The Hypocrites," " His House in
Order," " A Wife Without a Smile," " Trelawney
of the ' Wells,' " " The Importance of Being Earn-
est," " Chantecler," " The Tyranny of Tears "—
the plays of such as Ibsen, Shakespeare, Pinero,

Rostand, Barrie, Fitch, Chambers, Galsworthy, Jones, Wilde and Ade as opposed to the Belasco catalogue of William C. De Milles, Roi Megrues, Edward J. Lockes, John Meehans, Lee Arthurs, Wigney Percyvals, Willard Macks, Richard Walton Tullys and Victor Mapeses.

And Charles Frohman was and is not the only one. Winthrop Ames, who has been producing plays but a very short time in comparison with the lengthy career of Belasco, has in that brief period achieved a vastly more important position for himself through the presentation of such works as " Anatol," " Strife," " The Pigeon," " Prunella," " L'Enfant Prodigue," " Old Heidelberg," " Rutherford and Son," " Sister Beatrice," " The Thunderbolt," " The Piper." . . . William Faversham, during his few years as a producer, has done " The World and His Wife," " The Faun," " Othello," " Julius Cæsar," " Herod " and " Getting Married," an honourable record marred only by the *flon flon* called " The Hawk." True enough, these producers have also on occasion presented plays quite as seedy as those presented by Mr. Belasco, yet such plays have in their repertoire been the exception, certainly not, as with Mr. Belasco, the rule. Harrison Grey Fiske has given the public twice as many substantial plays as Belasco. George Tyler has given the public three times as many substantial plays as Belasco. And what is more, these plays have been produced with a skill always equal to and often greatly superior to the productions of the latter. It will probably be agreed, for instance, that the latter's most adroit presentation of a good play was his production of " The Concert," indeed a brilliant endeavour. Yet it will doubtless also be agreed that Faversham's production of " Othello," Fiske's production of " Where Ignorance Is Bliss " and Ames' productions of " Strife," " The Piper " and " The Thunderbolt " were considerably better even in such matters of casting and detail in which Mr. Belasco is believed to excel. Again, was Belasco's production of " The Darling of the Gods " in any way superior to the Fiske production of " Kismet "? Again, was Belasco's production of Hopwood's " Nobody's Widow " in any way superior to the Selwyns' production of Hopwood's " Fair and Warmer "? A few prettier lamps, maybe, but what else? Still again, was Belasco's production of Hurlburt's " Fighting Hope " in any way superior to the Nethersole production of Hurlburt's " Writing on the Wall "? And still again, is Belasco's current production of " Little Lady in Blue " in any way superior to Tyler's production of " Pomander Walk "? Or, in truth, as good?

To compare Belasco with such men afield as Antoine or Stanislawsky or Reinhardt — a fruity frolic of the newspapers — is to compare Holbrook Blinn with Max Maurey, Ned Wayburn with Meyerholdt or Butler Davenport with Victor Barnowsky. (Indeed, I do Mr. Wayburn, at least, something of

an injustice. Mr. Wayburn has brought a great deal
more to the music show stage than Mr. Belasco has
brought to the dramatic.)   Such comparisons are of
course altogether too absurd to call for serious notice. These producers are as far removed from
Belasco as is Mr. Ziegfeld from Al Reeves, or as is
Arthur Hopkins from Corse Payton. A mere
glance at their records, records brave with the
production of fine drama, development of fine acting
and successful research and innovation in stagecraft,
is sufficient to shrivel to the vanishing point even
the best of Belasco's achievements. Beside such
men, beside even such second-rate producers as
Granville Barker or von Fassmann or Roebbeling,
Belasco is a schoolboy in the art of the theatre.
And beside the inventiveness and imagination of
such as Marstersteig, Gordon Craig, Adolph Lin-
nebach, Livingston Platt or Hagemann, his inventiveness and imagination seem so much chintz. . . .
But these are facts to be found by the bad sailor in
the most accessible books of reference and I pose
as no apothecary of news.

Mr. Belasco has contributed one — and only one
— thing for judicious praise to the American theatre. He has brought to that theatre a standard of
tidiness in production and maturation of manuscript,
a standard that has discouraged to no little extent
that theatre's erstwhile not uncommon frowzy hustle
and slipshod manner of presentation. But what
else? His plays, in the main, have been the senti-

mental vapourings of third and fourth-rate writers. He has produced none of the classics; he has produced not a single modern first-rate British play or French play or German play; he has produced but two Austrian plays and one of these he deleted of its two most striking factors; he has encouraged no young American talent and those young Americans whom he has encouraged, he has encouraged to write not dramatic literature but so-called sure-fire shows, lending to their manuscripts his fecund aid in devising superficial hokums and punches and other such stuffs of the two dollar vaudevilles; he has developed, in all his career, but one actress, Miss Frances Starr; he has developed, in all his career, but a single actor, David Warfield — and this single actor he has long since stunted by casting him year in and year out in revivals of the lucrative trash of Lee Arthur and Charles Klein.

Upon what, then, does his eminence rest? The circusing, after the manner of Oscar Hammerstein, of an inferior actress who had come before the public notice through a sensational divorce case; the promulgation, as original, of a system of stage lighting that had been in use a long time before all over Germany and had already been borrowed by producers in the theatre of Russia; the promulgation, also as original, of a so-called ultra-realismus in stage settings which dates back to Charles Kean in the 1850's and which was elaborated to very nearly its present painful proportions by Otto Brahm in

Berlin, if I am not mistaken, as far back as 1888 and carried even further two years later in the Moscow Art Theatre; the divulgation, also as original, in 1902, of a scenic treatment of such a play as " The Darling of the Gods " already familiar to youthful students of a stage that years before had been occupied by Franz Ebert, Adolph Zink and the other imported lilliputians in an extravaganza called " The Magic Doll."

I have been Mr. Belasco's guest in his theatres these many years. He has, with unfailing courtesy, regularly invited me to review his efforts and, with an equal courtesy, has uniformly assigned to the reception of my tender upholstery a most comfortable and well-placed seat — unlike the rude Mr. John Cort who always, with shrewd and uncanny precision, sits me in an ulterior pew without any stuffing in it and, to boot, directly behind a very fat gentleman guest who is given, particularly at tense dramatic moments, to stupendous and disconcerting nose-blowings. I admire Mr. Belasco as a showman — he is probably the best and certainly the most successful in the Anglo-Saxon dramatic theatre. Indeed, if ever I write a bad play, I promise him the first refusal of it. I admire him for having gauged the American *esthetik* as probably no other showman since Adam Forepaugh and Barnum has gauged it. And I admire him, further, for having done several really good things really well. But, though he has been ever to me an urbane host and though

ever he has subtly flattered my sense of humour by
hesitating to bid me inspect his " studio " or his
first-edition E. Phillips Oppenheims or his collection
of Byzantine soup ladles, I cannot but believe, albeit
unmannerly, that he has by his many counterfeits
worked a vast and thorough ill to the American
playhouse and its drama. And I cannot but further
believe that his legend is ending to the brightening
of a new and more understanding dawn in the native
theatre.

" Little Lady in Blue " is, in many of its manifestations, a typical specimen of the Belasco dramaturgy. It is artificial, not in the properly appropriate sense that such a play as Jerome's " The Great
Gamble " or Chesterton's " Magic " or Besier's
" Lady Patricia " or Eleanor Gates' " We Are
Seven " or Wilde's " The Importance of Being
Earnest " is artificial, but in the sense that such
things as " Brown of Harvard " and the Owen
Davis *demi-drame* are artificial. And not merely
artificial, but worthless. A pale distillation of
the more flavourless juices of Louis N. Parker,
the comedy (an early nineteenth century fable) has
been designed, it would seem, for the mere exploitation of a so-called star actress. Thus, it provides that actress, as its heroine, with the familiar
opportunities to prove to the audience in due succession (1) that she can speak French (in this instance, however, the quality of the lady's *merci* is
considerably strained) ; (2) that she can speak Ger-

man (at least to the extent of pronouncing " fertig "
as if it were " fatigue ") ; (3) that she is virtuous;
(4) that she can sing; (5) that she can play the
piano; (6) that she knows how to wear pretty
frocks — in short, that she can do everything but act
comedy.   For Miss Frances Starr, a most agreeable
and proficient interpreter of certain dramatic rôles,
is apparently no more suited to act comedy than I
am suited to act Little Eyolf.   The net result
of the lady's attempt is little else than a composite imitation of Maude Adams and Patricia Col-
linge.   The net impression of the play is of " Pomander Walk " written by Catherine Chisholm
Cushing — on a rush order.

II

Still another play designed and set forth with
obvious frankness for the exposition of three prepossessing frocks containing one prepossessing
young lady is Mr. Hulbert Footner's " Shirley
Kaye."   In the first act, a mauve crêpe mousseline
and the prepossessing young lady encounter an un-
couth basso who hails from the baggy trouser belt
and despises the women of the Idle Rich.   In the
second act, a cream-coloured peau de soie with a
black velvet rosette and the prepossessing young
lady, looking pensively out of the richly portièred
French window in the direction of the baggy basso,
suddenly fling an impatient gesture toward the lavish
chamber and, in voice vibrant with pent-up emotion,

Legend's End   81

tensely exclaim " All-this-*suffocates*-me!" And in
the last act, a black lace over yellow charmeuse and
the prepossessing young lady sit on a bench beside
the baggy basso and, with eyes fastened wistfully
upon the grate-fire, exchange views with the baggy
basso on the one they love, both parties eventually
discovering to their own and the intense astonishment of the audience that it is each other they have
all the while been alluding to.

Mr. Footner sketches his characters by engagingly
simple means. His Westerners indicate their rug-
gedness by saying " Hell " and making comical remarks about the butler. His Eastern society characters establish their hauteur and breeding by saying
such things as " I do not possess that book " in
place of " I haven't that book " and by sitting up
as straight as pokers. Part of the play has to do
with the outwitting of a man of affairs by the prepossessing young lady, who contrives to get hold of
his proxies or something of the sort for a railroad
directors' meeting. This brewed much airy and
superior spoofing from the cave-men of the press,
who professed to no belief in such feminine virtuosity. This spoofing I might persuade myself to
digest with greater conviction were it not for the
circumstance that these very same gentlemen in
their very same reviews of the play showed that
they had succumbed completely to the very same
prepossessing young lady, Miss Elsie Ferguson, and,
succumbing, had been outwitted by her into believ-

ing that she was an actress of high rank.   The truth
is that this Miss Ferguson is anything but a performer of the first water: she lacks variety, flexibility
of voice, precision in enunciation and fluency of gesture among other essentials.   But the truth also is
that she is so very pretty, so very alluring and so
thoroughly winning that she is quite able to outwit,
for the time being, the critical sense.   And when I
say the critical sense, I allude not only to the critical
sense of my confrères of the daily journals but also,
and probably more particularly, to my own.

III

In the criticism of Miss Maude Adams, it has
become a kind of *lex non scripta* that one must ever
be exceeding chivalrous and speak nothing that is
not good.   Miss Adams occupies in the theatre the
place that a wife occupies in the home: no matter
how tired one becomes of her, no matter how much
one becomes irritated, with the passing of time, by
her eccentricities and her mannerisms, it is a law of
social conduct that one keep up a show of loving
her and refrain from saying aught ill for the public
ear.   Miss Adams and the tradition associated with
her name have these many years succeeded in making
a gentleman even of me.

I have known all along, of course, that she is
a pretty poor actress as leading actresses go, and
all along I have felt uncomfortable, as have many
others, when she has spoiled so many truly beautiful

lines by accompanying them with that peculiar neck-
twist, that little semi-upper-cut gesture and other
such idiosyncrasies of hers. But, following the ritual, I have regularly maintained a polite silence and
have, with the rest of them, professed to be en-
thralled by the " dauntless frailty," the " brave wist-
fulness," the " odd, half-strangled utterance," the
" throwing up of the head with that half-defiant gesture " and all the other of Miss Adams' attributes,
qualities and trickeries. And what is more, so in-
sistent is the thing, I am not even now going to write
the truth about the lady. For what the use?
After all, there is something rather fine about her,
if not as an artist, at least as an institution of our
theatre. Her name and position, in these days of
a stage so promiscuously adorned with boudoir alum-
næ and Wall Street ingénues, are of a pretty dignity.
To her ears, the tin-din of Broadway seems not to
have penetrated. She has played and played only,
during the real years of her career, the plays of fine
artists. From all the cheapness, all the shoddy
press-agency, all the trashy appurtenances of the
show-shop, she has firmly and consistently drawn
aside her skirts. And in a theatre from which, by
Sunday night " benefits," actors' dancing clubs, syndi-
cated beauty talks and Red Cross balls, all remote-
ness and illusion have been made to vanish, such a
figure as this — one of the few, few figures it has
— cannot but be regarded with respect and held
high in esteem. And I am not sure but what, after

all, criticism may not fairly be conscious of such items, however seemingly foreign their nature.

It is this Maude Adams, I suppose, rather than the Maude Adams we watch play before us, that makes such as I eager to fib eloquently in her behalf as an actress. And, for one, I am glad to be a party to the polite misdemeanor.

Barrie's " A Kiss for Cinderella," Miss Adams's 1917 offering, though not without its several typical Barrie conceits and lovely touches, fails to arouse my enthusiasms. On all sides I have read and heard tell of its " unalloyed charm," its " gently pathetic fancy," its " heart-warmed, moist-eyed delicacy," its " wistful loveliness " and all its winsome et ceteras, but I am unpersuaded. At no point save in its first act does it approach to the stature of Miss Gates' " Poor Little Rich Girl," which it in content closely resembles. Much of it is of an aridity difficult to reconcile with the name of its author and in the matter of imagination generally it is not only beneath the Gates' play but beneath Paul Apel's " Hans Sonnenstösser's Trip to Hell," a play of fabric similar to " The Poor Little Rich Girl " which was done abroad at an earlier date. The general effect of the Barrie play is of flat near-beer. The Barrie imagination has here taken flight as without a propeller. There is a loud inaugural buzz of engines, the beginning of a graceful mount, a wild indirection, a looping of loops, a sudden stopping — with the moon still a million miles away.

Barrie, alas, is not always Barrie. Under the circumstances, therefore, the criticisms which hail the play and its author with ecstatic whoops put me in mind of one of Harry Tate's vaudeville acts I once saw in the old Tivoli music hall. . . . Tate, wondrously figged out as an aviator and surrounded on the field by a crowd of hysterical admirers, is beheld seated with majestic mien in an aeroplane, ready for a great flight. The engines start an enormous clatter; Tate pulls his cap tighter over his ears; and his hysterical admirers set up a great shouting. The din is terrific and all is ready for the wonderful volitation. The machine, however, though its engines continue to make an awful noise, refuses to budge. But the hysterical admirers are not to be denied. They promptly lie down on the ground on their Little Marys and, looking up at the stationary machine and their beloved hero, wildly wave their hats up at him as if he were really soaring high above them. . . .

THE FOLLIES OF *1917*, B. C.

WHERE once the casual dominie, come incognito to the city for a fly at forbidden thrills and clandestine joys, was wont covertly to patronize the "Follies," a more sagacious creature he now hastens his steps towards the latest Biblical play and thereat and openly achieves for himself a threefold physiological inflammation and emotional bedevilment. For he has come to appreciate, this sly dog, that where it is a matter of what Mr. Frank Tinney calls "the genuwine hot stuff," the average so-called religious play makes one of the Ziegfeld exhibitions seem in comparison as tame as kissing one's grandmother.

By the simple device of changing the locale from Paris to Jerusalem, calling François something like Parsodias and Fleurette Borsippa or Jezebel, and liberally sprinkling the dialogue with thees and thous, the canny theatrical manager is able not only to get away with an unexpurgated version of a "Girl with the Whooping Cough," but, what is more to the point, able to hocus into his auditorium the vastly lucrative and sometime coy church element. For that other element, that element of more wonted theatrical predilection, the element in New

York made up largely of Broadway vestals and
Forty-second Street Platos, the announcement of a
new Biblical play has come to be particularly rich in
promise and fruity in expectations. For the Biblical play, in the theatrical argot of sensational sex
punch, has — as these snoopers are well aware —
long since taken the place left played-out and vacant
by Charmion, Anna Held's eyes, Brieux and the
Medical Review of Reviews, Al Reeves' Beauty
Show, Paul Potter and the Princess Rajah.

The average Scriptural or religious play is built
on the astute managerial theory that the best way
in which to inspire an audience with pure and lofty
thoughts and so bring that audience under greater
submission to the will of Almighty God is to show
the audience a ballet of semi-nude women, a scene
in a pagan boudoir in which the hero is elaborately
seduced by a passionate Babylonian lady, and either
a flock of live sheep or the spectacle of a team of
horses toting a papier-maché chariot over a tread-
mill. Where a farce by, let us say, Mr. Avery Hopwood, which causes the tender churchgoer to shield
his eyes with his hands, shows nothing more epizoo-
tic than a married woman flirting with a man not her
husband (both parties being fully clothed), the usual
religious play, which he swallows whole, is pretty
certain to disclose at least one spectacle of lavish
concupiscence and wenching set in a frame of wholesale dishabille.

The essential commercial stratagem for oiling the

churchgoer's hypocritical alimentary canal for the
sufficiently smooth reception of the business is amaz-
ingly facile of execution.   All that is necessary is,
first, to have the hero hold up his hands in horror
when the undressed ballet wiggles its torsos and
shakes its legs in the wild bacchanale (this salves
sufficiently the conscience of the churchgoer), and,
second, to wind up the elaborate half hour's incales-
cent orgy of seduction with a minute or two bit showing the grievous repentance of the hero.   Which,
of course, to the soul with a sense of comic values,
is much like passing out pamphlets at the conclusion
of an half hour's crescendo hoochee-coochee exhibition proving by some vague scientific gentlemen that
the hoochee-coochee is a preventive of appendicitis.

For years I have been wrought by the regimen of
my professional office to attend these Biblical and
religious exhibitions and, with but two exceptions, I
have yet to lay eye to one to which the citizen — I
here use against our theatrical gentlemen their own
fatuous phrase — " might take his wife or sister or
sweetheart."   From Henry Arthur Jones' " Saints
and Sinners," with its clergyman's daughter deflow-
ered by an army captain with whom she continues to
live in sin, to " Marie-Odile," with its rape of the
ingénue; from " Michael and His Lost Angel," with
its duet of seductions, to the carbonaceous contor-
tions of Pauline Frederick in " Joseph and His
Brethren;" from the temptations of the flesh in
" The Christian " and the courtesan market of " The

Sign of the Cross " to the stripped Adam and Eve
in the " Creation " of Coney Island; from the er-
rant nun of " Sister Beatrice " to the Iris Bellamy
air of John Luther Long's " Kassa "; from the
prostitution of Wilkie Collins' " The New Mag-
dalen " and Stuart Ogilvie's " Sin of St. Hulda " to
the street-walker and big-busted Passion of Hobart's
neo-morality " Experience "; from the biological ex-
cursions of Lady Sybil in " The Sorrows of Satan "
to the harlotry of Wilson Barrett's " Daughters of
Babylon," you will find quite the measure of lust of
such as Georges de Porto-Riche or the Wedekind of
" In Full Cry," from whose plays the ecclesiastic
retreats with fingers clasping the nose. . . .

But this is no new thing. The two leading alle-
gorical personages of the so-called Moral Plays —
the religious drama of the sixteenth century — so
one learns from " The Trial of Pleasure " (1567),
" The Three Ladies of London " (1584), " All for
Money " (1578), and " The Three Lords, etc."
(1590), were, respectively, Concupiscence and In-
fidelity.

The Biblical play most recently offered the churchgoer is named " The Wanderer " and is a version by
Mr. Maurice V. Samuels of Schmidtbonn's " The
Prodigal Son," originally produced by Reinhardt in
Berlin. What we envisage here, according to the
program, is the parable of the prodigal son as narrated in the Gospel of St. Luke. But what we actually envisage here is the parable of the prodigal son

as narrated in the Gospel of Florenz Ziegfeld. In testimony whereof I take the liberty of quoting the following affidavit culled from the leading metropolitan theatrical newspaper:

FUSSING "THE WANDERER" GIRLS

A favourite pastime these nights is to hold hands with the young women in "The Wanderer," who are obliged at the conclusion of the wild dance in the second act to fall prostrate over the edge of the stage, with their arms and heads waving in the faces of front-row patrons.

The legs, arms and shoulders of the frolicsome dancers are bared, and the spectacle of these young women all but falling into the laps of those in the front row appears to be alluring to even the most hardened first-nighters. Indeed, many of the male patrons of art á la Manhattan regard the number as providing a medium of horse-play such as is introduced in the "Balloon" number in "The Midnight Frolic."

Mr. ——, who is always alert to the best in the drama, occupied a seat in the first row on Friday night, and when a blonde young thing, stretched out on her back, waved her hands in his face, he slipped a cigar into one of them and a cigarette into the other.

In place of Miss Kay Laurell in her birthday suit, that erstwhile irresistible drawing-card of the "Follies," the management of this Biblical play offer by way of similar tremor and by way of inculcating in the audience a noble religious feeling, Mr. William Elliott without his clothes on. For this coup I have endeavoured to find some justification in a copy of the Bible which my friend Mencken obligingly cab-

baged for me out of a room in the Prince George
Hotel, but my search through the paragraphs from
eleven to thirty-two in the chapter fifteen has proved
without fruit; and I must so make up my mind that
the *capriccio*, like most such things in these Scriptural plays, was a something devised merely for profane box-office purposes, for all the world like the
Sadie Martinot dido in " The Turtle." Here, however, I beg of you please not to mistake me. If out
of my professional duty I have to deposit an eye on
such spectacles, I confess I would from a standpoint
of pure esthetics, if nothing else, somewhat rather
see the average young actor without his clothes on
than with the sort of clothes on the average young
actor is in the habit generally of wearing.

My point, though, is not this. What I object to
is the condonation of promulgations of nudity in a
Biblical play and the condemnation of the selfsame
thing in a music show. Why the city officials profess
to be shocked at the sight of the chorus girls' mere
bare knees in the Winter Garden — and command
the Shuberts to order thick stockings forthwith —
and why these same Solons profess to be exalted at
the sight of bare knees — to say nothing of bare um-
bilici and bare spank-spots — in any other stage exhibition so long as it elects to nominate itself a Biblical play is assuredly a subject for the student of the
higher philosophy.

If you say to me that it is all a matter of time,

place and the audience's mood and that nudity is less
nudity in a religious play than in the Winter Garden,
I answer you that the theory is, truth to tell, very
catchy, but that, further than this, it is of the juiciest
of pharisaisms.   I should like to believe that Miss
Olive Thomas coming out on the stage of " Ben-
Hur " in sitz-bath attire provokes in me a holier and
more godly impulse than when she comes out on the
stage of the " Follies " in the same garb, but I confess that my mind is in such matters a reluctant ves-
sel.

The old story of the artist's model being one thing
to the eye of the artist and quite another to the mis-
creant peeking in at the window fails, at least in the
way sometimes offered, to fit the theatrical case.
Were these so-called Biblical or religious plays works
of art, or even second-rate works of art, one might
take another view of the situation.   But they are,
more often than not, the veriest pot-boilers, poised
shrewdly against the portly purses of the pews.   In
the first-rate religious plays — plays like " Androcles " or Brieux's very beautiful and compelling
" Faith " or Andreyev's incisive " Savva " — one
will find no such palpable and tawdry box-office bait
as scenes in Babylonian bagnios or hip-wriggling si-
rens or naked actors or soft-pillowed debauchery.
The commercial failure of these respectable works
of dramatic art and the commercial failure before
them of like honourable efforts would seem, somewhat sadly, to indicate that the type of pewman who

patronizes the playhouse is an even greater hypo-
crite than some of his critics have brought us to believe.

"The Wanderer" bears approximately the same
relation to a religious spectacle that Mr. William A.
Sunday bears to Cardinal Gibbons.

SLAPSTICKS AND ROSEMARY

IT is the custom of the respected dramatic critic at least once a year personally to recall with a great show of wistful affection this or that performance of a day now long passed into that star-haunted attic of memory. The performances thus still vividly recollected with a mellow head-shaking pathos are in general associated with the names of Lester Wallack, Ada Rehan, Lotta Crabtree, Mary Anderson, Ellen Terry and, in the instance of the very young critics, Edmund Kean, Farren, Macready and Rachel. Only the other day, indeed, did my esteemed colleague, Mr. Walter Prichard Eaton, lament typographically the thought that Charlotte Cushman was no longer with him (and us) to dazzle the boards with her still brilliantly remembered talent. And, of course, it is almost impossible in the *Evening Post* to distinguish which is the dramatic department and which the obituary.

Although not yet old enough to wear rubbers when it rains, I too am able from out the past to conjure up the still trenchant pictures of celebrated mummers of another day. Not a few of those the mere thought of whom is sufficient to extract a tender tear from my brothers' eyes, mine eyes, too, have rested on. Noble artists some of them, I venture; yet my theatre, alas, was to be the theatre of another epoch. I envy, indeed, the critical perspicacity and precocious powers of analysis that were enjoyed by Mr. Eaton while he was still in kilts — we are practically of an age — but I am forced into the unprofessional admission that, at ten or thereabouts, I was a not particularly reliable critic of acting. I recall, for instance, merely that Mary Anderson had the sniffles at the matinée when first I, yanked thither by my governess, saw her and that she seemed to be almost as pretty as my mother in her newest ball gown. And my chief lingering youngster's impression of Duse as Tosca is of a sort of Theda Bara. For a truer estimate of that actress's celebrity I am therefore constrained to study such of my colleagues as the enthusiastic Mr. Wollcott of the *Times*, who — though considerably younger than I — was apparently already a sophisticated and not unexcellent critic while I was still yelling whenever the family tried to wash my ears.

My boy memories of the theatre are vastly less informative, vastly less dignified, memories. In place of the probably edifying exhibition of acting given (*circa* 1877) by Miss Rose Coghlan as Clarissa Harlowe, I somehow seem to recall more lucidly Della Fox rolling down De Wolf Hopper's extended legs in " Wang." In place of what was unquestionably a fine bit of acting by Tommaso Salvini in " La Morte Civile " (*circa* 1889), I seem

to remember the toboggan in the second act of
Hoyt's " A Midnight Bell." And in place of some
probably admirable work by Booth and Barrett, it
would appear that my acuter recollection is of the
funny scene in " The County Fair " where Neil Bur-
gess, dressed up like a woman, shocked the country
folk when he leaned out of a barn window upon the
lower half of which a billposter had pasted the legs
of a chorus lady in tights, and of an awfully cunning
girl in Henry V. Donnelly's stock company named
Sandol Milliken. I do not remember very much
about John Hare's doubtless first-rate performance
which I saw at the Garrick overseas in 1890 or about
Richard Mansfield's doubtless memorable performance in " Don Juan " which I saw the following year
in the Garden Theatre, New York (I was just nine
then), but memory lights up at the mention of the
unknown actor in a ten-twenty-thirty melodrama
called " The Ensign " who, in the rôle of an unpol-
ished American seaman, facing the modish and contemptuous British villain on the deck of a United
States man-o'-war, boomed in the fellow's teeth:
" We ain't got no manners, but we kin fight like
hell! "

And so, too, does rather memory quicken at the
mention of Franz Ebert, the tiny comedian of a
troupe known as " The Lilliputians," at the trick
scenery of the Byrne Brothers' " Eight Bells " and
Charles Yale's " Devil's Auction," at Charley Bige-
low and Lillian Russell in " The Princess Nicotine,"

at Digby Bell in " The Tar and the Tartar," at Cora
Urquhart Potter's wonderful brown hair and
Vashti Earl's wonderful blonde hair and Christine
Blessing's big blue eyes and Thomas Q. Seabrooke
in " The Isle of Champagne " and my first sight of
Denman Thompson and the scene where E. S. Wil-
lard mixed up the name Lucy with the letter he was
dictating in the first act of " The Professor's Love
Story " (I was about fifteen then) and Katherine
Florence's make-up in " The Girl I Left Behind
Me " and the exciting fire-station scene in " The Still
Alarm " and a very bad play named " Gloriana "
(which I then admired) and Camille D'Arville in
" Madeline or The Magic Kiss " (they gave away,
I recall, pictures of Miss D'Arville on celluloid but-
tons as souvenirs) and Robert Downing's biceps and
the minstrels Barlow and Wilson and Virginia Earl
as the lunch counter girl in Hoyt's " A Hole in the
Ground " and Gus Williams in " One of the Finest "
and Gladys Wallis and . . .

And a burlesque show containing Watson, Bickel
and Wrothe and called " On the Yukon " in the old
Star Theatre of Cleveland, Ohio, some two decades
and a half ago.

Indeed, I do not know but what, among all my
early memories of the theatre, this memory of a
twenty-five-cent burlesque show isn't quite the most
energetic. A distressing fact, surely, and one most
profoundly lacking in official solemnity, yet a fact at
once eminently frank and proportionately certain.

The Bickel I have never forgotten: he is to me at this late day still the funniest low comedian on our stage. Nor the show itself have I suffered to fade. I laugh at it yet as memory echoes its primitive, but withal positive, Elizabethan unities of slapstick, bladder and squirt-gun. A droll masque, if ever there was one; its humours broad of girth, its mien robustious, its cabotinage simply killing. And thus came it about recently, upon reading my twenty-nine and thirty year old colleagues' fond memories of Shakespearian performances given in Daly's forty years ago, that I, too, looked backward upon the tender rosemaries of my boyhood, summoned again unto my fancy the ne'er to be forgotten reminiscences of days now long gone into lavender and, so mellowing, sought again to evoke the past with all its sweet keepsakes theatric, all its affectionate recollections. Two nights I gave over to a reunion with my retrospects: one at the very Daly's ever so proficient in distilling the homesick critical tear; one at the Columbia Theatre. And jolly good nights, in faith, were they!

Here were the good old days all over again — particularly at Daly's, where the stage was now given over to no less a band of troubadours than " Joe Freed and His Heart Charmers," as the billing is. Who Joe is, I know not, but his show, believe me, is a topper. True enough, it should, in the vernacular, be pulled — it is somewhat more *calorique* than the Russian Ballet or " Homo Sa-

piens " or even Mr. Belasco's "Marie-Odile"—
but, posture as you will, it is full of more rowdy guf-
faws, more loud porpoise snorts, than any show I
have seen in seasons. In the first place, the two
comedians are named August Beerheister and Heinie
Hopslinger, which is in itself sufficient to indicate the
vasty promise of the evening. Mr. Beerheister
wears a pair of enormously spacious trousers and a
diminutive brown pancake hat while Mr. Heinie
Hopslinger, in view of his obviously Teutonic nomenclature, treasures a clever surprise for the audience by appearing in Hibernian make-up. Thus
equipped, the comedians march down to the footlights, take a good look at the spectators and then,
facing each other, proceed, in the most ludicrous
manner you ever saw, alternately to crack jokes and
each other over the head. Observes Mr. Beerheister, "So you iss a member uf der union?"
Whereupon his colleague thus: "Don't you call
me a onion" — *swat!*

The roguish persiflage ended, Mr. Beerheister
decides to call up ooo nutting on the telephone and
invite his lady friend, May Rose, over from Hobo-
ken to dine with him. Miss Rose enters immediately, seats herself and calls for the menu, to which
Mr. Beerheister aptly rejoins, "Uf course, me 'nd
you!" Miss Rose, in adjusting herself, has draped
her skirt over one knee and Mr. Beerheister, in
bending down the better to observe the lady's ex-
posed limb, falls precipitously off his chair. Mr.

Hopslinger, with a saucy grimace, has meanwhile become a waiter and bids the fair one order. " I'm not hungry," drawls the lady, " so you may bring me merely a couple of oyster cocktails, some horace dovers, a planked shad, a nice big thick porterhouse steak with French fried potatoes, a salad or two, a slice of cramberry pie — *and* a cup of corffee." But, protests Mr. Beerheister, fanning himself with the dinner card, forasmuch as he has with infinite droll- ery been surreptitiously counting his funds while the lady has been ordering and has found himself pos- sessed of but thirty-eight cents, " ain't you forgotten something? " Whereupon the lady, suddenly re- collecting, retorts oh yes and orders Mr. Hop- slinger to fetch her a bottle of " Pommeroy brute."

Mr. Hopslinger meantime has gone over to tel- ephone the order to the chef and has suffered a dis- charge of flour in his face from the aperture in the instrument. While he is yet wiping the flour out of his eyes, Mr. Beerheister, somewhat impatient, ap- proaches the 'phone, seizes the receiver, shouts " Hello " and is jocosely floored by a stream of water. Mr. Hopslinger by this time has contrived to brush the flour off his countenance and, walking to the hotel desk, gaily drinks the ink, wiping his mouth with the blotting pad.

Approaches now an elegant gentleman in evening clothes, coat fastened in front with a loop. The two comedians contemplate the splendid fellow in awe as nonchalantly he counts over a huge roll of bills

which he holds in his yellow chamois gloved hand.
Presently, the elegant gentleman drops one of the
bills and Mr. Beerheister falls upon it. "What!"
thunders the elegant one in a pink tenor, "would
you demean yourself for a paltry one thousand
dollar bill?" Mr. Beerheister, arising, is properly
ashamed of himself. "Oh," says he, "I didn't
know it wassa poultry bill." "Anyway," observes
the elegant gentleman, "it has now been contami-
nated from contract with the germs on the floor."
Whereupon he calls "Boy!" and when in response
a chorus minx in a toga of transparent green gauze
appears, bids her gingerly carry the bill off and throw
it in the ash-can. Mr. Beerheister promptly makes
off after the hussy. "Where is you goin'?" inquires
Mr. Hopslinger. "If you wanta find me, you kin
haf me paged at th' ash-can," calls Mr. Beerheister
over his shoulder, thus not observing whither he is
going, bumping with a thud against the side of the
proscenium and landing emphatically upon what he
drolly describes as his "roundhouse."

At the Columbia, nothing less than "The Golden
Crook Extravaganza Company" and — mind you
— with Billy Arlington! Here the two comedians
are of the hobo gender and are named respectively
Prince Oswald and Dudley Dustswinger. Both are
clad in amazing pants sustained by a single sus-
pender, and undershirts. Prince Oswald wears a
frowzy stove-pipe hat; Dudley Dustswinger a felt
bonnet garnished with holes. The scene, according

to the play-bill, is " the reception room of the Midnight Club," an institution that resembles murally a holiday box of drugstore candies.   The comedians come down to the very edge of the footlights, Prince Oswald bearing a stalk of celery.   " You know, Oswald, I seen a lot o' monkeys in m' lifetime, Oswald, but you ain't like a monkey at all, Oswald.   Monkeys is *intelligent* animals."   Zowie goes the celery in Mr. Dustswinger's face !   " You have grocery insulted me," retorts Mr. Dustswinger, eating the celery.   The scene darkens and an actor made up as Satan appears in a red light.   " Who are you? " inquires Prince Oswald.   " I," responds the other in sepulchral tones, " am — the — devil."   " *Oh,* is *that* all? " drawls the Prince, " then go ter hell." The evil one, paying small heed to our comedian's whimsy, bids of Mr. Dustswinger his greatest wish. " I wish fer a beautiful woman to love me," replies Mr. Dustswinger, not unintelligently.   " So be it," says the devil.   " Look ! "

Mr. Dustswinger, with an undulating mazurka of the neck, follows the devil's finger and observes, in the open window, a girl in pink tights.   " Is she real? " he asks.   " See for yourself," suggests his Satanic Majesty.   Mr. Dustswinger approaches the window with a great show of timidity and, by means of a couple of pokes, satisfies himself of the lady's actuality.   The devil pulls the curtain.   " Aw, Mr. Devil, please let me see her again," beseeches Mr. Dustswinger.   " So be it," reiterates the other —

and again the window-shade is raised and again the
now beaming Mr. Dustswinger reassures himself of
the vision's reality by coyly pinching the vision in the
leg. The devil, however, brushes the impudent Mr.
Dustswinger aside and draws the curtain. "But,
Mr. Devil — good Mr. Devil — won't yer please
let me kiss her just onct?" implores Mr. Dustswinger. "So be it," again from the other and Mr.
Dustswinger rushes to the window, pulls up the
shade and kisses — Prince Oswald who has sneaked
off unobserved during the colloquy and taken the
vision's place.

The comedians now get out a banjo and a violin.
The taller of the two, Prince Oswald, who wears
the stove-pipe hat, seats himself with the banjo and
crosses his long legs high above him. Dustswinger,
violin to chin, stands beside his chair. The lights
are lowered and they begin to play the venerable
sob-siphon from "Cavalleria Rusticana," Mr. Dustswinger drawing out to its full every sad note and
employing the return trip of the bow to push the
stove-pipe hat off his colleague's head.

It subsequently develops that Prince Oswald is possessed of a consuming thirst and craving for liquor.
But he has only two cents. "Hello, Sam," he says,
moving toward the barkeeper; "I'll betcha two cents
I kin drink a glassa whiskey quickern you kin." The
wager is laid. Prince Oswald pours himself a gi-
gantic beaker and the great contest is on. The barkeeper finishes his small glass at a gulp. Prince Os-

wald continues drinking slowly until the last drop is
gone.   "You lose," says the barkeeper.   "Well,
kin you beat that!" exclaims the Prince, giving the
audience a cherubic wink.

Enters now our genial friend Dustswinger with a
jug.   "Fill this up," he orders the barkeeper.   The
latter fills the jug.   Dustswinger starts to make off
without paying.   "Here you, gimme back that jug if
you ain't goin' to pay," commands the barkeeper, taking the jug rudely from Mr. Dustswinger and empty-
ing it of its contents.   "But kin I have the jug
back?" questions Dustswinger humbly.   The barkeeper gruffly thrusts it back in our friend's hand.
Whereupon our friend, with a ludicrous nudge at the
audience, takes out a hammer, breaks open the jug,
extracts a sponge and treats himself to a fine tipple.

It is now Prince Oswald's turn and, coming con-
fidentially down into the footlight trough, he whis-
pers to the audience how he used to love his beautiful school-teacher, how he brought her a little peach
as a present one day, how she took him on her lap
and thanked him, how he next brought her a big apple and how she took him on her lap and this time
not only thanked him but kissed him — and how he
then began saving up to buy her a watermelon!

And so it goes.   The dear old quartettes in the
purple Prince Alberts still sing about the River
Shannon and the good-old-U. S. A.   The comedian
still dances with the fat lady, one hand on her neck,
the other debonnairely on her bass-drum.   The so-

ciety lady still interprets her lofty social status with
a wholesale and not entirely discriminate use of
" whoms," and lorgnettes the presuming comedian
into a humiliated silence by proclaiming that he is
" beneath content." And every time any one comes
out to exude a sentimental song the lights are still
dimmed and the spotlight is still turned on. But
vulgar if you will, the laughter is still there in these
lowly masques — more laughter than you will
find in a year's round of the loftier music shows
which have substituted a Broadway and Forty-second
street species of what they call refinement for the
honest old shirtsleeve stuff of the Miners. If, my
friends, you want to renew the days of your boyhood,
the days when all you actually knew about Ada
Rehan was that her picture came in packages of
Sweet Caporal cigarettes and could be traded with
the neighbour's kid for one of Corinne in tights (provided you added a couple of agate marbles and a
slingshot) — if you want to live those days over
again, go to a burlesque show.

The best thing about George M. Cohan's " Revues " is this very quality of boyish bladder-bur-
lesque with which he perfumes his buffoonades.
Mr. Cohan is ever successful in his efforts of this
species because he frankly addresses himself to the
youngster in us. He knows just as well as you and
I that we will laugh harder and longer at the spectacle of a pickle-herring smearing shaving lather all

over another pickle-herring's face, neck and ears, poking some of it in the latter's eyes and then licking it off the fellow's face and eating it than we will laugh at, say, any two dozen alleged verbal witticisms of the average modern day librettist. And he knows equally well that we cannot for the dignified life of us refrain from laughing at the ceremony of the zany who, in making his lordly adieux, trips over the mat and lands kerplunk on his et cetera, so he includes the stratagem in his harlequinades along with such of its sister stratagems as the comedian who tumbles out of his chair in his attempt to get a better view of the contents of a lady's stocking (*vide* Joe Freed and His Heart Charmers) and the amorous old beau who flirts even with the small statue of Venus (*vide* Al Reeves, *et al*).

There are, in a general way, but two grades of emotion in a theatrical audience: the fifteen-year-old emotion and the thirty-five-year-old emotion. The first is the quality of the music show audience; the second the quality of the drama audience, at least in some communities, if not in New York. (In New York, to be regarded as at all successful a play must make its appeal to the majority. It so must reflect that majority's attitude, opinions, philosophy, thought. And at least four out of every five such persons believe that bock beer has something to do with a goat!)

It is a ridiculous enterprise to attempt to cater to the thirty-five-year-old emotion in the music hall.

The music hall is the playground of youngsters, whether they be youngsters in fact or youngsters with beards matters not.   And George Cohan realizes the truth of this.   Accordingly, in his shows, he provides us with all the things we relished in the days when we all broke our front tooth on the candy called " Iceland Moss " and scratched our pencils on slates to see the pigtailed beauty at the desk across the aisle shiver.   Cohan is the Peter Pan of Broadway.   And so in his latest burletta, he gives us again the actor dressed up in a dog outfit that we clapped our hands at in the pantomimes of the long ago, the Judge of the court who uses his gavel as a drumstick and, when summoning the court to order, raps out a rat,tat,rat-tat-tat on the bench, and all the complemental loved ones of our boyhood.   But more than this, he has negotiated in the latest edition of his revue what amounts to a genuinely clever and entirely compelling *reductio ad absurdum* of the conventional modern musical comedy, employing for his purpose such devices as the use of the numbers 1, 2, 3, 4, 5, 6, 7 in the place of the equally unimportant words of the average song-show lyric and — as a climax — a youngster of ten to do effectively all the patriotic song business and hair-tossing dances out of which the George himself has made a fortune.

PANTALOONS A-POSTURE

THUS dulcetly the mimes when lifted the curtain on Mr. Cyril Harcourt's drama, " The Intruder " :

RENE LEVARDIER.   I shall leave by the ten o'clock train for Fontinblow.
PAULINE [*his wife*]. What! You are going to Fontaineblue to-night?
GEORGE GUERAND [*her lover*]. But I did not believe there was a night train to Fountainblah.

For a study of contemporaneous mummering, would that an evening before this stage had been yours! You would have been fetched, I promise you.   You would have seen artist and artiste act the play almost entirely with the eyebrows. You would have seen the leading lady interpret deep nervous emotion with the upper portion of her corset. You would have heard allusions to the Pont Noof and you would have seen the actor who played the thief adjust his hat to his hip and, with feet akimbo, defy the hero who was standing beside him by addressing his remarks hotly to the head usher. You would have seen the leading lady, grief stricken, sink into a chair, clasp 'kerchief to mouth and move her head slowly from side to side like Mr. Montague Glass'

108

Mozart Rabiner. You would have seen the actor playing the husband halt long enough at the door on his exit to give the audience an eye: thus registering suspicion. You would have seen the actor playing the lover halt long enough at the door on his exit to give the audience the same eye: thus registering alarm. You would have heard an allusion to the cohan-seerage and you would have seen the actor playing the husband indicate doubt by biting the right corner of his lower lip and the actor playing the lover indicate defiance by taking his hands out of his pockets.

In short, you would have been reminded of the fireside story of the local actor, who, at the last moment called upon to substitute in a play adapted from a foreign source, rushed out upon the stage the opening night and proudly negotiated " Oui, oui, monsieur " as " Owie, owie, monster! "

In no other profession in the world, of course, is there so much incompetence as in acting. Not even in dramatic criticism. The reasons for this incompetence are familiar to readers of Diderot, Coquelin, Lewes, Walkley, George Moore, Anatole France, Tree and such others as have treated of the subject. But some of these reasons, though familiar, are not as sound as they might be. Tree, for example, himself an actor, argues, as did Coquelin before him, that the little knowledge which is supposed to be dangerous in most walks of life is the desideratum of the stage artist — the little French, German,

Italian, music, etc. And then, following up this
spruce brain manœuvre, the gentleman observes that
where education tends to the repression of emotion,
the actor lives and moves and has his being in its
expression. Mr. Tree here obviously waxes ridiculous. To argue that education is not necessary
to an actor in that it will interfere with his expression of the emotions, to argue that he may the
better express them if he does not know thoroughly
what he is talking about, is to argue that Robert G.
Ingersoll was less successful in impressing his audience than Robert Downing. A farce actor or a
melodrama actor may, of course, be at once an ig-
noramus and a successful stage performer. But
small wonder (realizing most actors believe with
Mr. Tree) that such as Ibsen and Shakespeare and
Hauptmann are so regularly murdered in their
tracks! Indeed, no better proof of the vacuity of
Mr. Tree's belief may be had than in Mr. Tree's
own performances.

Even where the actor is not possessed of a thorough education, his histrionic eminence in the community depends largely upon his cajoling that community into believing he is possessed of such an education — as witness the case in our own community
of Mrs. Fiske. Sarah Bernhardt is a great actress
because she is an educated woman. True, the
greater the idiot, the more vividly he may express
such physical emotions related to amour and the
chasing of a lady around the room as are part and

parcel of the Sardou species of drama; but the mental emotions of the more modern dramaturgy require certainly for their expression something other than mere ear-wiggling and leg work.

The difficulty with the actor, however, is not that he is not, generally, an educated person, but that, generally, he has not even a vague smattering of the minor knowledges necessary to his art. The average actor or actress on our own stage, for example, cannot pronounce correctly three simple words in French, German or Italian, cannot play, even amateurishly, the piano, does not know how to handle a foil, cannot dance two steps of the minuet, cannot read even the first measure of so incomplex a composition as Liszt's "Von der Wiege bis zum Grabe." The average actor thinks of his newly acquired rôle principally in terms of the clothes it will permit him to wear. Twenty years ago a dramatist could rely, in part at least, upon his actors. Glance at the plays of the period and you will find trivial stage directions and scant instructions as to costuming. To-day Shaw's stage directions to the actors occupy as much space in a play manuscript as does the acting play itself. And Barrie's are often almost as long as Shaw's.

Walkley says that an actor must be impressed by the outward and visible signs of things rather than by the things themselves. It is true that an actor is so impressed, but this does not, assuredly, argue that he should be. What Walkley should have said was

that a theatre audience is impressed by the outward
and visible signs of things rather than by the things
themselves and that, this being the case, the actor —
being by nature of his craft a lazy fellow — takes
the same easy course so to impress his audience.
To contend that this is, therefore, just what the actor
ought do — and that is but fair to allow him to do
it — is to contend that the best actor is that actor
who interprets not the rôle written for him by the
dramatist but the audience's composite idea of the
rôle written for him by the dramatist. And to make
this contention is to speak in terms of mob popularity, which popularity is, of course, ever vitally at
odds with art of any kind — even with what Moore
called the lowest of all the arts, acting. The plain
truth, patently enough, is that the actor bears the
same relation to an artist that the phonograph bears
to Madame Sembrich. The artist is contemptuous
of the crowd. The only actor in America who is
contemptuous of the crowd is Mr. Arnold Daly.
And Daly, by that mark, is the only actor in America who approaches to the rank of an artist. And
Daly, as actors are regarded by the theatregoing
crowd, is not what is known to them as a successful
actor.

The actor thinks in terms of what his audience
will think. Mr. William Faversham had once the
impertinent intelligence to portray Iago as he himself thought that character should be portrayed and
his audiences, who had been used to the rubber-

stamp notion of Iago, felt themselves slighted and would have nothing to do with the characterization. Other actors, playing like merchants the safe side, merely sell to their audiences the characterizations of the rôles and the appurtenances thereto that the audiences are accustomed to. Let an actor playing an English character correctly recite the word specialty as speciality and, as was the case with Miss Grace George last season, the audience will promptly snicker its distrust. Let an actor playing a judge enact the rôle in a make-up resembling Mr. Justice Freddie Kernochan in place of the customary make-up resembling Russ Whytal and he will be a gloomy failure in the audience's eye.

I cannot believe, for all that has been said and said eloquently to the contrary, that the numskull makes the best actor. It is to me inconceivable that Havelock Ellis, incog., could not have played the doctor in " Damaged Goods " very much better and very much more convincingly than the actor who did play the part or that Finley Peter Dunne couldn't have played the Irishman in " General John Regan " several times better than Mr. Charles Hawtrey.

Yet, in spite of all these remarks, picture to yourself the most intelligent and best actor in the whole world playing John Gabriel Borkman. Picture this actor in the midst of a superb performance. Picture him captivating the most intelligent audience ever gathered together into a theatre. Picture his keen strokes of characterization, his perfect articulation, his own clear mentality gleaming through the Ibsen script. *Then — suddenly — picture, in the very midst of this remarkable impersonation of the rôle, the great actor accidentally splitting his pants!*

And, having succeeded in picturing this, you have succeeded co-ordinately in picturing the tumbling to earth of every fine theory of the art of acting ever written — including particularly this, my own.

THE BLACK ART

JUST as the operas of the Italian Gasparo Spontini were found to sing better (if the phrase be allowed) in German than in the tongue in which they were originally edited, and as the " Tosca " of Sardou has found its better expression in the musical habiliments contributed to it by Puccini, and Molina's prose " El Combidado de Piedra " its poetic juices in the instruments bequeathed it by Mozart — and as, on the other hand, despite the then so-called golden voice of Bernhardt, the transplanted drama of Wildenbruch could never be made to " sound right " in the French — so do we find now, and probably not without some trace of stomach-ache to certain venerable and delicate systems, that the mighty melodious line of Shakespeare becomes more musical, more lyrical, in the palate of an Ethiopian than in the palate of a Caucasian.   That Shakespeare in the Teutonic is a more tuneful fellow than in the English is pretty generally agreed.   But that Shakespeare for his finest effect, his most superb beauty, must look to the super-Pullman-porter or elevator chauffeur is surely a nosegay to stagger the vanity, confound the complacency and lance the pride of the white man.

Yet in a performance of " Othello " given by our
mezzotint brothers at the York Theatre in commem-
oration of the Shakespearean tercentenary, the fact
was established with a vitality that first baffled, then
put to rout, the plump resistance of sovereign snick-
ers and sardonic elevations of the nose.   Under the
direction of a Mr. R. Voelckel and with a company
headed by Mr. Edward Sterling Wright, an actor of
esteem in dusky art circles, the familiar tragedy was
read with a singular impressiveness and an ear-
haunting tonal quality.   I have, in my day, heard
" Othello " from many tongues in many lands, but
never, unless my ears deceive me, have I heard a
reading now more liquid and silver, now more full-
throated and golden, than this reading of the
Moor's fable by these ambitious darkies.   Here
was the music of the prose voiced not in the dry
semi-cackle of the Haymarket and up St. James's
way, nor the sometimes monotonous ventriloquy of
the Volksbühnen, nor the messy twang of Longacre
Square.   There was from this stageful of blacka-
moors something of the violin, the alto-saxophone,
something of the muffled drum, the harp, something
even of the sacring bell, the octavin keyed in B flat,
the grand piano, the mèscal.

Their articulation — as is, of course, ever the case
with the negro — was of that middle ground 'twixt
speaking and singing (the articulative quality, to wit,
of a pretty young girl's " I love you "), the sort of
articulation that, better than any other, is suited to

the delivery of such a word weaver as Shakespeare.
Gone from this reading were all those familiar mummer tonsil qualities, all those little artificialities, that
steal from the poet's lines their rippling loveliness
and inject into them, in place, the air of studied
phrase, of sedulously practised mouth-pursings before a pier glass. The sound of Shakespeare and
the sound of sometimes excessively sibilant Anglo-
Saxon speech took on, from the lips of these niggers,
something of the soft fluidity of French, of the musical dropping of the harsh " e " and the " a " of an
article before the vowel-beginning noun. For the
ugly " I," we had the symphonizing darky " Ah ";
for the unmusical " my " of the text (or the cor-
ruptly synonymous " me " of the white actor), the
liquid " mah." Consider, in example, the speech of
Desdemona:

> " Something, sure, of state
>   Either from Venice, or some unhatch'd practice
>   Made demonstrable here in Cyprus to him,
>   Hath fuddled his clear spirit; and, in such cases,
>   Men's natures wrangle with inferior things,
>   Though great ones are their object. . . ."

Picture to your ear the speech as it comes into
contact with the tympanum from Anglo-Saxon lips,
with its succession of hissing S's, its coarse " shure,"
its burring R's in " great ones are their," its horri-
sonous conflict of R sounds in the brace of words
" natures wrangle." Then dream to your hearing
the speech from black lips:

Something, shua, ahv state
Eitha fromm Venice, aw some unhatch'd practice
Made d'monstrable heah in Cyprus to him,
Hath fuddled his clea' spirit; and in such cases,
Men's nat-youahs wrangle with infe'ior things,
Though great ones ah thei' object. . . .

The " s " sounds remain, true; but the black " s "
is, as we know, a more dulcet " s " than that which
emanates from Anglo-Saxon teeth.

To turn to another phase of the presentation, we
may discover such euphemists as will, not without a
genial jocosity, point out that " Othello " interpreted
by a corps of decided brunettes must perforce be little else than a burlesque, a thing of freak, forasmuch as thus, at the very beginning of things, is Desdemona's father deprived of his objection to his
girl's alliance with a cullud gentleman.   A licorice
Desdemona, obviously (according to the contending
critics) being scarcely a persuasive protagonist and
one hardly the species to register in the audience's
heart a sensitive agitation before the spectacle of a
miscegenative marriage.   Here we enjoy one of the
perfectly patent, facile, and yet intrinsically silly arguments ever seized upon by hair-trigger Hazlitts.
It should assuredly be a no more difficult task for an
auditorium to imagine the black Miss Margaret
Brown as the white Desdemona than it should be for
an auditorium to imagine the white Mr. Robert
Mantell (face made familiar by the protracted
press-agency of countless photographs) as the black

Othello. If a mere matter of ten cents' worth of make-up paint is sufficient to subvert and destroy the effect of a great tragedy by the world's greatest dramatic poet, then may God have mercy on our souls!

A negress playing Desdemona and a negro playing Brabantio are — at least as I see it — not more out of the imaginative key than a white woman playing the Japanese Cio-Cio-San in " Madame Butterfly," or the Brahman Lakmé, or the African Selika in " L'Africaine " — or a white actor playing a black rôle in Sheldon's " The Nigger," or a Japanese in " Typhoon " (consider as revelant in this case the semi-similar note of race antagonism between the white race and the yellow), or an Indian in " The Heart of Wetona." If a white actress can smear her face with dark yellow powder and play " The Octoroon " convincingly, for the life of me I can discover no good reason why a dark yellow actress cannot smear her face with white powder and play Desdemona convincingly. As a matter of record, I experienced vastly less difficulty in imagining Miss Margaret Brown as an Italian than, in the past, I have experienced in imagining the Yankee Mr. John Cromwell of Miss George's Playhouse troupe as an Englishman, Mr. Seymour Hicks (in " Broadway Jones ") as an American, Madame Suzanne Després as the Danish Hamlet, Miss Constance Collier as the Athenian Thaïs — or any one of a half dozen of our warped and ancient women stars as a delectable young fowl for whom the leading man was rampantly willing to sacrifice his career, his fortune and his life.

We grant readily that women can cope and have coped successfully with the imagination in male rôles (" L'Aiglon," for instance, or " The Prince and the Pauper ") ; we grant readily that a piece of canvas with a window and a door painted on it can successfully placate the imagination as the exterior of a house; we grant readily the fourth wall convention, and the theory that two persons conversing with each other always face Mr. J. Ranken Towse, and that when a man wants to smoke there is always a match handy, and that the sky has wrinkles, and many similar things.   Should it therefore be so difficult a joust to coax the imagination to grant that a coloured girl can play Desdemona ?

In this connection, parenthetically, does not the eyebrow suffer a lift when one ponders as to what the more intelligently critical of our dark fellow-citizens must think when they look upon the stage from their gallery exile and observe white actresses like Mrs. Craig, Emma Dunn and Beverly Sitgreaves playing the rôles of negresses — and Mr. William Harris, Jr., casting an entire play dealing with the black race with white actors ?   Must not such castings seem quite as fantastic to them as does the casting of a black girl for Desdemona seem to the less intelligently critical of our white fellow citizens ?

These coons, indeed, deserve a very great credit

for their dignified contribution to a tercentenary celebration that, on the part of some of their paler
brethren, was marked by a sterling display of hypocrisy and snobbery — and, in the instance of at
least one lordly impresario, brilliant incompetence.
Some of the histrionism revealed by them was, it is
quite true, almost as bad as some of that observed in
Mr. Percy Mackaye's so-called community masque
" Caliban," and it is further true that some of the
gentlemen of the cast gave an exhibition of gestures
which for sweep, multiplicity and grandeur has seldom been excelled — even by Thomascheffsky's company in the Ghetto — yet the fact remains, pretty
or no, that this negro Wright's interpretation of
Othello and this negress Brown's interpretation of
Desdemona are not only in many ways as good but
indeed considerably better than certain conspicuous
and blazoned white interpretations of two other celebrated male and two other celebrated female
Shakespearean rôles that during the last span of
moons have been vouchsafed us under the holiday
cloak of the memorial festivities. Let me therefore
recommend that you visit the theatre when this
Wright troupe of black Shakespeareans comes your
way, *i.e.*, if it doesn't happen to be a warm day.

THE CASE FOR BAD MANNERS

THE lot of the American who elects to write for the American stage is, to say the least, not a happy one. By craft a dramatic critic, I am frequently given to speculation what I would do — how I would feel — were I myself to become a playwright and, so becoming, be compelled to bear the injustices that certain of my colleagues in the critical robes are in the habit of doling out, regularly and sourly, to the native-born dramatic writer. These critical injustices — injustices uniformly permitted to go on their way unrebuked because of that mental laziness which passes current and is mistaken for critical *esprit de corps* — I shall forthwith present and essay to puncture.

The first smart of the lash which the American playwright is made inevitably to suffer from critical hands has to do with what one of the critics — otherwise a discerning fellow — has named " our comedy of bad manners." Let an American playwright present a dramatic manuscript in which there are exhibited a number of characters possessed of bad manners and upon him will descend the aggrieved Hazlittry like so many hungry wolves, yowling " bad manners " at the top of their lungs and la-

menting in equal fortissimo that our American playwrights are in no wise to be compared with the English playwrights in the stage matter of polite deport-
ment and suave conduct.   This is for the most part
stuff and nonsense.

If the American society play is, in good truth, approximately as " society " as the S. P. C. A., it is
certainly not the playwright's fault so much as it is
America's fault.   If one demand of the American
playwright that he hold the mirror up to American
nature, why in the next breath berate the poor fellow
because the mirror reflects American nature instead
of Sir George Alexander's?   There is no reason
why a comedy of bad manners may not be as good
art as a comedy of good manners.   The whole business is apparently but a piece of carefully thought-
out affectation on the part of the critics who hope so
by posturing a modish aloofness and sovereign *savoir
faire* and *vivre,* to create in the criticized a feeling
of large awe.

The comedy of bad manners is well known, recognized and properly eulogized and appraised abroad.
A gentleman is not afraid to be seen speaking to his
valet on the street.   A snob is.   The manners of
Pinero's " Preserving Mr. Panmure " are manners
quite as bad as the manners of Tarkington and Wilson's " Man from Home," yet nobody howls down
Pinero.   To ask the authors to make a comedy of
manners out of such a play as " The Man from
Home " is as reasonable a request as to ask a char-

woman to wear an evening gown when she scrubs the
floor.   Bad manners may be dramatized in terms of
good manners no more than a Civil War theme may
be dramatized in terms of a pillow-fight.   The comedy of bad manners is an established institution in
France and in Germany.   Why, in the name of all
that is honest, should we not also permit our own
playwrights to write such comedies?   The author
of " Snobs " was ridiculed for writing such a comedy when such a comedy was precisely what he was
trying to write: a comedy of American bad manners.
Why demand of our writers that they dramatize,
and dramatize only, not what is, but what should be?
Why not allow them, if they choose, to dramatize
nature rather than man-millinery?

The difficulty here is not so much with the American playwrights as with the American producers
who, when they put on one of these American comedies of bad manners, generally cast the play with
English actors.   No wonder the result is so often a
jocose dido.   No wonder the result is not a straight-
forward, honest and honourable comedy of bad manners but, rather, a mongrel and irrelevant something
in which a character with a broad *a* and a pink hand-
kerchief up his cuff is made to boast vulgarly to another monocled character of the incomparable virtues of his home town, Toledo, Ohio.

Fulda's " Jugendfreunde " is a very good comedy
of German bad manners — and the Germans gladly
admit it.   Capus and Coolus and Bernard have

done several very good comedies of French bad manners — and the French gladly admit it. Shaw's plays and Brighouse's are full of bad manners — and the English are delighted with them. Why shouldn't an American playwright be given an equally fair chance — a much fairer chance, indeed, since the comedy of bad manners is certainly more accurately and essentially a thing of the American soil and of Americans than it is of France or England or Germany?

Furthermore, good manners are not so dramatic as bad manners. The thing is simply a matter of practical theatrical economics. An amusement-seeking audience is vastly more entertained by a character who eats elaborately with his knife than one who eats in mannerly fashion with his fork. A man gorging twenty lamb chops and using only his hands in the strategy is, in terms of the theatre, certainly a more entertaining creature than a man eating but one with the proper weapons. The same argument holds true in the matter of drama as an art — and not merely, as above, as a box-office proposition. The bad manners of the American Tom Barry's " The Upstart " are better art than the good manners of the British Somerset Maugham's " Caroline," and Barry's play is the very much better play.

Two thirds of the Russian drama is drama of bad manners. The comedy of Molière will be found to contain quite as copious a share of bad manners as the comedy of such of our American playwrights as

George M. Cohan who are the critics' favourite targets. Mr. Langdon Mitchell's excellent comedy "The New York Idea," generally regarded by the critics as one of the best examples of the American comedy of good manners, exhibits quite as many instances of bad manners as does Mr. Hulbert Footner's exceedingly poor comedy, "Shirley Kaye," regarded by the critics as one of the best examples of the American comedy of bad manners. Manners, good or bad, have little or nothing to do with the case. It is not the manners, but the manner in which the manners are written, that must count with the critic.

More often than not it is the actor who is responsible for the transforming of an American playwright's good comedy of bad manners into a bad comedy of bad manners — and so confounds and confuses the more gullible critic and causes blame to be lodged upon the playwright.

Let us, in this relation, consider the following bit of the garden scene — polished, well mannered — from Pinero's "Gay Lord Quex." I quote from the book of the play.

QUEX [*with tender playfulness, first glancing at the sleeping Lady Owbridge*]. And so all these good things are to befall me after to-morrow?

MURIEL [*in a low voice*]. After to-morrow.

QUEX. When I approach, I shall no longer see you skim away into the far vista of these alleys, or shrink back into the shadows of the corridors (*prosaically*) — after to-morrow.

MURIEL. No — not after to-morrow.

QUEX. In place of a cold word, a chilling phrase, a warm one — after to-morrow.

MURIEL. I am going to try.

QUEX. If I touch your hand, you'll not slip it behind your back in a hurry [*touching her hand*]?

MURIEL [*withdrawing it*] Not after to-morrow. [*She sits; he stands behind the stone bench, leaning over the back of it.*]

First, imagine this scene, if you please, acted by finished and cultivated players.

Now, imagine the scene, if you please, played — as it would likely nine times in ten be played — by our average café-trained Broadway mummers:

QUEX [*with a large artificial gardenia in the lapel of his conspicuously new evening coat and with a broad black ribbon draped diagonally across his shirt-front; with tender playfulness registered by toying with the lower button of his cream-coloured silk waistcoat, and indicating with his thumb the sleeping Lady Owbridge*]. 'nd so ahl these good things er to befall mi after to-morrow?

MURIEL [*in a low voice, looking to see whether* QUEX *has stepped on the train of her gown*]. After two-morra.

QUEX [*flashing a beautiful gold cigarette case and extracting a cigarette*]. When I approach, I'll no longer see you skim away into the far vistar of these alleys, er shrink back into the shades of the corridors [*in a hoarse voice, gazing at her intently*] — after to-morrow.

MURIEL. No — not after two-morra.

QUEX [*drawing forth a beautiful platinum match safe, extracting a match, poising cigarette in his mouth, striking match on back of bench and lighting cigarette. After a puff or two*]. In place of a cold word, a chilling phrase, a warm one [*replacing match safe and cigarette case in his pocket*] — after to-morrow.

MURIEL [*giving her gown a little pat to settle the skirt*]. I'm going to try.

QUEX [*throwing his cigarette circumspectly into the wings and watching to see whether a stagehand has been careful to extinguish it*]. If I touch your hand, you won't slip it behind your back in a hurry [*seizing her hand*]?

MURIEL [*pulling it away and looking at it*]. Not after two-morra. [*She carefully adjusts her skirts so they will not become mussed and sits; he stands behind the stone bench, leaning on it with one elbow and with his free hand smoothing back his hair.*]

To blame the playwright, under such circumstances, for being a priest of bad manners is akin to blaming the bass-drum in the orchestration of one of Irving Berlin's compositions for one's ear-ache.

But the injustice to the American writer of plays does not halt here. When an American like Miss Margaret Mayo, for example, writes a risqué farce like "Twin Beds," the majority of her critics are disposed to hurl at her the stereotyped argument that, in risqué writing of this kind, it requires a Frenchman's delicacy of touch to make the theme inoffensive and acceptable. Here, also, we encounter a typical specimen of native critical fluff. If anything, Miss Mayo writes her risqué farces with the two-fold delicacy of a Frenchman. At the hands of Hennequin or Veber or Sacha Guitry or Paul Giafferi, for instance, a farce like that named above would be twice as broad, twice as vulgar, as the American playwright's.

When one bears in mind that it is a fixed tradition
of the American farce stage (1) that babies are the
result of clandestine kisses, (2) that a man is always
horrified and greatly distressed when he finds himself locked in a hotel room with a pretty girl, and
(3) that when a young unmarried couple find themselves compelled to remain over night in an isolated
inn the clerk always takes them for man and wife,
to the horror of the young man — when, as I say,
one bears this inviolable and bizarre ritual in mind,
one may well realize that most of the Gallic farce
themes are already automatically deodourized and
delicatessened before the American playwright is
permitted to touch them. When the American
Miss Mayo's " Baby Mine " was produced in Paris,
the Frenchmen, alarmed over its delicacy, injected
a goodly dose of more obvious naughtiness into it.
Hopwood's condemned farce, " Our Little Wife,"
were it rewritten or adapted by a Frenchman for the
Paris stage, would be deleted of its present delicacy
and made as dirty as a washstand in a sleeper on the
Southern Railway.

The American critic permits the American playwright little, if any, liberty in the matter of postulate or initial thematic premise — and that little he
permits him with the greatest condescension and reluctance. The postulate or the premise of an American's play must, by the critical voice, be ever probable, logical and consistent with the facts of life.
Otherwise the playwright's work is made a thing of

critical spoof.   Six out of eight of the metropolitan criticisms of Miss Clare Kummer's " Good Gracious Annabelle " attested to this peculiar point of view.   And the play, at that, was a confessed farce.

Mr. Edgar Selwyn told me not long ago that, to succeed in critical America, it was essential that a farce's first act convince its auditors of the sincerity (*sic*) of the farce and win the hearts of its auditors to the cause of its thematic protagonists.   Mr. Selwyn is undoubtedly correct.   But imagine such an imposition as " sincerity " upon a writer of farce — farce, a something designed merely to make people laugh and be merry.   Imagine critical rules for such a thing!   As well impose a strict technique upon a dialogue for Weber and Fields or upon the antics of a Marceline.   By such critical attitude, the American is discouraged, if not indeed altogether prevented, from writing brilliant, irresponsible, illogical, improbable things like Molnar's " Gardeo-offizier " and is forced instead into composing such logical, probable slobbergobbles as " In for the Night."

It is absurd to demand that the postulate of a play be logical and its theme in accordance strictly with the facts of life.   What, by such processes of ratiocination, would become of half the great or half-great plays of all time, from " Œdipus Rex " on? The stage is a stage, not a stern court of law.   To deny a playwright any premise he chooses to offer is to forbid him the first aids to satire and paradox, to the sprightly exercise of his imagination, to a foundation for a grade of humour somewhat above the humour of the Erie Railroad, chin whiskers and custard pies.

The American critical fraternity must answer some day for killing or attempting to kill, by injustices such as these, the aspirations and hopes of such promising young American writers of satiric comedy as Tom Barry, such genuine talents for delicate farce as Avery Hopwood, such keen appraisers of American bad manners as George Bronson Howard, such courageous and clear-visioned writers of honest crudities as the Edward Sheldon of " The Song of Songs." . . .

If, therefore the American dramatist, as Europe knows him, is a faint creature, a mere fellow for mock and nose-fingering, it may be that — in certain instances, at least — it is not so much his fault as some have been cajoled into believing.

In other and more frequent instances, however — ah! here is a different matter! Where the Hazlittry has been so often dark to the virtues of our genuinely talented writers of plays, it has on the other hand been equally so often quick to proclaim with high gusto the writers of plays who have no genuine talent whatever.

The result is plain.

The Charles Rann Kennedys and the George V. Hobarts swarm the Broadways of the United States and up and down the Rialtos are heard loud the

voices of the George Broadhursts and the Willard
Macks. But to find a real dramatist, a dramatist
capable of writing adult plays for well-educated,
well-travelled, well-fed adult Americans, one must
indeed stop long and look till astigmatism sweeps
the eye and listen — and listen to the cables.

THE VAUDEVILLES

HAVING, for some time past, been subject to a notion that my periodic allusions to vaudeville may, after all, have been slightly too acescent — that possibly the thing had improved and was no longer the snide numskullery it once had been — I lately discharged the required fee and took roost upon a seat in the cardinal vaudeville hall of the metropolis. Imagine my surprise when I discovered — I may as well confess it forthwith and frankly — that I had, in truth, been mistaken; that I had been out of touch with the vaudevilles for a sufficient term to render my remarks at once inappropriate and unfair; that, in short, I had stated the case against vaudeville from the plane of a too ancient prejudice. For I found that vaudeville, judging it from the exposition thereof on its principal New York stage, is not only not so bad as I in my sciolism and ignorance had believed it to be, but that it is a blamed sight worse.

The arterio-sclerosis, the vacuity and the stupidity of this species of professional entertainment is beyond the comprehension of even the assiduous patron of the Broadway drama. Burlesque, beside it, is a high art. And Broadway drama of the

typical sort in which the hero is unable to prove
an alibi and clear himself of the charge of murder
because on the night in question he was with
Madame Purée de Saint Germain and chivalrously
declines to compromise that lady, is a product of
God-given genius.

By way of emphasizing the impartiality and the
gospel of the foregoing paragraphs and dismissing
at once the allegation that I am constitutionally incompetent to judge vaudeville — an allegation eminently true — I shall remove the personal element
from a consideration of what took place that evening upon the platform, shall set down simply the
facts and shall so permit the reader to compose his
mind for himself.

When I entered the hall, the first three numbers
on the bill — always the weakest numbers on a
vaudeville programme, according to the vaudeville
purveyors' own code and testimony — had already
spent themselves.   What followed, therefore, in the
purveyors' minds and to the purveyors' intentions,
must have been the strongest.   The first of these
strong features (headliners, I believe the designation is) to assess the vision was a so-called hobo
monologist, by name, Mr. Wills.   This Wills gentleman had his face smeared with bluish grease-
paint and Hess' No. 8½ to suggest the need of a
shave, had his person encased in exaggeratedly tat-
tered apparel and had a couple of a dozen medals
pinned upon his bosom.   Thus Mr. Wills: " I got

some telegrams here I jest received. I'll read 'em to you. Here's one from Harry Thaw: 'The future looks black for me. I'm goin' to live in Pittsburgh!' Here's one from a friend o' mine in Rooshia: 'I saw the Tsar at the opera last night. He was in a box with his wife, the Tsardine.' Here's another one from the Austrian general Rushemoffski: 'I chased the enemy at the point of the sw-aw-rd for three miles and, gettin' near him, I cut off his retreat.'"

After winding up with a *mot* concerning the slowness of the trains on the Erie Railroad, Mr. Wills proceeded to relate the tale of how he had boarded a street-car that contained seven policemen and a blind man and how, upon leaving the car, he had found that one of them had robbed him of his watch. He next remarked that war preparations must certainly be going on in this country as he noticed some labourers were already digging trenches in Forty-second Street and that Forty-second Street was all torn up about it. Waiting patiently for the laughter at this sally to subside, the gentleman then observed that he had that afternoon gone into a saloon for a "smile," had poured out a very large drink of whiskey and had been told by the bartender that if that was a smile, he (the bartender) would have to go out of business if Mr. Wills took a laugh. When he came out of the saloon, continued Mr. Wills, he saw two ladies pass with their skirts raised above their shoe-tops. One

of them had on green stockings, said Mr. Wills,
and the other had on red, white and blue stockings.
He did not know which one to look at, said Mr.
Wills.   Then, said Mr. Wills, he concluded to look
at the lady with the red, white and blue stockings
and so see America first.   The Wills gentleman concluded with a parody on " The Rosary," which,
being a jolly novelty, chaffed the Ford automobiles.
   Following Mr. Wills, came one of " society's
favourite dancers," a Miss B. Glass, and with her a
collaborative colleague in the shape of a Mons.
Rudolph in a dress-suit with a large artificial gardenia
in his buttonhole and patent-leather hair.   Mons.
and his partner first negotiated a waltz in a migra-
tory spotlight, next a military gavotte diligently pat-
terned after a similar dance in one of last season's
musical comedies and concluded with what the play-
bill described as " Miss Glass' revival of the cake-
walk," but which seemed to be more revival than
cake-walk.   After the period provided for recov-
ery and known in the theatrical parlance as the inter-
mission, a couple of gentlemen in evening clothes
became visible.   Following some stepping of the
familiar kind, one of the team remarked that he
was going across the street to buy a box of cigarettes.
This left the first gentleman free for a *pas seul.*
Then the second gentleman returned.   " Let's make
a night of it," proposed the first gentleman.
Whereupon (music cue) and the second gentleman
something after this fashion:

No more bright lights fer me,
No more gay life fer me,
I gotta home in the country sweet,
I gotta wife that's fine and neat,
I gotta boy — he's just so high —
He is the apple of my eye,
They are waitin' at home fer me,
They are waitin' to greet but me.
You can have your bright lights,
Oh, those Broadway night lights,
But my wife and my kiddie fer me!

Upon the applause, the gentlemen reappeared at the right of the stage, locked arms, tipped each other's hats, twined arms quickly back and readjusted hats upon each other's heads — and lockstepped off.

Next, what the programme announced as a melodramatic sketch. A young man, it appeared, had stolen money from the bank. " Gosh all hemlock! " ejaculated a " rube " character, supposed to be a director of the institution, " I doan't see why. I've watched that there boy sence he wuz knee-high to a grasshopper and I doan't understand it nohow! " Entered a sputtering " German " character, also supposed to be a director. " Mein Gott, iss de bank boosted? " Entered an old deaf character, also supposed to be a director. " Good morning," said the rube character to the deaf character. " Eh? " asked the deaf character, placing his hand to his ear. " Good morning," repeated the rube character. " Eh? " asked the deaf character. And so on

forte, piu forte, fortissimo, fortississimo, until —
" Aw, *sit down!* "

The young man was called in. " Why, oh why,
did you do it? " Pause. Then —" I'll tell you
why I did it! I did it because my wife and my
baby were starving — yes, *starving!* You didn't
pay me a living wage and — and — I had a *right*
to the money! " Entered wife. " He didn't mean
to take it; did you, Dick? Here's the money. He
didn't mean to keep it, he didn't mean . . ." The
young man stood in the corner, head down, his fingers
toying nervously with the brim of his hat. He now
grasped his wife in his arms. " It'll be all right,
dear, it'll be all right. Don't worry, I'll take care
of you and the baby, so help me God I will."

" Mein Gott, der bank is saved! " ejaculated the
German character.

" Eh? " inquired the deaf character, placing his
hand to his ear.

" And the boy's salary — the salary that wuz
wrongfully kept from him — amountin' to $4500,
shall be given to him at once. I knew him, gosh all
hemlock, sence he wuz knee-high to a grasshopper
and I knew he wuz all right! " exclaimed the rube
character.

And so, curtain.

Now —" Vaudeville's Pet Singer," one Miss La
Rue Dresses by Hickson. At the left, professor at
the piano. At the right, gilt chair. In the centre,
spotlight. In the centre of the spotlight in the

centre, the thrush. A comely person in all directions save the larynx. The lady's coup: "My
Leetell Grey Home in the West."

And then — the sound of mechanical birdies singing behind the drop. And then — soft lights
and low. And then — Harold Bell Mendelssohn's
"Spring Song" from the union. And then — up
the curtain and: "The Six Diving Lilies." Six damsels in polychromatic Oluses. Six damsels reclining
languorously in a pink and yellow woodland dell.
Six damsels, one after the other, performing nata-
torial *roulades, folliæ di spagna* and such like an-
chovies. And the six selfsame damsels who were
visible in the days before advanced vaudeville for
one dime at the Marcus Loew moving-picture
depots!

There, in full, the evidence. One thing, however, seems certain. Vaudeville has advanced — in
prices.

A FEW PAGES OF DESTRUCTIVE
DRAMATIC CRITICISM

THE fresh-as-a-daisy temper of the theatrical courtship of the native cockney emotion continues to be reflected in plays like Mr. Austin Strong's "Bunny," the theme of which was already ancient when Bhasa used it in the second century of the Christian era in the Sanskrit drama "Mrichchhakatika" (*vide* von Schröder's "Indien's Literatur," Lecture 43), and in music show libretti like "Stop, Look, Listen," the vernal guffaw wooers in which are the comedian who observes emphatically that he is through with women for good and all, who — while he is yet speaking — eyes a likely minx crossing the stage, thereupon says "excuse me," turns around and follows her into the wings; the rattling off by a character of an interminable string of Chinese, the query as to what the character said and the comedian's retort, "he said 'no'"; and the apothegm on poison ivy.

Add to the picture, in a dramatization of W. B. Maxwell's "The Devil's Garden," the scene of cross-examination in which a husband discovers that his wife has been monkeying with some one else — a scene bijoued with such passages as "Will, let go my shoulders; you hurt; I'll answer all your questions in the morning"; —" No, I think I'll have the answers *now*"; —" You're lyin', woman"; —" I won't pretend any more"; —" I did it for your sake, Will, as God sees me, I did it for your sake, only to help you! I couldn't get the help unless I sacrificed myself to save you"; and —" We'll begin at the beginning, and I'll have the truth, I'll have it to the last word if I have to tear it out of your bosom."

Add, further, some dialogue artificially draped together by Mr. Henry Arthur Jones for the purpose of permitting Mr. Otis Skinner to lean over the back of a chair with hat tilted jauntily across eye and walking-stick pointed with grandiose flourish at the villain.

Add, still further, some more musical comedies in which ("Katinka") the star pantaloon makes a joke about listening to some one eat soup and, when two armed Ethiopians threaten him, observes that the future looks dark; and in which ("Very Good Eddie") the humour embraces such penoche as "Are you against matrimony?" "No, I'm up against it," and such jocosities as kissing good-bye to a five-dollar bill about to be loaned to a friend.

And — the panoramic impression begins to be complete.

In the panorama there are, true enough, here and there visible fleeting instances of something or other soundly good, yet the circumstance obtrudes that the theatre of the period is still anything but lively in imagination, anything but green in fancy. Do I seem again to be entering into several pages of what the yokelry condemns for destructive criticism? If so, let us appraise the annoyance.

What, after all, the philosophy of this hyperorthodox prejudice against what the contemporaneous whisker so calls destructive criticism? Destructive criticism is the drill master of progress. Smashing a popular, and therefore probably imbecile, theory on the nose and advancement are twins. From Christopher Columbus, who cracked the shell of the popular theory that the earth was flat, to Bernard Shaw, who handed the popular Sardou theory its burial certificate, the history of destructive criticism and the history of enlightenment are complemental. The attendant theory that fellows like Columbus and Shaw have not been destructive critics since they substituted by their own hand something better for that which they destroyed is sister nonsense. If Columbus had promulgated the theory that the earth was round but had himself been unable to prove it — if the truth of his theory had been forced to wait for attestation until a hundred years after his death — Columbus would still have been a path clearer. The same with Shaw. The same, indeed, with any other exponent of so-called destructive criticism, whatever his especial field of enterprise — from Theodore de Bèsze who in " De Haereticis a Civilis Magistratu Puniendis " wrote destructive criticism of the quality of economic mercy and so, in a way, philosophically, logically and ethically made possible the tonic execution to-day of such gentlemen as Policeman Becker, to Johannes Schlaf and Arno Holz who, though themselves unable forcefully to invest the drama with the quality of consistent naturalism, yet by their destructive criticism of the existing theory cleared the way for such as Hauptmann. Who have been the destructive critics? Such men as John Goodsir who destroyed the flubdub enveloping cellular pathology and upon whose devastating arguments the modern anatomists have builded their wisdom. Such men as Andrew Gordon who laughed at the nursery notions of his colleagues in electrical science and who, laughed at by them in turn, has now been born anew and with magnified brilliance in the brain of Thomas Edison. Such men as Peri who, protesting in favour of poetry against the despotism of music in the matrimony of the arts, reveals himself as ancestor of Richard Wagner. Such critics as the Honourable Jim Huneker who destroyed the cult of Bronson Howard and the Augustin Daly marionette market in terms of at the time unheard-of Continentals, and Frank Harris who exploded much of the Shakespeare hocus-pocus. . . .

On the other hand, of what species the constructive gentry, the great building forces who have been smiled upon and tea'd by pretty actor ladies, shaken of jolly hand by smooth managers, quoted fulsomely in the New Republics and the hotel parlours? William Winter, who interprets art in terms of morals, who for many years has written seriously that the true purpose of the drama is to portray merely the sweet episodes of life and that by this measure such dramatists as Hervieu, de Curel, Ibsen, Strindberg, Hauptmann and Brieux are artists inferior to Sydney Grundy, Louis Tiercelin, H. V. Esmond, Louis N. Parker, James A. Herne, Frances Hodgson Burnett and Madeleine Lucette Ryley. J. T. Grein who, reviewing, on January 5, 1902, a play called "Frocks and Frills," wrote: "Herein are we introduced to the amusing mysteries of a fashionable dressmaking establishment and when there a beautiful woman like Miss Ellis Jeffreys removes her bodice and exhibits a camisole of delicate lace, a climax is provided which should be sufficient to draw the town"— and who, reviewing "Mrs. Warren's Profession" a few weeks later, wrote "It was an uncomfortable afternoon and I cannot withhold the opinion that the representation was entirely unnecessary and painful." Irenæus Prime-Stevenson who writes of the great genius of Meyerbeer. John Runciman who greases Purcell at the expense of Bach. Ashley Dukes who applies butternut oil by the wholesale to Maeterlinck; and P. P. Howe who smears Granville Barker, as dramatist, with melted opera caramels. The critics who hail the genius of Tagore and Alfred Noyes and Ridgley Torrence. Heinrich Dorn who upheld the popular musical tra-

ditions against Wagner. Such comedians as Charl-
ton Andrews who execute such sweetmeats as " the
most typical exponent of such national drama as
America thus far boasts is Mr. David Belasco " and
talks of a play by Sudermann called " Die Heimat."
Such professional yum-yum mongers as those of several of our leading news brochures who, like the
gentlemen above, mistake indiscriminate praise for
constructive criticism, confound flattery with critical
fecundation.

As against such gooroos of glucose, I stand,
please God, a sniper. That no theatrical person —
whether manager, actor or playwright — ever pays
the slightest attention to anything I say — save possibly to allude to me now and again as an old grouch
— I not only appreciate, but also expect. So far
as I know, nothing I have ever written by way of
criticism — and I have been at the job now for more
than twelve years — has ever disturbed in the least
the prosperous mediocrity of our theatre. Mr.
Augustus Thomas is still the dean of American playwrights and, as the dean, still writes " scientific "
dramas (" The Soul Machine ") in which he seriously advances the doctrine that a person may be
placed under the spell of hypnosis at long distance.
Mr. David Belasco is still the foremost artistic conscience and wizard of realistic detail in the American
theatre and, as such wizard of realistic detail, still
lights his stage (" The Boomerang ") from above
— it being a peculiarity of nature that the sun al-

ways enters a room through the ceiling instead of,
as is commonly believed, through the windows.
And advanced vaudeville audiences still laugh themselves half to death at the mention of the necessity
for donning ear-muffs when eating blueberry pie.

It is one of my deepest regrets that I was not
born a constructive critic. I long for the grin of
public approval. My hand is lonesome for the
jovial shake, my back for the commendatory pat.
If, as some one has said, whom the gods would
destroy they first make popular — then give
me *fraternité* or give me death. But, alas, so intrinsic in me is the impulse to the contrary, the
impulse to proclaim the flaw and withhold the squirt-
gun of eau de cologne, that I myself am powerless
against it. I have never written a single paper of
dramatic criticism, a single short play, a single short
story, a single musical composition, a single book
or edited a single number of a magazine that has
been able, upon careful scrutiny, to withstand my
own searching and sinister eye. There is ever something about my labours that grossly displeases me;
that — after a re-perusal — seems a bit crude, even
a bit ridiculous; that does not bear truthful raid by
an intelligent destructive critic. The theory, so
frequently quoted by disgruntled clowns, that " he
who can, does; he who can't, criticizes," is, as I
have frequently observed, a theory appurtenant to
the notion that Rudolph Friml is a greater man than
W. J. Henderson.

Consider, in the light of destructive criticism, such a play — already alluded to — as Mr. Henry Arthur Jones' " Cock o' the Walk." The work has been denounced in some quarters on the ground that it was patently written to order to outfit the person of a star actor. Such criticism is, of course, thoroughly unjust: many excellent plays have been written in just such manner. Elizabeth commanded Shakespeare to write more than one to be acted by her favourite mummers at court festivals. And the poet himself now and again wrote voluntarily to the measure of the minstrels of his Globe Theatre. Molière not only wrote " Le Malade Imaginaire " to fit himself but, so Schlegel tells us, went so far as to act and draw his last breath in representing the imaginary invalid. Shaw, by his own confession, wrote at least three of his plays with star actors in mind. Goldoni wrote for the company of Sacchi in Venice, and Hoyt wrote " A Contented Woman " for his wife, Caroline Miskel. The list is long. It includes D'Annunzio, Rostand and Wedekind; Hubert Henry Davies, Haddon Chambers and Barrie; Schnitzler, Max Dauthendey (*voila* Tilla Durieux!) and Sheldon's " Song of Songs." The critical hostility to Mr. Jones's play should be, not that it was written to order to fit Mr. Otis Skinner, but that, having been written to order to fit Mr. Otis Skinner, it should fit Mr. Otis Skinner let us say at least twice as well as if it had not been written to order to fit Mr. Otis

Skinner — which, save in the most obvious externals, it does not.   As it is, Mr. Jones's play gives its star performer not one-half the opportunities he enjoyed in " Your Humble Servant " (also a made-to-order job) and not one twentieth the opportunities he enjoyed in the dramatization called " The Honour of the Family " (also a made-to-order job).

If, on the other hand, Mr. Jones desires that his play be considered uncommercially, be considered alone for its intrinsic, as opposed to its extrinsic, qualities, then destructive criticism must be visited upon Mr. Jones to the effect that he has, in this work, attempted an excursion into theatrical satire à la the Shaw of " Fanny's First Play," the Rittner of " The Man in the Prompter's Box," the Bahr of " The Yellow Nightingale " the Ettlinger of " Hydra," the Barrie of " Alice-Sit-By-The-Fire," *et al.*, to which exalted form of humour Mr. Jones would seem to be unsuited.   Mr. Jones proudly exposes such dialogue as " if you wish to keep these silly matinée girls out of your theatre, my dear Conyers, just try giving them a good play " and (in retort to a deaf bishop's complaint that he cannot hear the actors) " You are to be congratulated," and imagines it to be fresh, bouncing satire when, in point of fact, it was old stuff when Sheridan wrote " The Critic "— to say nothing of when it was used in varied form by Mr. Philip Bartholomæ in the prologue to " Kiss Me Quick " and in the prologue of the Winter Garden show in which was the tune

" Sumurun "— I forget the name of the thing. No man who could write a " Mrs. Dane's Defence " is likely to write satire. The scene between the vain actor-manager and his foolish girl admirer in the second act of Mr. Jones's play (a scene in which the actor for whom the play was written takes no part) is the one really good spot in the manuscript. It has about it a sly and knavish air that recalls some of the grace of " Rebellious Susan." But otherwise, the manuscript is small potatoes.

" Bunny," the late Austin Strong play mentioned in my isagogic remarks, was one of those become irritating contraptions: " a play with a Dickens air." It was the familiar lifeless, quasi-literary, nineteenth century confection of second-hand-book-shop, quiet-lane-in-small-town-near-London, June-morning, male-Bianca-for-hero — wherein human nature is seen as in a reading glass. Mr. Strong's manner of writing is polished and his imagery (as, for example, his address to a young lady that she " is like a bright flag flying in the breeze ") is of course measurably superior to the usual Broad-way imagery in a like situation —" your hair is like spun gold "; " your eyes are like stars in two mid-night pools "; et cetera — yet his characters seem but so many actors dressed up like Chauncey Olcott and in imminent danger of losing their sideburns.

Turning to the dramatization by Miss Edith Ellis of W. B. Maxwell's novel, " The Devil's Garden," the vacuity of what is locally regarded as constructive

criticism may be nicely appreciated.   Let us, accordingly and by way of illustration, criticize the play
thus " constructively ":

In the first place, allowing for the fact that the
Maxwell tome was a loudly overestimated mumbo-
jumbo, the dramatization, again allowing that the
novel possessed meat for the stage, failed of prosperity for various clearly definable reasons, the chief
of which was that the dramatist allowed the most
interesting elements of the novel's action to transpire
in the intermissions.

In the second place, the dramatist eliminated the
satyric Barradine, the most piquing protagonist of
the earlier evening, in her very first act.

In the third place (as I, in a misguided moment, have pointed out elsewhere), she showed
clearly in this same act that Mavis Dale was so
deeply in amorous thrall to her husband, so eager
again to regain his love, that even were Dale, immediately the curtain lifts upon Act II, to confess the
murder to her, he would be at once freely forgiven
and set at peace.   Thus, as early as nine o'clock, was
the audience robbed of any sense of future conflict.

In the fourth place, the character of Nora, the
young gypsy, and the personage of the play next in
interest to Barradine in the eyes of the audience,
was not disclosed in person until the third act and
then with so small a measure of preparation that the
compelling scene wherein the girl throws herself,

screaming for physical love, upon the throat of Dale, went for dramatically nothing.

In the fifth place, the events growing out of this scene, events in which the spectators had been made to become keenly interested, were not only not visualized, but almost entirely set aside by the dramatist as being of no value to the play's thematic evolution.

In the sixth place, the dramatist's comedy relief was a thing at once miss-fire and distinct from her story.

In the seventh place, the lapse of ten years between Acts II and III divided the manuscript into two separate plays but weakly bridged together.

In the eighth place, the minor characters such as Barradine and Nora were revealed by the dramatist as mediums of much more forceful and vital drama than the selected protagonists, husband Dale and wife.

In the ninth place, the dramatist, choosing Dale as her main protagonist, elected to play upon the man's struggle with his conscience when, Maxwell or no Maxwell, the man's struggle with his flesh disclosed itself, even in flashes of her own stage manuscript, to be thrice as dramaful.

In the tenth place . . .

But why continue?

Such widely practised and endorsed " constructive " criticism is so easy and, while so superficially plausible, reasonable and sound, yet at bottom so empty. For every such apparently tan-

gible argument against elements in this particular
play and for every such seemingly sound argument
accounting its failure and so working constructively
in behalf of future dramatic manuscripts of a like
species, I can summon up contradictory arguments
(also seemingly sound), together with concrete illustrations, which will not merely belie my initial arguments but which will probably prove the truth of the
reverse of them to the entire satisfaction of every
one concerned.

For example, I have pointed out Miss Ellis' generally granted mistake in having obliterated her most
interesting early-evening figure in her very first act.
Such an argument is pure critical flub-dub. Ibsen
did the same thing — and critic nor public has ever
found fault with him for it — in " Little Eyolf."

For example, I have noted, as have many of my
colleagues, that the dramatizer sprang the Nora-
Dale scene upon her audience suddenly and without
preparation and so caused it to miss its proper effect. Nonsense pure and simple. What of the un-
prepared-for scene between the thug and the Salvation Army girl in the second act of Shaw's " Major
Barbara," quite the most effective dramatic scene in
the whole play?

For example, as against the criticism of heavily
lugged-in comedy relief in itself largely distinct from
the play, what of the heavily lugged-in, equally distinct, but yet highly amusing comedy relief of Mr.
Broadhurst's successful " Bought and Paid For "?

For example, in controversion of the criticism that, through the lapse of ten years in the middle of her play, Miss Ellis deleted her manuscript of the necessary vital consecutiveness, consider a similar lapse (doubled and more indeed) in the matter of this consecutiveness in the prosperous Bennett-Knoblauch play " Milestones."   Consider, similarly, such plays as " Madame X " " Merely Mary Ann," et cetera.

So far as minor characters being figures more interesting (at least, while upon the stage) than the also present leading protagonists, cast an eye upon the waiter in " You Never Can Tell," the Mexican in " Arizona," the poet in " John Gabriel Borkman," the girl artist in " A Man's World," the Millie James character (you recall it, though I forget the name) in " Lover's Lane," the Bill Walker of " Major Barbara," the burglar in " A Gentleman of Leisure," Nutty Beamer in " Young America," a half dozen characters in Shakespeare. . .

As to the charge that the dramatizer reserved the most interesting elements of the novel for the intermissions, ponder upon the circumstance that the dramatizer of " Ben Hur " did the same thing — and made a fortune.

As to the perfectly apparent passion of mate for mate and the equally apparent readiness eventually to embrace the offender, no matter what he has done or does (with the attendant diminution of the booby spectator's sense of physical conflict and suspense as to the play's outcome) — turn to such box-office

belles as " The House of Glass," " The Family Cup-
board," et al.

And so with the rest of the blooms of such constructive analytical criticism. Whether addressed
to a question of art or to a question of popular success, criticism of this sort is not only valueless, but,
by virtue of the circumstance that it seeks to impose
upon drama a firm formula, a changeless set of rules
and regulations, deleterious. The simple truth
about such a play as " The Devil's Garden " is that
it failed (whether the view critical be from the point
(1) of sound merit or (2) financial popularity) because it was neither (1) mentally, nor (2) physically,
stimulating.

WHY SCHMIDT LEFT HOME

WERE Mr. George M. Cohan's farce-comedy "Broadway Jones" to be translated almost literally into French and presented in Paris as having been written by a German playwright and were then the hornswoggled reviewers for the Paris newspapers the next morning to observe that the play was at once a typical specimen of German humour and the work of an obvious rank amateur in matters appurtenant to the stage, one might perhaps permit oneself at least a homœopathic chuckle. Were an even more celebrated German's farce-comedy to be translated almost literally into English and presented in New York as having been written by a British playwright and were then the hornswoggled reviewers for the New York newspapers the next morning to observe that the play was at once a typical specimen of English humour and the work of an obvious rank amateur in matters appurtenant to the stage, one might permit oneself a snicker no less. This snicker, therefore, out of a magnanimous and an unselfish nature, let me now and here pass along.

Stolen deliberately and almost word for word from Lothar Schmidt's "Das Buch einer Frau"

155

(The Book of a Woman), as that piece was done four years ago in the Königgrätzerstrasse-Theatre of Berlin, there was produced not long ago in the Princess Theatre in New York City a play called " Such Is Life "— with the name of Harold Owen, an Englishman who collaborated in the writing of the melodrama " Mr. Wu," set down as sole author.   Save for such minor alterations as the substitution of an allusion to Edinburgh for one in the original manuscript to Hamburg and the giving of the characters British, in place of Teutonic, names, the Schmidt play and the play blithely presented by the Englishman as his own were identical.   The play divulged in the Princess Theatre, therefore, was — and I overstate the case in not the slightest degree — a typical German farce-comedy written by Schmidt who is one of the most popular, most widely known and most adroit playwrights in the modern German popular comic theatre.

Presently about fifty-three years old, Schmidt (whose plays are acted all over the Empire and its neighbour, Austria, and who has been translated onto the Russian stage and, in several instances, the stages of other European countries) belongs to that familiar group of comedy writers that includes such men as Rittner, Molnar, Otto Erler, Felix Salten, Sil Vara, Karl Ettlinger, Otto Ernst, Karl Rössler and Otto Gysae: a group which, while here and there many comedy pegs below the Thoma-Schnitzler-Bahr group, is still many rungs higher than that embracing such writers as Robert Faesi, Otto Schwartz, Paul Apel, Otto Soyka, Vosberg, Otto Falkenburg, Ludwig Bauer and Hans Müller, though the latter are witty fellows all of them. Among Schmidt's better-known pieces of farce-comedy writing, to recall a few to your notice, are " Die Venus mit dem Papagei " (Venus with the Parrot), " Nur Ein Traum " (Only a Dream), " Entgleisung " (Off the Rails), " Fiat Justitia," " Christiane " and the comedy which Mr. Owen has translated as " Such is Life," to wit, " The Book of a Woman." Further to establish the relative theatrical importance of Schmidt — and probably the simplest way in which to bring with conviction his popular Continental eminence to the local notice — it may be chronicled that he demands an exceptionally high royalty — a no less lofty revenue, indeed, than Bernard Shaw — which is to say, fifteen per cent. of the gross box-office takings, a rate noticeably above the customary five, seven-and-a-half and ten with which the attorney for the usual writer for the theatre is well satisfied.

So much for the facts. Keep a firm grasp upon them, if you please, while we proceed now to go 'round the curve.

Of this celebrated German comic writer and of his typical German farce-comedy, clumsily disguised as " ' *Such Is Life,*' *an English farce-comedy, by Mr. Harold Owen,*" what did my good fellow, M. De Foe of *The World,* find? Let us observe. Thus, M. De Foe (with Italics by the entire company) :

" Harold Owen, the English author of ' Such Is Life ' also wrote ' Mr. Wu '. . . . so it cannot be argued that he is wholly without experience in writing for the stage, *an inference naturally to be drawn from the tedious proceedings at the Princess Theatre . . . ' Such Is Life' . . . an English war-time comedy. . . . The author might possibly be at better advantage in writing narrative fiction.*"

And my good fellow, M. Broun, Hazlitt to *The Tribune,* what of M. Broun? Thus, *f. quanto possibile,* M. Broun: " The fact that such a play can achieve production should be most encouraging *to every young author.*"

And my good fellow, M. Darnton, Lewes to the *Evening World,* what of M. Darnton? Thus, *tepidamente,* M. Darnton — " feeble English comedy."

And my good fellow, M. Woollcott, Lamb to *The Times,* what of M. Woollcott? Thus, with punditic scowl, M. Woollcott — " mildly nonsensical bit of English humour."

That " The Book of a Woman " is, in fine truth, the least meritorious of all Schmidt's plays and that there is no particular disposition here to question the local appraisal of its worth, cannot avail to obscure the succulent give-away which my learned confrères, through the piece, achieved for themselves. So to mistake an intrinsically typical modern German comedy for an English comedy — the humours of the two nations are, of course, quite entirely different; so to imagine one of the leading popular comic writers of Germany " without experience in writing for the stage ": and so further to confuse

and disorder, confound and jumble, is surely a something to give one a crick in the upholstery.

"A critic," Huneker has written, "will never
be a catholic critic of his native literature or
art if he doesn't know the literatures and arts of
other lands. We lack æsthetic curiosity. Because
of our uncritical parochialism, America is compara-
ble to a cemetery of clichés." The " Such Is Life "
episode brings to mind the native critical obfuscation,
in like quarters, when two years ago Mr. Edward
Sheldon presented his dramatization of Hermann
Sudermann's novel " Das Hohe Lied " under the title
of " The Song of Songs." The local reviewers,
with two exceptions (both men of Continental training), seanced themselves into a spirituelle conclusion
that Sheldon had so gutted the German novel of its
philosophy that Sudermann, had he had the oppor-
tunity to see the dramatization, would never have
recognized it as having been made from his book.
When, as a matter of record, Sudermann had not
only seen the dramatization, but had expressed to
Sheldon his profound admiration for the faithful-
ness of the young American's work.

To proceed in the matter of the disguised Schmidt
comedy, the critical gentleman on the staff of *The
Dramatic Mirror,* on the other hand, saw in the play
" the smart *French* attitude towards love and marriage "— and so further contributed to the gaiety of
the guessing contest. The reasons for this general
critical confusion go, of course, very much further

back than " Such is Life ": they go back to the large
local fundamental unacquaintance with Continental
drama, its philosophies and humours, its viewpoints
and its technics.   The local criticism is, in the main,
builded upon traditions of such philosophies and humours, such viewpoints and technics — traditions frequently false — rather than upon the modern gos-
pels.   For example, what the average American
critic believes to be the modern French attitude in
comic writing is in reality the modern German attitude.   Schmidt's farce " Only a Dream " is an infinitely more " Frenchy " farce (from the American
point of view) than, for example, Sacha Guitry's
" Petite Hollande "— which (from the American
point of view) has to it a sort of German air.   Such
German comedies as the " Lottie's Birthday " of
Thoma and the " Little Prince " of Misch might
seem, to the American mind, to have been written respectively by the French Max Maurey and the
French collaborators Maurice Hennequin and Pierre
Veber; while such French pieces as Mirbeau's and
Natanson's " Le Foyer " might seem, to the same
mind, to have been written by a German of the school
of Wedekind — or at least of Turszinsky and
Jacques Burg.

What Frenchman of to-day has written a farce
with so Gallic a viewpoint (locally speaking) as the
" Blue Mouse " of the Germans Engel and Horst,
well remembered by American audiences; what German of to-day has written a farce with so German a

point of view (also speaking from the local plane) as the " Petite Fonctionnaire " of Alfred Capus? One speculates, indeed, into what category our critics would have put such a play as Anthony Wharton's " Irene Wycherley " had it been produced in New York under another title and signed with the name of a Norwegian playwright. Or what would happen were Björnson's " Geography and Love " put on next month in the Princess Theatre as " ' The Chart of Armour ' by François Deauville and August Düsseldorf " ?

The difference between the French attitude in matters of amour and the German attitude is to no little extent exactly the opposite of what is locally imagined. That is to say, the respective attitude of the *bon vivant,* the worldly fellow, the Heliogabalus of France and of Germany — and let it be remembered that it is with such sophisticated characters that the typical farce-comedy of both Paris and Berlin more often deals. (Or at least what may in each instance fairly be taken as the typical farce-comedy.) The Frenchman of this sort in his affairs of the heart has in him more of the Viennese than has the German: he is, for all that the Anglo-Saxon believes to the contrary, a highly sentimental and anything but light-hearted fellow. He loves in the moonlight, where the German loves in the sun. He coos his *je-vous-aimes* in the key of B flat, where his neighbour to the North laughs his *ich-liebe-dichs* in d f dd. The door-slamming, wardrobe-hiding, under-the-bed-diving French lover of the Anglo-Saxon notion is no more the French lover than the Irish Shaw's Blanco Posnet is an American cowboy. Nor, to point the fact more pertinently, is he the typical lover of typical French farce, as those who know their Rip and Bousquet, their De Flers and De Caillavet, their Romain Coolus, their Bernard and Athis, their Sacha Guitry (in his more recent years) and their Benière properly appreciate. He is no more typical of the French lover or of modern French farce as Frenchmen know it than an American society man by the late Paul Armstrong was typical of an American society man — or than the Italian Bracco's " Comptesse Coquette " is typical of Italian farce, or the British Pinero's " Wife Without a Smile " is typical of British farce, or the German Blumenthal and Kadelburg's " Is Matrimony a Failure? " is typical of German farce, or the French Desvallières and Mars' " Never Again " is typical of French farce, or the American Hatch and Homans' " Blue Envelope " is typical of American farce.

When the domestic thinkers speak of typical French farce and the typical viewpoint of such farce they speak of the typical French farce and viewpoint not of to-day nor of yesterday, but of twenty and twenty-five years ago. *Tempora mutantur* — and farce and viewpoint, messieurs, change with them. The modern German viewpoint in love matters is the French viewpoint of twenty and thirty years ago;

the modern French viewpoint (I speak, of course, as life is reflected in the respective dramatic mirrors) is the German viewpoint of day before yesterday. The German beau has dressed his heart in lingerie; the French beau his in medicated flannels.

As to what is locally regarded as typical English humour. Judging from the reviews of " Such is Life," the local estimate of typical English humour as being largely a matter of obvious puns is derived in the main from animadversions upon the subject in *Puck, Judge* and our other uncomic papers. The pun, of course, as students of international humour know, is less typical of modern English humour than of modern German humour. The pun is the chief weapon of the modern German Tingel-Tangel, or cabaret, as it is of the modern German music show libretto and, in many instances, of second-grade farce. (The French, too, are theatrically much more taken with punning than the English: the Paris revues, libretti and short farce pieces are full of plays on words.) Several years ago, when the farce " Mon Ami Teddy" was translated into German and exhibited in Berlin, the German translator laboriously edged fully half a dozen exotic puns into the manuscript and gained thereby from his German audience fully half a dozen extra chuckles.

The modern English stage piece is free from punning: the English have long since lost their palate, it would seem, for such patent jocosities. Is there, for example, so much as a single pun in the rank and

file of the British farces and comedies of Pinero or
of Hubert Henry Davies or of Shaw or of Henry
Arthur Jones or of Barrie or of Maugham or of
Jerome or of Roy Horniman or of Cicely Hamilton
or of Anstey or of Sutro or of Besier or of Arnold
Bennet or of Maurice Baring or Keble Howard or
Gertrude Jennings or R. C. Carton or Cyril Harcourt or Bernard Fagan or George Rollit or Anthony Wharton or Horace Annesley Vachell or of
any other such British playwright, important or unimportant? In six years of playhouse rounds in
London, I heard but three puns, two in shows at the
Alhambra, the third in a musical comedy at the
Adelphi. And in many more years of reading, I
have encountered less than eight or ten puns, at the
most, in British play manuscripts. Nor is the typical English humour of Wells and Chesterton, to
speak beyond the theatre, any more a humour of
puns than the typical English humour of W. W.
Jacobs and Neil Lyons — or the typical (and excellent) English humour of *The Sketch* and *The Tat-
ler, Punch* and *Tit-Bits* and *London Opinion.* The
typical English humour, contrary to being a thing
for specious mock, is of a high order. The English, above the Germans and the French, it is interesting parenthetically to note, have produced by all
odds the best humour out of the grim materials of
the present war.

I regret that I have no more leisure to waste
wherein further to illuminate the darkness of the

local Hazlittry as that darkness cast its shadows upon the Lothar Schmidt play and the qualities which that play brought under the notice of the intramural criticism.

The simple truth about the play was probably this: (1) It was, true enough, not a good play though even had it been a good play it would not have been susceptible of proper enactment by the English actors assigned to its interpretation, for English actors can no more play German farce than American actors can play French farce or German actors American farce. Just as the American actor lacks the deftness and polish for French farce and as the German actor lacks the speed and brashness for American farce, so is the English actor deficient in the gusto and stomach essential to German farce.

And (2) the first act was played in high lights (afternoon) where it was plainly necessary to its effectiveness that it be played, as originally, by the lamplight of evening (the humour of the transparent door episode was otherwise lost entirely).

And (3), Mr. Owen garbled amateurishly the translation of two of the wittiest passages in the Schmidt manuscript.

And (4), the play, a moderately quick farce, was interpreted in the tempo of Stephen Phillips' "Herod."

And (5), the actors were, with the exception of Mr. Gottschalk, so very bad anyway that they would have ruined any play.

II

Coleridge observed that the true stage illusion as,
for instance, to a forest scene, consists not in the
mind's judging it to be a forest, but in the mind's
remission of the judgment that it is not a forest.
The true stage illusion as to melodrama consists not
in the mind's engaging with it as drama holding the
mirror up to nature, but rather as nature holding
the mirror up to drama.

Properly to place oneself in a receptive mood before a melodrama, it is essential that the mind be
cajoled into surrendering for the time being its sense
of comedy.   Otherwise, of what avail or plausibility such effective melodrama climaxes as that of the
Guignol's " Vers La Lumière," in which an English
officer sinks to death in a bed of quicksand over
which, but a moment or two before, the villain has
airily promenaded in safety?   The melodramatic
mind must believe temporarily in Santa Claus, in
ghosts, in the theory that a woman's wit is ever superior to a man's, in the notion that all noble fellows,
great lovers and valiant heroes in real life are
Irishmen, in the theory that murder is never com-
mitted anywhere save in a darkened room (prefer-
ably a library), and that children are always kid-
napped during thunderstorms.

With the mind so persuaded, Mr. Bayard Veiller's melo-piece, " The Thirteenth Chair," provides
a lively theatrical evening.   Writing after the for-

mula practised auspiciously in the Rue Chaptal, the
author has contrived as good a show of its kind as
was his eminently successful " Within The Law."
This Veiller, indeed, would seem to be the most
adroit fellow in the matter of melodramatic stage
trickeries since the expert William Gillette. Like
the clever band of Frenchmen who compose melodramatic pieces for the playhouse of Maurey —
such men as André De Lorde, Serge Basset, Lèon
Marchès and Gaston Richard, Eugène Morel, Elie
de Bassan and the like — Mr. Veiller is a sufficiently
penetrating physician to the mob spine to appreciate the larger modern theatrical value of tricky
" props " over the botanical oratory favourite of the
melodramatic yesterdays. Two of his most effective
stage moments in his latest piece follow the recipés
practised respectively at the Guignol four years
ago by François de Nion in " La Matérialisation de
Miss Murray " and a couple of years before that by
Robert Francheville in " La Porte Close ". . . .
The door that slowly and mysteriously opens, apparently without human agency, is a device that
never fails on the melodrama stage.

So intriguing is the major portion of Mr. Veiller's melo-piece that it seems something for regret
he did not exercise the precaution to spare his audience its present final disappointment over the dubious legerdemain with which he solves his plot. The
ease with which the presently confusing elements
might have been explained away to the satisfaction

of the skeptic yokel is quite obvious, even to one like myself whose trade lies far removed from play-making. The spiritualistic medium, Mr. Veiller's central character, confesses throughout the earlier portion of the melodrama that she is able easily to deceive her clients by more or less simple stratagems. When, however, at the play's climax the medium is called upon to compel the villain to confess to the murder, her (and Mr. Veiller's) ingenuity fails and, to the sad let-down of the play, she abjures chicanery and trusts for assistance, with much pathos via the face muscles, to God and the spirits.

Now while what follows is all very reassuring to the faithful, it comes as something of qualm to the other nine-tenths of the audience. This qualm might have been prevented — and most readily — had the author merely caused the medium, previous to entering into her final trance, to whisper an in-audible something to the young hero and then caused the young hero, whose presence in the scene is not needed, to leave the stage. This would suffice again to plant trickery in the audience's mind and yet not diminish in the least the present suspense of the situation. And when then the door opens mys-teriously and when then the knife tumbles from the ceiling the audience might be spared its present skep-ticism as to the spirit *flon-flon* and convinced to the greater prosperity of the ticket rack that a human hand (or a black thread) had had something to do with the currently unconvincing door-opening and that the butler, rather than Little Laughing Eyes, had stamped on the floor above and so dislodged the dagger.

These are, one appreciates, trivial things for the critic to treat of, but one is speaking here less of drama and dramatic literature than of the show-shop. And Mr. Veiller's melodrama as it stands, with half its motivation entrusted to Kellar and the other half to Providence, is, while a very good show despite its last act wabbles, still a trifle like kissing a girl who has been eating onions. To make the kiss pass for nectar, the man must also eat onions. A Hermann the Great, after entertaining his audience and gaining its rapt and willing attention for two hours, could not well hope to retain that audience's favour were he suddenly to turn down his sleeves and begin acting a scene from "The Servant in the House." That, briefly, is what Mr. Veiller has attempted. Yet, on the theory that a palatable dinner is not entirely to be spoiled by a leaky demitasse, "The Thirteenth Chair" is probably certain to satisfy the majority of its partakers. It is as greatly superior as theatrical entertainment to the late Richard Harding Davis' "Vera, the Medium," as it is inferior to Chesterton's "Magic."

THE DRAMATIC CRITIC AND THE
UNDRAMATIC THEATRE

IN the several seasons theatrical passing now
into history, no more droll entertainment has
been vouchsafed the people than the vehement
resuscitation of the ancient repartee as to the status
in the playhouse of the dramatic critic. In the badi-
nage, almost every one from Mr. Abraham Erlanger
down to the Court of Appeals has participated, and
the net result has been, if not entirely convincing, at
least provocative of a wholesome and genuine amusement.

Not the least chic feature of the enterprise has
been the perfectly straight face with which the parties on both sides of the fence have gone about the
discussion: though one must of course allow that
farce is thus best conducted. And not the least wistful feature of the business has been the balmy ignorance with which both sides have issued their respective most flooring grunts — to say nothing of
the attendant inconsequences. In an attempt to
bring light out of chaos, let us therefore endeavour
to engage the question with an eye cool and impar-
tial.

This question, despite the gaudy bosh with which

it has been enveloped by the parties thereto, whether
managerial or critical, is, at the bottom, one of ab-
surdly facile decipherment. Stripped of its fine
feathers and obscuring indignations, it presents itself, quite nude, as merely this: Is there a place on
Broadway for dramatic criticism? The reply to
which simple question, equally simple, is: No.
And the seeming assumption on the part of a number
of our managers that there is, in their theatres, a
place for such criticism is, to say the least, in view of
the circumstances not wholly unimpudent.

I speak, of course, of criticism, not of mere journalistic reporting. That there should be no place
in these or any other theatres for mere journalistic
reporting is altogether too clear to every one (save
possibly the editors of the newspapers) here to require argument. To report the result of a first
night performance, particularly on Broadway, is to
report a murder in terms of the flowers placed by
relatives on the deceased's coffin.

Every such first night is a bouncing success. The
sedulously trained usher claque, the passionate am-
bassadors from the Lambs' Club, the actors and
actresses out of work who have got in free and who,
either because they feel applause is therefore ex-
pected of them or because they once acted with one
of the actors and, though feeling him a shrimp in the
art, yet deem it but in accord with the corps colours
that they lustily clap him,— these go to constitute
what must by the honest reporter be termed " an

enthusiastic audience." I have been going professionally to the theatre in New York for more than twelve years and I tell but the simple truth when I say that in all that time I have, with but a single exception, never once attended the opening of any play, however bad, whereat the congregation was not clamorously encomiastic. To report premières by such tokens is, therefore, to report so many corpulent fabrications. And not to report première performances by such tokens is to take a step toward decent dramatic criticism. And to take such a step toward decent dramatic criticism is to make oneself, as I shall attempt to show, even more inappropriate and exotic to the surroundings.

Mr. Clayton Hamilton, who is a married man and consequently has much more time to figure out such things than I have, has deduced that, in a Broadway season, but one play in every twenty-three is worth even a portion of afterthought and that, so, " a person of intelligence and taste who casually takes a chance on going to a play is likely, twenty-two times out of twenty-three, to have his intelligence insulted and his taste offended." Allowing for Mr. Hamilton's somewhat overly elaborate bull-fiddlings upon the words " intelligence " and " taste," the substance of his findings remains still intact and of an infectious probity. In the last half dozen years, I doubt if there have been more than five or six plays out of all the many hundred-odd presented in each season that have merited approach by the

critic seriously interested in drama. The rest?
Trick melodramas, fussy farces, mob mush, leg
shows. A few of them amiable enough pastime
— as kissing the maid or becoming wistfully al-
coholic is amiable pastime — but certainly not approaching to an art calling for sober thought and
criticism. Where there is no art, there is no call
for criticism. It is as ridiculous to write criticism
of a drama by Mr. George V. Hobart as it is to
write criticism of the moving pictures. (The latter
are the result of a circumspect elimination of the
principal attributes of four of the arts and a clever
synthesis of the scum: they have removed style from
literature, speech from drama, colour from paint-
ing, form and the third dimension from sculpture.)
The theatre managers are, therefore, so far as
I am able to make out, not only clearly justified,
but absolutely merciful, in barring critics from their
houses if so they choose. Why a hard-working,
obtuse manager with a wife and several children and
a chorus girl to support, should have his livelihood
imperilled by a dramatic critic who, however otherwise well-educated and well-trained, probably doesn't
know whether the sound of galloping horses is re-
produced by hollow cocoanuts or scooped-out can-
teloupe, is a problem to confound any fair-minded
man. The manager is, self-confessedly, a trades-
man. Why I, or any other critic, should be permitted by him to chase away his customers is no
clearer to me than why the same manager, or any

other manager, should be permitted by me to hang around the newsstands and chase away prospective buyers from the newsstand impresarios of publications containing my criticisms — of the manager.

The manager whose stage is quite frankly given over to yokel-yankers should promptly invite all critics out of his theatre. But no. What actually does he do? He bids the critic sit upon his article, having so insinuated in advance to the critic that the aforesaid article is a drama worthy of the critic's consideration, and then, when subsequently the critic tells the truth about the article, he froths at the mouth, sputters, writes letters to the landlord of the critic's gazette and bids the critic thenceforth begone from his show-house gate. I personally have enjoyed such romantic adventures, even as have numerous of my colleagues. Several years ago, you will recall, I was invited by the management of the institution to write my impressions of the Princess Theatre as an American Antoine *et* Guignol. I wrote them. Promptly the management responded with an emotional brochure to my friend and financial manager, Mr. John Adams Thayer. Having derived a good belly-laugh out of the *papier*, Thayer, being an unselfish fellow, despatched it by Roscoe, the office lad, to my chambers that I, too, might profit of its mirth. And I, being not less of generous heart, subsequently printed the libretto for the delectation of my readers. I had written merely what seemed to me to be wrong with the conduct of the Princess stage, an opinion not long afterward substantiated by the sudden explosion of the enterprise, a stupid and unnecessary failure. Hence the pardonable questions: (1) Why was I, a professional critic, invited to write the truth about the Princess Theatre and (2) why, when I did so, did my hosts seek to take me to task?

Last year, upon being invited by a manager to review a performance by Miss Phyllis Neilson-Terry and to record my impressions of the lady's talents, I wrote (having already observed the lady's antics through an half dozen London seasons) that the lady in point was a fourth-rate performer and one quite apparently maladroit and rudderless. Whereupon the manager, his illusions evidently somewhat annoyed, invited me into his auditoriums no more. Until a recent month, that is. Again was I bidden, why I know not, to inspect the workings of the same fourth-rate actress in a piece called " The Great Pursuit "— and again, in all honesty, I found the fourth-rate actress to be quite as convincingly fourth-rate as she was the season before and the seasons before that. And (belated 'tis true) the majority of my colleagues found — and wrote — the very same thing. The question that currently disturbs my slumbers is, therefore, this: Will the manager now exclude me from his auditoriums once again — and with me, the majority of my colleagues — or will he hie himself into an umbilicular contemplation and doze to the conclusion, albeit mayhap reluctant,

that when I wrote the original criticism which earned
his ill will, I wrote simply what at the time seemed
to me an eminently well-studied, careful and equita-
ble opinion — although, alas and unfortunately, a
not sweet one — that my motive was merely the
usual and incomplex motive of serving, as best I
humbly may, the causes of a respectable American
stage and its drama, and that, had he at the time
viewed me possibly less as a Villista or Hohenzol-
lern and more as a favourer who was trying to help
him and by helping him, so too the producing theatre
to which he is a party, he might not only have rid
our stage of another hypocritically glozed British
facemaker, but also — and this will indubitably
capture him with a more benign magnetism — might
have saved himself a lot of money?

Hall Caine's cheap melodrama, " Margaret
Schiller," produced in the New Amsterdam Theatre
by the Messrs. Klaw and Erlanger, elicited, almost
without exception, the combined and deserved snick-
ery of the reviewers. And, shortly afterward, its
withdrawal was made necessary. Yet what the
attitude of Mr. Erlanger toward the very critics
he had invited to express an opinion on the piece?
I have been privileged a glance at one of the gentleman's *billets-doux*, addressed to the proprietor of
the journal of one of the critics, and I quote there-
from a sentiment : " Hall Caine is one of the greatest writers living, and who is (naming the critic)
to say he isn't? (Again naming the critic) ought

to stop criticizing and go to sweeping up the streets!" Need I go on? What chance in our theatre does dramatic criticism of an intelligent gender or drama stand with such an attitude behind it?

Yet assuredly such a species of criticism should have a place in our theatre. God knows, our theatre needs it! What of a theatre in which the leading manager believes — and doubtless honestly — that Hall Caine is a great writer? What of a theatre whose dean of playwrights, so regarded and hailed, cabbages without credit a tale of Guy de Maupassant and exploits it as his own under the caption of " Rio Grande "? What of a theatre whose leading actress, so proclaimed, is accorded that rank and the added laurel of intellectuality by virtue of the fact that she cartoons her almost every comedy rôle and declines to submerge this great and aloof intellectual personality of hers in her almost every dramatic rôle — an actress who, in any other country under the civilized sun, would be named a caricaturist? What of a theatre whose leading histrionic guest at and celebrant of the late Shakespearean festival displays his critical powers thus in a volume called " Thoughts and After-Thoughts ": " I contend that ' Henry VIII ' is not a symbolic play!" And thus: " As, however, this play (Maeterlinck's ' Les Aveugles ') contains thirteen characters, of which twelve are blind, it would be superfluous to discuss it as an acting drama!" I reveal but two sample gems.

The truth of the matter, however, is that, to a not inconsiderable degree, the American theatre has taken its place alongside the honk-a-tonk, the cabaret, the Midway Plaisance. Where, now, its one time dignity, its importance? Once — and not so long ago — a place of amusement, recreation and stimulation for ladies and gentlemen, it has, with a few noteworthy exceptions, become a sort of stamping-ground for the culling of membership to Broadway dancing clubs, a place of labour for moving picture actors temporarily out of work, a clearing-house for the lack-lustre dramatic imaginings of hack novelette writers and ex-actors. The charm that was the theatre, even ten years ago, where is it now? Small wonder such a critic as Huneker could not be dragged into a theatre to-day with a team of oxen or the promise of a quart of Pilsner!

And so I say that, under the circumstances, the present-day manager is not only astute, but entirely justified, in his barring of this or that possibly somewhat too intelligent commentator from his theatre. True, such barring would still leave a sufficient supply of critics on the job, at least in New York; but perfection is a part of few schemes.

Mr. William A. Brady, a vastly more perspicacious fellow than some like to believe, not long ago remarked that he himself did not understand why people longer give a continental about the theatre as we have it on Broadway. Mr. Winthrop Ames, rather than assist in the further corruption of the national taste by producing more of the Broadway slopdramaturgy, when nothing really good presented itself to him preferred to keep his theatre dark throughout an entire season. Mr. John D. Williams, sickened by the pish put out on the Broadway stages week in and week out, put on Galsworthy's " Justice " in order, as he expressed it, that he might personally enjoy at least one respectable piece of dramatic writing before the year ended. And after Williams had dug down into his own pocket and got the play ready for production, it was only after great difficulty (he believed for a time he would have to abandon the enterprise altogether) that he could obtain a New York theatre for its exhibition. " The public don't want such gloomy stuff," observed the stenographers who had been sent to Baltimore by the Messrs. Dillingham, *et al.,* to report on the play; and it was only the sympathy of Messrs. Cohan and Harris that stood between the Galsworthy drama and the storehouse. Mr. George Tyler said, less than three-quarters of a year ago, that never in the history of the American theatre has public taste been at anything like the low ebb it is at present. " And never, as a consequence," he continued, " has the general grade of dramatic fare been of so mean a calibre. The reason is not far to seek, for there are to-day a mere handful of managers and producers who are interested in the theatre, who love the theatre, who respect the theatre. It was not so in other days. True enough, a man-

ager may love the theatre and have, at the same
time, a respectable eye to the box-office.   But to-day,
with a few exceptions, a manager's love never gets
nearer the theatre as an institution than the sill
across which his treasurer sells tickets — to Tyson."

There are managers and there are managers.   It
never has been and probably never will be necessary for the Bradys, the Ameses, the Williamses, the
Hopkinses, the Cohans and Harrises and the Tylers
to go officially into the critic-barring business.

And yet — let us be fair — there are occasions
when even such managers as these would be doing
the drama a pretty service were they to exclude from
certain of their representations critics (albeit fellows intelligent, honest and discerning so far as they
go) of a grown exceeding common species.   I allude
again, of course, to the type of critic of the school
headed by the late Mr. William Winter, the critic
who regards and appraises every dramatic offering,
however intrinsically with or without merit, from the
plane of a provincial morality.   Had I been Mr.
A. H. Woods, I should have excluded from my
theatre, upon my presentation of Mr. Sheldon's admirable dramatization of Sudermann's " Song of
Songs," at least two metropolitan professional play
reviewers who are notoriously infected with an ob-
streperous blue-nosed hostility to any play that
voices a philosophy of life more daring than that
of " The Cinderella Man."   Such critics are a men-
ace not only to the manager, but to the public.   And

so, too, might my sympathies have been found with the Shuberts when their presentation of a clever Viennese satiric farce comedy — already greatly tamed in adaptation — was denounced by several of my horrified spinster colleagues on grounds of a shoddy Anglo-Ohio morality. Not indecent, mind! That is, patently, a considerably different thing. Had I been in the Messrs. Shuberts' place, such putz-pomade dispensers would henceforth have been promptly disbarred.

To return, momentarily, then, to dramatic criticism.

The theory, favourite of theatrical managers, actors and a certain species of playwright, that criticism should ever, even when of soundly adverse content, be of gentle and ladylike mien, is nonsense pure and simple. To accomplish its end, criticism, when seeking to correct an evil, should and must be hard, unflinching. To inject an alloy of honeysuckle into such criticism is but to inject into it personal feeling. It is not necessary or fitting that the surgeon, knife ready, first kiss his lady patient, however much the lady patient may be reassured by the act.

And not merely is this true in the case of dramatic criticism; it is even truer in the commoner appraisal of purely theatrical materials. Such an actor, for example, as the one in a recent exhibit who pronounced it " seckatary " should be consigned promptly to the firing squad. No additional evidence of the fellow's treachery should be required.

Any one so incompetent in his profession as to be guilty of so unsightly a misdemeanor, however intrinsically trivial, should expect small consideration.

True enough, such duties are not altogether pleasant. It is a not particularly jolly profession which calls upon its practitioner to prick the artistic pretences of gentlemen who, outside their labours, are doubtless excellent and convivial souls, and of ladies who, outside their stage antickings, are doubtless good wives and mothers. But the critic has naught to do with such meditations. I myself, for example, am personally not at all a bad sort of fellow. Yet having on one occasion published a book which failed to satisfy my own critical demands, I felt honestly compelled to write and print (under a pseudonym) a criticism of both the book and myself, the which perfectly just criticism, upon subsequent reading, impressed me as exceedingly harsh and unfriendly — if not, indeed, positively vicious.

AMERICA'S MOST INTELLECTUAL
ACTRESS

BY pursuing to no little degree the pattern of the Duke in Chesterton's play "Magic" ("Speaking of the Magna Carta," the Duke would say, "just look at Vegetarianism!"), it has come about that Mrs. Minnie Maddern Fiske has established herself, among all the ladies on the American stage, as the leader in thought, the first in intellectual endowments and deliberative attainments. Like the Duke, it has long been the custom of Mrs. Fiske when approached with a question as to her opinion on, let us for example say, the quality of Hermann Heijermans' play, "Op Hoop van Zegen," to lift an eyebrow and observe, "Ah yes, my friend, Hermann Heijermans' play, 'Op Hoop van Zegen'— just look at that poor horse being beaten by that cruel beer-wagon driver!" And while it may be true that a rude fellow here and there has professed to detect no particular connection between such philosophies and a vigorous intellectual drive, the fact remains that by the parties to the American theatre and by nine-tenths of the American public generally, their fair exponent is held in veneration as one of the first minds of the native stage, one of the native stage's most museful students, and, in finality, the native stage's one and only real female intelligence.

News of Mrs. Fiske's stunning mentality and penetration came first to my ears, I recall, in the long ago years when I was yet a youngster in kilts and bangs: the long ago years of Allen and Ginter's cigarette pictures of Pauline Hall in tights, of homeric gumdrops that cost a penny and might, before eating, be bounced up and down on the end of a long rubber, of the mysterious and carefully hidden "Bel Ami" in the paper covers with the picture of the handsome Lothario in evening clothes leaning over and kissing the languorous hussy on the shoulder-blade — the long ago years when the conductors on the horse cars always wore in their lapels a small pink rose made of celluloid.

As I say, it was in these remote days that first I was apprised of the Fiske acumen, of the Fiske brain manifestations and phenomena. And so, growing up, there followed me through adolescence and into my maturer years a great awe for this astounding theatrical cerebralist, and an even greater awe for the thoughts and ideas that were held to emanate from the dorsal side of her cerebrospinal axis just behind the corpora quadrigemina. Quite true, time and again after I had arrived at the advanced age where it was no longer necessary for the professor to put Mrs. Rorer's Cook Book on the piano stool that I might reach the keyboard, a gipsy doubt, a cruel suspicion, was wont to assail me and bid me pause. But search assiduously as I would through Lorillard Spencer's *Illustrated American, The Criterion,* and kindred periodicals of the day, nothing could I find to disprove the Fiske mental estate. Quite true also, neither could I find anything to prove it, but said I to myself there is doubtless no need to prove it: it is no doubt so self-evident that it needs no proving — like the fact that two plus two equals four or that the earth is round or that a straight line is the shortest distance between two points or that F. Marion Crawford's " Saracenesca " was a great novel to press four-leaf clovers in.

Did I essay to discover in this gazette or that a dazzling opinion from the profound Fiske on art, the drama, literature, what not, did my investigation prove fruitless. Not a syllable, not a word, had the lady written or spoken for publication. I asked questions. Mrs. Fiske, they told me loftily, never gives interviews; she never expresses opinions; she is a dignified actress, a great intellect. But, I wanted out of silly boyish curiosity to know, how then does any one know she is a great intellect? This question, I discovered, carried with it what was regarded as a measure of impertinence and ill-breeding and was, like the question on grandma's false teeth and the symbolism of the staircase business in " Sapho," a cue for the application of a hair brush to a ludicrously unrelated portion of the anatomy. As

I grew a bit older, I was informed on many subjects
that had been to me mysteries: my parents explained
to me that babies really didn't, as I had supposed,
grow in cabbages, that the world really wasn't coming to an end when it got suddenly dark out-of-
doors, that if I was sick or tired and didn't feel like
saying my prayers it was quite all right as there
wasn't any God anyway — and all that sort of thing.
But there were no parents, there was no Wedekind
in the neighbourhood, there was no one to enlighten
me in the pesky Fiske logogriph.

And so the years passed. At the age of seventeen, thirsting still for a drink of wisdom from the
deep Fiske fount, I contrived by dint of great enterprise to learn that Mrs. Fiske loved dumb animals.
Ha, methought, at last a bit of light, a scent, a token.
I would now, at least, learn what the celebrated
thinker thought about animals. Perchance, here
was a new theory of biological evolution, mayhap a
new Darwin! I pursued the clue relentlessly, un-
remittingly. And, lo, five years later, at the age of
twenty-two, I learned — what? From a copy of the
New York *Herald*, a newspaper of those days, the
astonishing philosophy that Mrs. Fiske had said the
day before that she believed a teamster who failed
to equip his horses with spiked shoes for slippery
pavements should be either heavily fined or sent to
jail!

But did my allusions die? Nay, nay. I bided my
time. This, I reckoned, this love for dumb animals,

might after all be only a sideline, a temperamental
fillip, an artist's idiosyncrasy, and in the lady doubtless there was treasured still great wisdom of the
quality I had heard tell in my childhood. I sub-
scribed to a clipping bureau. Several years later,
I received a clipping. It was headed, " Mrs. Fiske
on Ibsen." At last! I cried. The silence had been
broken! The oracle was about to speak! The
pearls were about to be cast! I read. A press-
agent's story of two or three sticks in which the only
words credited to Mrs. Fiske were these jewels:
" Ibsen is a wonderful dramatist. His characters
live. His plays will live for all time. They are
classics." . . . When I recovered, the nurse was
bending over me and assuring me that if I took my
medicine regularly I should be out in about four days.

More years went the way of years. And coming
into manhood I heard still on all sides of me and
read still in the many public prints of America's
great intellectual actress. But though my explora-
tions were still indefatigable and nothing if not sed-
ulous, nothing could I contrive to excavate that
might show just why the good lady was so regarded,
that might disclose her ideas on this subject or that,
that might reveal her philosophical attitude toward
life or art or morals, or, indeed, anything save that
S. P. C. A. was a worthy organization and that it
was cold-hearted to make a horse work when it was
suffering from diabetes and incipient blind staggers.
Subsequently, with the coming into general use of au-

tomobiles, even the lady's latter philosophies appeared no longer in the prints — and all was darkness. Until recently —

Now at length, after the impenetrable silence of years, has the foremost intellectual actress of the American stage deigned to impart to the public a few of the choicest secrets of her brain. These inmost secrets, into which we shall presently inquire, have been whispered to our ears through the medium of the pages of the *Century Magazine,* and they represent presumably, in the mass, the great lady's carefully treasured and until now withheld theatrical *esthetik,* philosophies and poultices. What the amazing nature of these ideas? Their eye-opening revolutionary bulk? Their crack and snap, bite and sparkle, force and sharpness? Let us see.

No. 1. An article entitled " Mrs. Fiske Punctures the Repertory Idea." Great Thought No. 1 in Article No. 1: " Bosh! Do not talk to me about the repertory idea. It is an outworn, needless, impossible, *harmful* scheme."

Possible answer to Mrs. Fiske's Great Thought No. 1, Article No. 1: (*a*) the repertory idea brilliantly worked out by the National Theatre in Stockholm, Sweden; (*b*) the repertory idea brilliantly worked out by the Comédie Française under Perrin and Claretie and by the Odéon under Antoine; (*c*) the repertory idea brilliantly worked out by Mrs. Horniman in her Manchester theatre; (*d*) the repertory idea brilliantly worked out in the Abbey

Theatre, Dublin; (*e*) the repertory idea brilliantly
worked out in the Berlin Hoftheater under Lindau,
in the Lessing-Theater under Brahm, in the Schiller-
Theater under Löwenfeld, in the people's theatres
of Hamburg, Cologne, Düsseldorf and a half dozen
other German provincial cities; (*f*) the repertory
idea brilliantly worked out in the Michel Theatre
of Petrograd and in the Moscow Artistic Theatre
under Stanislawsky and Dantschenko; (*g*) the repertory idea brilliantly worked out in the Teatro Espa-
ñol of Madrid under Fernando de Mendoza.

Possible catechism for Mrs. Fiske in relation to
Great Thought 1, Article 1: (*a*) Just how has
the repertory idea been harmful in the above instances?; (*b*) needless?; (*c*) impossible?; (*d*)
Name one non-repertory theatre more successful, artistically or commercially; (*e*) Name one non-repertory theatre *as* successful, artistically or commercially.

Possible reasons for Mrs. Fiske's inability to reply satisfactorily to inquiries relating to Great
Thought 1, Article 1: (*a*) Mrs. Fiske judges the
repertory idea entirely from its several Anglo-Saxon
failures, brought about by incompetent planning and
careless extrinsic and intrinsic direction; (*b*) Mrs.
Fiske argues " This is an age of specialization, and
in such an age the repertory theatre is a ludicrous
anachronism," Mrs. Fiske thus showing that she
somewhat curiously believes art to be measured by
and predicated upon the whims and mandates of a

particular age or time — that this being an age of specialization in prose drama, the poetic drama of Shakespeare is therefore ludicrously anachronistic — that the specialization of Mrs. Fiske in the instance of such a play as " The High Road " and in the production and ensemble enactment of that play was less an anachronism than, a greater artistic feat than, and one-tenth as enjoyable an exhibit as, any one of the plays produced a year ago by the repertory company of Miss Grace George.

Personally, I agree thoroughly with Mrs. Fiske that there is much to be said against the repertory system. What I am endeavouring here to bring out, however, is that the arguments (or more accurately, the mere grunts) which the dear intellectual lady lodges against the repertory system are the weakest and silliest sort of arguments — that her surface opinions may be basically sound, but that the reasons she exhibits in support of these surface opinions are no reasons at all.

In further instance of the manner in which Mrs. Fiske argues against the repertory idea, we find her observing, with the air of one who has just fetched a climacteric wallop, that one of the finest arguments against the idea was to be had in the success of Mr. Barker's repertory company at Wallack's with " Androcles " and its subsequent failure with " The Doctor's Dilemma " due to the inability of two actors in the company, who had done well in the former play, to interpret satisfactorily the rôles to which

they were assigned in the latter! Imagine the condemnation of a whole system — of the entire repertory idea the world over — in terms of the failure
in a single play of a couple of actors — one of whom,
Miss Lillah McCarthy, is, to boot, acknowledged to
be as inferior a performer as the English-speaking
stage is blessed with. One might as well, and with
an equal infatuation, use as an argument against the
whole system of specialization in the theatre the
wretchedly cast and enacted "Morris Dance,"
which this same Mr. Barker produced independ-
ently of any repertory scheme.

"What may be good for France or Germany,"
agrees presently the lady, still speaking of the repertory idea and side-stepping friskily, "is not neces-
sarily good for us Americans. The repertory idea
is more feasible in a country where a long-developed
art sense is stronger among the playgoers, who can
thereby discard what is bad and recognize immediately what is good." Here we engaged some difficult plumbing. Mrs. Fiske has already argued with
great eloquence that the repertory idea is (1) bosh,
(2) outworn, (3) needless, (4) impossible, and
(5) harmful (the latter italicized), but is now beheld donning a gas mask, pirouetting on one toe
and arguing lucidly (1) that, inasmuch as the repertoire idea is bosh, outworn, needless, etc., etc., it is
feasible only in civilized theatrical communities, (2)
that, since it is feasible only in countries where a
long-developed art sense is strong, the repertory

idea is therefore harmful; and (3) that it is an impossible and needless idea because the American playgoing public is not up to it.

One grows dizzy, so vivid and sharp is the logic. The argument is of a piece with a contention that anything which is above the grasp of a group of Cheap Jacks and numskulls is by virtue and because of this fact at once a thing of bosh, and needless, outworn, impossible of execution, and harmful. The repertory idea therefore takes its place, in the mind of our good lady, with such analogously needless, outworn, impossible and harmful bosh as the art of Cézanne, the music of Dvořák, the drama of François de Curel, the satire of Anatole France and of Ludwig Thoma, the poetry of Hugo von Hofmannsthal and the prose literature of Anton Tchekhov. In the Fiske philosophy, we find, indeed, nothing less than an apotheosis of the drama of Helen R. Martin over the drama of Jean Baptiste Poquelin, the art of Penrhyn Stanlaws over the art of Antonio Correggio, the science of Doctor Grindle over that of Doctor Loeb, and the musical performance of the Jazz band in Reisenweber's restaurant over that of the Boston Symphony orchestra. . . . Had Mrs. Fiske lived in the early years of the eighteenth century, one would doubtless have found her among those who fought tooth and nail for the works of the Italians against the work of Johann Sebastian Bach.

We proceed now to Article No. 2, " Mrs. Fiske

on Ibsen the Popular," and to *l'Idée Piquante* No. 1 in Article 2, to wit, " Stuff, my friend, and non-sense! Oh, I have no patience with those who de-scend upon a great play, produce it without under-standing and then, because disaster overtakes it, throw up their hands and say there is no public for fine art. How absurd! In New York alone there are two universities, a college or two, and no end of schools. What more responsive public could our producers ask? "

Molnar's " Where Ignorance Is Bliss " is prob-ably not a great play, but it is at least a very fine play. It was produced in the city of two univer-sities, a college or two and no end of schools, with complete understanding and meticulous care by Mrs. Fiske's own husband. Disaster overtook it in four short days . . . Mrs. Fiske is indeed hard on poor papa!

Where, to continue, may one inquire of Mrs. Fiske, was this public for fine art more recently in the instance of Mr. Faversham's excellent Shake-spearean presentations? For Arnold Daly's excel-lent presentation of Bahr's " The Master "? For Reicher's excellent presentation of " The Weav-ers "? For the excellent presentations of the Ridgely Torrence plays, and Brieux's " The Incu-bus," and Percy Mackaye's " The Scarecrow," and " The Yellow Jacket " when it was first shown, and Patterson's " Rebellion," and Stephen Phillips' " Herod," and Hervieu's " Know Thyself," and Pi-

nero's " Thunderbolt " and " Wife Without a Smile,"
and Synge's " Playboy," and Chesterton's " Magic,"
and Shaw's " Fanny's First Play," and Birmingham's " General John Regan," and Lennox Robinson's " Patriots "— or, to descend in the scale, for
even such plays as " Rutherford and Son," " The
Faith Healer," " The Upstart," " The Younger
Generation," or Besier's " Lady Patricia " which
Mr. Fiske produced so beautifully for Mrs. Fiske,
which Mrs. Fiske played so well and which failed
pretty dismally to attract the attention of the city
of two universities, a college or two and no end of
schools?

The truth, of course, is that, despite Mrs. Fiske's
pleasant optimism, eight out of every ten young
gentlemen in our American universities and colleges
— to say nothing of our foreign universities and
colleges in New York City — prefer " The Follies "
to Ibsen as they prefer the histrionism of Miss Ann
Pennington to that of Mrs. Fiske.   And the notion
that they do not in actuality practise this preference
is, for all one professes to believe to the contrary,
somewhat prettier than it is true.

Idée Piquante No. 2 :   " For the many false, but
widespread, impressions of Ibsen we must blame
. . . the innumerable little essays on his gloom and
none at all on his warmth, his gaiety, his infinite
humanity."— Mrs. Fiske's eyes sparkled, according
to the interviewer, as she continued —" When will

the real book of Ibsen criticism find its way to the shelf? "

One may answer pleasantly for Mrs. Fiske's information — and to allay her curiosity — that the real book of Ibsen criticism will find its way to the shelf some eighteen or twenty years ago in the writings of Georg Brandes, some seventeen years ago in the writings of Litzmann and some sixteen years ago in the fourth volume of the " Dramaturgie des Schauspiels " of Heinrich Bulthaupt, to say nothing of in the remote future of a half dozen years ago in the case of Otto Heller's " Henrik Ibsen: Plays and Problems " and Bernard Shaw's " Quintessence of Ibsenism "— and in the even dimmer future of a number of years before that in the case of James Huneker's " Iconoclasts " and Josef Hofmiller's " Zeitgenossen "— and in the future of even longer ago still in the writings of Edmund Gosse, William Archer, P. H. Wicksteed, August Ehrhard, U. C. Wörner, Julius Elias and possibly C. H. Herford.

Mrs. Fiske proceeds next to deny emphatically that Ibsen is parochial. Here, say what you will, one must allow the lady a point, a *touché* on the right side of the jacket. That one has never heard any one claim that Ibsen was parochial may, of course, in certain too captious quarters be held against the lady — but *place aux dames, messieurs!*

Amazing Discovery No. 3: " Hedda Gabler is a universal character."

No. 4: "To read 'Borkman' in the light of
some knowledge of life is to marvel at the blending
of human insight and poetic feeling."

No. 5: "Ibsen gives us in his plays only the last
hours."

The latter is presented by Mrs. Fiske as an original and searching deduction. Upon it, indeed, her
interviewer in rapt astonishment comments, "It was
putting in a sentence the distinguishing factor, the
substance of *chapters* of Ibsen criticism! Here
were set forth *in a few words,* etc., etc." . . . The
same thing was said of Ibsen and his plays many
years ago by Huneker and before Huneker by Walkley and long before Walkley by Henrik Jaeger.

We come to Article No. 3, "Mrs. Fiske to the
Actor-in-the-Making" and deduce at once there-
from this syllogistic pearl: (1) "Acting is a science"; (2) "Acting is a thing of the spirit, a con-
veyance of certain abstract spiritual qualities, a
matter of the soul"; (3) Therefore, "Consider
your voice; first, last and always your voice. *It is
the beginning and the end of acting!*"

Thus we are told that though acting is an exact
science, a thing of the soul, etc., etc., yet "with the
voice good and perfectly trained an aspirant to high
histrionic place may forget all the rest. It (the
latter) will take care of itself." One may perhaps
be pardoned, therefore, for expressing a wish to
have seen Robert G. Ingersoll play Hamlet, to behold the Silver-Tongued Orator of the Platte in a

performance of Torvald Helmer, to sneak a look at Burton Holmes in the rôle of Drayman Henschel . . .

Over Article No. 3 there is need to tarry not longer. A smack, a taste, suffices. And we so pass on to Article No. 4, " Mrs. Fiske Builds a Theatre in Spain." This, a treatise on endowed playhouses. In reply to the query as to what she would do were she given five millions of dollars to spend on such a theatre, Mrs. Fiske, speaking of such a theatre, observes, after the formula of our dear Duke, " I should give a million to certain humanitarian cults, a million to Eva Booth to spend among the poor she understands so well, and, of course, I could easily spend the other three million in one afternoon in helping on the effort to make women see that one of the most dreadful, shocking, disheartening sights in the world is just the sight of a woman wearing furs."

Failing to find any good argument in Hazlitt, Lamb, Lewes, Archer, Hagemann, Magnin, Turner, Duruy, Schlegel, Collier, Sainte-Beuve, Beaumarchais, Genest, Filon, Montague, Shaw, Symons, Barre, Federn or Lanson wherewith to confound this telling, well rounded and constructive reasoning in the matter of the endowed theatre, there is left nothing for the critic to do but allow Mrs. Fiske her point, and pass on to the lady's consideration of the question of a national theatre.

Commenting on Mr. E. H. Sothern's proposal

for such an endowed theatre in the nation's capital,
thus Mrs. Fiske: " I suppose that most Frenchmen could get to Paris once a year or so to the
Comédie Française, and certainly a theatre in the
Strand is within reach of all the people in little
England; but neither the New Theatre that was nor
Mr. Sothern's dream playhouse that is to be could
be called a national theatre when most of the people
in the nation would never see even the outside of it
in all their days."

How many Frenchmen who can get to Paris and
the Comédie Française once a year or so actually
do get to the Comédie Française? For one provincial, one *patapouf*, from Lyons or Marseilles or
Bordeaux who visits the Comédie Française, there
are several thousands who, on coming to their capital,
make a bee-line for Ba-Ta-Clan or the Olympia
music hall. The Comédie Française has been made
a national theatre not by the people of the French
nation, but by the people of Paris. . . . Is a theatre
in the Strand or a theatre in the ulterior and not too
comfortably accessible town of Manchester the real
national theatre of England? . . . Is a national theatre a matter of a convenient real estate site or a
matter of national literature?

But let us permit Mrs. Fiske to continue: " The
national theatre must go to the people. The national theatre, dear child, will not be a theatre at
all, but a travelling company!" Which, in view of
the failure outside a few large American cities of

such excellent travelling companies as have presented
to "the people" such few specimens of typical
American dramatic literature as "The Easiest
Way" and the like, makes for a happy prospect
indeed. What the use of endowing, however richly,
such a travelling theatre? A national theatre without an audience would certainly not amount to
much; and one can no more through ample moneys
endow the native yokelry with a taste for fine drama
than one can endow that same yokelry with a taste
for fine literature by giving away free copies of the
works of Joseph Conrad. The true national theatre is a theatre not for the nation's heterogeneous
mob tastes, but a theatre for the nation's discrim-
inating and best tastes. Does Mrs. Fiske not know
that the national theatre even of such a nation as
Germany is to be found in Berlin — not in the *En-
semblegastspiele* nor in the so-called *Wandertheater*
that travel up and down the land and that for many
years have been doing precisely what Mrs. Fiske
—"with hand raised in prophecy," writes her interviewer — now and here announces as the dream out
of which, and out of which only, a national theatre
may be born?

There is much more that is sweet for one's tooth
in this essay on the ideal national theatre, but this
all must be left for another day. And so, to Article
5 and final, "Mrs. Fiske Goes to the Play." And
so, in this article, to the following insurgent statement: "How unthinkable that any one who looks at

all beyond the hour of his death could be concerned
with anything less personal and momentous than the
fate of his own soul, could be anything but utterly
engrossed by the intense wonder and curiosity as
to what his life hereafter would be! *There* is something interesting. The great adventure!"...
Boy, page Mr. Maeterlinck. If he isn't around,
see if you can find Mr. Tolstoi. And if you can't
find him, go into the café and locate Mr. Arnold
Bennett.

" I am not sure that even our dear Mr. Lewes,"
observes Mrs. Fiske further along, " realized why
he had been led to think so often that the actor was
the less exalted and less creative artist. I suspect
it was because he had seen most of them in Shakespeare. . . . None could be compared with Shakespeare; yet, in the estimate of the actor's place in
the arts, they all *have* been compared with Shakespeare!"

One must regret that Mrs. Fiske has read her
Lewes so carelessly. Our dear Mr. Lewes, as the
lady affectionately calls him, saw the actors of whom
he wrote in many rôles other than those of the great
poet. He appraised Edmund Kean (pg. 15) in
the rôle of Massinger's Sir Giles Overreach and
(pg. 20) in the rôle of Colman *fils'* Sir Edward
Mortimer. He appraised Charles Kean ("I must
confess," said Lewes, "that it has never been an
intellectual treat to me to see Charles Kean play
Shakespeare's tragic heroes ") in " The Corsican

Brothers " (the Boucicault translation of the French potboiler) pg. 26 — and also in " Pauline." He too appraised Fechter in " The Corsican Brothers." He appraised Rachel in the tragedies of Racine and Corneille (pp. 36-41) and in Madame Girardin's " Lady Tartufe " (pg. 42). He appraised Edmund Kean in the drama of Sheridan Knowles and Schiller; Macready (pg. 45) in the drama of Lord Byron, Bulwer Lytton and others; Farren (pg. 63 —) in the drama of Sheridan and Garrick and Colman, and in the translated French play " Secret Service," and in the rôle of Grandfather Whitehead, etc.; Charles Matthews in " He Would Be an Actor," " Patter versus Clatter," " The Day of Reckoning," " The Game of Speculation," in such rôles as Lavater, Mr. Affable Hawk and Sir Charles Coldstream in Matthews' own " Used Up "— in light farce and loud burlesque; Frédéric Lemaître (pg. 84 —) in Macaire, in Don César de Bazan, in the drama of Victor Hugo and the drama of the hack melodramatists of the day, in one melodrama so bad, indeed, that Lemaître knew his audiences would laugh it out of court and so acted it as a farce-comedy and made an enormous success of it; the Keeleys in John M. Morton's " Box and Cox," in " A Thumping Legacy," etc.; Madame Plessy as Madame Lecoutellier in Augier's " Maître Guérin," Bouffé in " Père Grandet," Got in " Le Duc Job," Delaunay in " On Ne Badine Pas Avec l'Amour," Montal in " Vingt Ans Après," Salvini in the drama

202 Mr. George Jean Nathan Presents

of Mr. Robert M. Bird of Newcastle, Delaware,
U. S. A. . . . And so it would seem that " our dear
Mr. Lewes," despite Mrs. Fiske's disbelief, after all
knew perfectly well what he was about when he esti-
mated the actor's place in the arts.

" But," continues Mrs. Fiske, undaunted, " there
are times when the actor as an artist is far greater
and more creative than his material, when he does
something more than ' repeat a portion of a story
invented by another,' as Mr. Moore has it. Yet
quite as distinguished a writer has said the least
gifted author of a play, the least gifted creator of
a drama, is a man of higher intellectual importance
than his best interpreter. Now, distinguished
though he be, this writer betrays himself as one untrained in the psychology of the theatre."

It may interest Mrs. Fiske to know that the opinion in point was coincided in and expressed by a
man indeed woefully untrained in the psychology of
the theatre. His name, Benoît Constant Coquelin.

" We actors," Mrs. Fiske then valiantly proceeds, " are time and again compelled to *read* values
into plays — values unprovided by our authors.
Think of Duse ! "

I trust I am not too impolite when I observe that
this is much as if George Jean Nathan were to say,
" We writers are time and again compelled to do
so-and-so. Think of Shakespeare ! "

Mrs. Fiske's rapturous Boswell now reads to her
what he alludes to as a " typically wild " bit of criti-

cism, to wit, " A good actor is one who is successful
in completely immersing his own personality in the
rôle he is playing," and bids thereon her opinion.
(What the typically wild myself actually wrote was
" A good actor is one who is successful in completely
immersing his own personality in the rôle he is playing. A star actor is one who is successful in completely immersing the rôle he is playing in his own
personality.") Retorts then Mrs. Fiske with a dry
air of finality, " There are, to that, seven answers.
Duse is one, and the other six are Irving, Terry,
Mansfield, Jefferson, Réjane and Sarah Bernhardt."
And lest you doubt the lady's authoritative judgment on these actors, I call your attention to the
very next page of the article on which you will find
this emblematic record : " I only saw Mansfield when
he was too young. I never saw him in his mature
years. I saw him in none of his great rôles. . . .
The critic of great acting is in danger. Personally,
I am cautious as a critic. I am careful not to give
an opinion on the work of an actor of great repu-
tation until I have studied him carefully many times."
Selah !

I find I have no space left wherein to expound
the Fiske intellectuality at greater length; wherein
to draw a parallel on the good lady's " original "
defence of actors who are said merely " to play
themselves " and what our dear Mr. Lewes said in
almost the self-same words on page 93 of " On
Actors and the Art of Acting "; wherein to draw

an amusing parallel on the quotations from Henley, *et al.,* which the good lady now and again drops in learned, off-hand manner into her Boswell's profoundly impressed ear and the self-same quotations which nightly she might be heard to recite in the acting rôle written for her by the author of the play " Erstwhile Susan "; wherein to draw further attention to the good lady's somewhat quaint opinions on music, art, literature and the theatre.   And so there is left nothing for me to do but now bid the jury, thus sketchily addressed, to leave the room and ponder the case.   Yet let me further bid the gentlemen of that jury hold against me not too hard if I have here and there, in the argument, appeared a trifle boorish and uncourtly to one who is doubtless a lovely and most charming woman.   I have not meant to be so.   And if, alas, I seem so to have been it is only because my pen is a clumsier and poorer thing than it should be, and I a less skilful fellow at the art of literary composition than on some far distant future day I may, God willing, be.

MYTHS OF MOMUS

ON the evening of August 14, 1916, two farces were presented in the Republic Theatre: one upon the stage, by Mr. Lawrence Rising and Miss Margaret Mayo; the other in the lobby, by the gentlemen whose profession it is to review the metropolitan dramaturgy. Of the two, the latter proved somewhat the more jocund.

The farce upon the stage of the theatre, dubbed "His Bridal Night," had as its theme the ancient caprice of mistaken identity; the farce in the lobby as its, the equally ancient caprice as to the incredibility and hence dubious theatrical practicableness of that theme.

The abounding persistence in contemporaneous circles of this phantasm, the notion that mistaken identity is too hollow a stratagem whether in actuality or in fancy to serve feasibly the amusement platform, obscures by its avoirdupois even the manifold beefy sister hallucinations that befog the Anglo-Saxon playhouse. And yet, as with the rest, what is there in it? The theatre itself was born out of an acceptance by its audience of the legitimacy of the theme. For, as any schoolboy or graduate student of the theatre at Harvard College can tell, the lead-

206 Mr. George Jean Nathan Presents

ing impulse given by Thespis to the drama (*circa* 536 B. C.) consisted in the adding to Dionysus' old dithyrambic chorus of a single actor who appeared successively in different rôles and who — as we discover in at least two suggestive instances — convinced his spectators even when he mistook *himself* for some one else.

From the very beginnings of the theatre to the present time, the theme of mistaken identity, against which the critical prejudice habitually waxes spoofish, has, whenever at all well handled, been a prosperous one. From 200 B. C. and the " Menaechmi " of Plautus (probably the first definite elaboration of the theme) to its appropriation in the sixteenth century in " A History of Errors " and from its subsequent reappropriation by Shakespeare in his " Comedy of Errors " to (in the early eighteenth century) its re-reappropriation in " Les Ménechmes " of Regnard — and through innumerable French, German and British farces of the nineteenth century " Pink Dominoes " order to such pasties of more recent years as the music show " Three Twins," the farce " A Hot Old Time," and the motion picture serial " The Iron Claw," the mixed identity story has been a cajoling and lucrative theatrical ware. I doubt whether, with the single exception of Molnar in " Der Gardeoffizier " (" Where Ignorance is Bliss "), there has been an instance where a skilled writer has failed to make money out of the whimsy. And even so, Molnar, though his play was too subtle to capture the Anglo-Saxon showgoer, gained an ample concrete reward for his use of the idea in his native Austria-Hungary. The theme, indeed, has in its many ways proved not less generally captivating, for all one hears to the contrary, than the Cinderella business. Whether handled by Mark Twain in " The Prince and the Pauper " or by Katherine Cecil Thurston in " The Masquerader " or by Anthony Hope in " A Prisoner of Zenda," it has ever resulted in a best-seller. Whether handled by William Gillette in " Too Much Johnson " or by Ludwig Fulda in " The Twin Sister " or by Shakespeare in " Twelfth Night," it has ever resulted in entertainment.

The current notion, therefore, that any theatrical piece having mixed identity as its thesis is a piece destined at once to be an ennui brewery and a dangerous theatrical investment is akin to the like current romance that good dialogue and lyrics are necessary to the success of a musical comedy. Beyond question, the best stage producer of the music show amongst us is Mr. Julian Mitchell — the best and the most successful artistically and commercially. And why is Mr. Mitchell the best and the most successful artistically and commercially? Simply because Mr. Mitchell is deaf as a post and so, being constitutionally unable to hear the lines or lyrics at rehearsals, pays utterly no attention to them and devotes his entire eye to the physical elements of the business in hand.

The first theory held by protestants against the theme of mixed identity is that mixed identity is too strainful upon the imagination, too singular and grotesque a conceit, to capture the conviction of a native theatre audience. . . . Yet this same theatre audience willingly takes for granted that no Frenchwoman loves her husband, that all bachelors habitually don dinner jackets even when anticipating a quiet evening alone in their apartments, that no woman is ever successful in hiding her past from the man she marries, that forests always grow in grooves and that falling snow never clings to any portion of a man's overcoat other than the shoulders!

The second theory is that the confusions of identity under the majority of circumstances exhibited upon the stage are in actuality impossible and so constitute poor meat for drama. But since the thesis of mixed identities is nine times in ten employed for mere purposes of loud farce — for mere slapstick pastime, as it were — it is as unreasonable to register such criticism as it would be analogously to urge against the slapstick itself that it is theatrically unfunny since in real life one is not accustomed to apply it abaft one's neighbour. The most amusing things of the farcical stage are and ever have been things entirely out of key with life and nature. Farce moves in a fantastic world, for in the fantastic reposes ever the largest mirth. The mugging mask of the roguish slave which filled the audiences at the " Adelphi " of Terence with loud chuckles, centuries later had the same effect even on the austere August Wilhelm Schlegel, so he admits, when he saw the piece produced in Weimar under the direction of Goethe.

From the innavigable yet compelling drolleries of Aristophanes to the wild casuistries of Etienne Girardot in " Charley's Aunt," from the so-called rope-dancings of Molière to the broken mirror scene in " My Friend from India " or the self-confessed madnesses of " Officer 666," the impossible and the comic are ever closely related. Too, aside from farce the argument against such a theme as mistaken identity is equally ethereal. There is no more good reason why this theme, even granting its intrinsic dubiousness, should because of this intrinsic dubiousness fail to capture the interest of a theatre auditorium than there is in a like possible contention against the validity of the ghost in " Hamlet," or the lighted cigar by means of which Mr. Gillette effects his escape from the gas-house in " Sherlock Holmes." It is, surely, as difficult to believe in ghosts as it is to grant that a lighted cigar would retain its vivid glow long enough to deceive the agents of Moriarty.

The third, and final, theory. To wit, that mistaken identity is a story too old longer to beguile or divert the modern time audience. This one of the convenient chatterings of indolent criticism. And at bottom, obviously, nonsense. The older a theme the more certain, as every one professionally connected with a box-office well knows, its drawing

power. The fact that this very farce, " His Bridal
Night," of which we are here writing, is in certain
directions (twin sisters, et cetera) basically like the
ancient " Bacchis Sisters " which Plautus cabbaged
from Menander three centuries before the birth of
Christ, does not per se argue against its box-office
magnetism any more than has the age of the idea
of Mr. George V. Hobart's " Experience " (fif-
teenth century and, specifically, the morality " Bien-
Avisé et Mal-Avisé ") or the age of the theme of
Molnar's " The Devil " (the twenty-sixth Coventry
Play) or the age of the idea of the Washington
Square Players' pantomime of the foods inside the
human stomach (" La Condamnation des Banquets,"
written by Nicolas de la Chesnaye four hundred
years and more ago) or the age of the idea of the
fire effect in a recent Winter Garden show (*vide*
the fire scene as recorded in accounts of " The
Prophets," acted inside a church in the early years
of the twelfth century) — any more, as I say, than
has the age of any of these militated against
their respective ticket-racks. The mistaken identity
theme is not a bit older than the theme of the Pixley-
Luders musical comedy " Woodland " (the " Birds "
of Aristophanes, 414 B. C.) which ran in New York
for six months and is still making money in the less
country-jake districts.

These myths of Momus, how loudly tinkle the
little bells upon their gaudy caps!

REALISMUS

IN any attempt to weigh the virtues or lack thereof of the quality known to the current theatre as realism, it is essential that prefatory note be made on the dubious chemistry of the very quality presented for appraisal. The shrewd disinclination of many of our writers on the theatre thus to disclose the intrinsic spuriousness of the subject about which they are preparing to deliver themselves is responsible not only for their incomes (which may not, unfortunately, here concern us) but, what is more important, for the hornswoggling of the all too-susceptible reader desiring respectable criticism with a flood of speciously convincing and basically preposterous ideas.

Here, probably, is to be discovered the most significant of all the reasons assigned for the mediocre intelligence and squinting viewpoint of the rank and file of our native theatre audiences. For, in the wide dissemination of theatrical falsehoods rests the real cause for the strabism that in this day operates so prettily toward the conservation of our drama's lack of ideals — to say nothing of its lack of ideas, of courage and of unsentimental sanity.

Therefore, before poising ourselves against a

discussion of the so-termed realism of the current
drama, together with its possible virtues and its possible vices and its effect, if any, on the general
dramatic movement of the time, it is, as has been
suggested, necessary that inquiry be directed into
the character and virginity of this so-called realism.
Obviously, we must know, in a discussion concerned
with realism in drama, if there is in the first place
any realism to be discussed.

By realism, the people of the theatre would seem
usually to mean the photographic depiction on the
stage of institutions, peoples and conditions that are
either sordid or, by Anglo-Saxon standards, morally irregular.   And thus it occurs — being seldom
contradicted by our critical guild — that this so-
called realism of our drama is, in any event, less
realism in the complete sense of the word than in a
narrow, back-alley sense.   If this strikes the ear as
somewhat nonsensical it becomes only necessary to
challenge: Name one American play character-
ized widely as realistic that has treated of other
than sordid or, by Anglo-Saxon standards, morally
irregular conditions.   Thus, our " realistic " plays
are plays like Walter's " Easiest Way," or, to bring
ourselves into smart descent, such trade goods as
some time ago enchanted the Broadway and Mul-
berry Street circles of New York City: such untidy
confections as " The Lure," " The Fight," " To-
day " and the like.

Where there is no honesty there can be no genuine

realism. And whereas such specimens as " The Lure," " The Fight," " Today " and so on are palpably dishonest — as we shall show — it must be plain that their much discussed and here and there widely proclaimed realism (with all its alleged inherent municipal and social corrective values) resolves itself into nothing more than machine-made proscenium sensationalism and box-office bait. And it must similarly be plain that whereas such " realism " is meretricious and consequently of large appeal to the low class of persons that, unfortunately, supports the American theatre with its regular patronage, it cannot fail to exercise a vitiating influence on what some of us optimists are pleased to allude to as the native drama. This, for two reasons. First, because we have in the United States at the present time a body of playmakers who, with but two exceptions, have their eyes set primarily upon the ticket rack and second, because, as a nation, we are to all appearances theatrically ignorant of the fact that realism is subjective rather than objective, that is, that the only dramatic realism worth discussing seriously is realism of thought, attitude and viewpoint, faithfully conceived and faithfully presented, rather than mere realistically smeared canvas. There is ten times more genuine realism in such a play (a comedy) as Brieux's " Les Hannetons " or in Galsworthy's " The Pigeon " (also a comedy) or in Bahr's " The Concert " (also a comedy) or in Fulda's " Friends of Our Youth " (also a comedy) or in Schmidt's " Only a Dream " (also a comedy), than in a score of melodramatic " Lures " and " Fights " with their sham spectacularized bawdy establishments, than in fifty " Todays " with their mountebank and absurd philosophies on modern American social, ethical and moral conditions.

Not, of course, that there is not a definite and sound realistic quality in such scenic pieces as " Salvation Nell " and the like: but the point to be made is that this realism is less dramatic realism than the extrinsic realism of slouchy clothes, paint and cheesecloth.   Realistic scenery and realistic depiction of types can affect the drama of worth as a whole finally in small measure unless with the realism of painted canvas and with the realism of types there be coordinated an element which shall bring out of these realistic garnishings a realistic purpose, a waterholding philosophy, a mental, rather than a purely ocular, emotion.   And the mental emotion thus produced in the auditor must be produced honestly.   It is the easiest thing in Christendom, remember, to stir up an American theatrical audience.   If there is an exception, it is to be found alone in the childish ease with which a metropolitan Gallic audience is to be inflamed through the medium of pieces possessed of a showy military flavour.   And even in the instance of this exception, there are many persons practised in the mechanics of the native theatre to shout rebuttal.   The much ridiculed, but invariably effective, promulgation in times of peace of the national

emblem in a certain lowly species of American entertainment, is an element here to be recalled. Ridicule
is one thing; fact is another. And, ridicule as much
as one cares to, it still holds that the American thea-
tre-attending audience is, in the great mass, ever
keenly sympathetic to so perfectly obvious a stratagem.

This quality of the native audience, this easily-
stirred, ever-ready-to-believe, débutante willingness
to lend ear and cheer to almost any piece of thematic
sensationalism, is something to be regarded as
nicely relevant to any inquiry into dramatic realism.
For in this attitude of the American audience reposes the danger that lurks in the exploitation of
such spurious, albeit spine-tickling and ocularly impressive, footlight " realism."

But, lifts a voice, are these " realisms " spurious? Let us observe in the cases of several of the
plays which succeeded in evoking argument and
achieving chronicle. Firstly, " The Lure," a play
the realism of which was endorsed on the ground
that through the divulging of its fact-nature to the
public, the need for investigation and reform must
be suggested to and felt by that public. This
" realism " concerned itself with the celebrated
mythology known as the " white slave traffic." The
play flaunting the " realism " in question was written
by its sponsor after he had failed (upon weary endeavour) to sell six or seven of his previous plays
on Broadway; was written deliberately, so the seem-

ingly authentic report has it, to *compel* a market by
virtue of its pseudo-sensational scene — a scene laid
in a bungalow of ill-repute.   Naturally enough, and
fairly enough, the reflection may here arise that,
even so, there may still have been an indirect sincerity, an indirect and unconscious integrity of purpose, discernible in the play.   But when we observe
that the events and incidents of the play which sought
to instil the " need for investigation and reform "
were based on wild exaggeration and fuddled hys-
teria, doubt tumbles to the ground.   Exaggeration,
true enough, has its authentic and entirely virtuous
place in drama — but the exaggeration must be
dramatic exaggeration, the exaggeration permissible
and often necessary to the demands of the stage for
the stage's complete effectiveness — not the exaggeration of actual conditions, not the gross distor-
tion of recognized facts.   If this latter be a legiti-
mate enterprise, then drama as a serious art — or
even as a form of easy amusement for partly intelligent men and women — must become nothing more
than a Punch and Judy show aided and abetted by
Paine's fireworks.   For all the primitiveness and
jejune thought of the Charles Klein melodramaturgy,
there yet remained in that dramaturgy a basic sincerity, an intrinsic probity.   Such plays as " The
Lure," however, arouse indignation on the part of
the easily impressed for a state of affairs that exists
(if at all) in such small part that it is negligible.
And it is the first rule of drama that where the drama

declares itself to be drama of vital blood and crusading heart, such drama must bear closely in mind the difference in the national social, moral and economic geography of mountains and molehills.

To illustrate. If there is dramatic justification in such exaggerations, why not a drama arousing indignation over dachshunds being allowed in the public parks because once in a great while it happens that one of the little angels goes mad and bites a child playing in the park? A far-fetched theme, yet basically and logically not a bit more far-fetched, not a bit less upright, than a theme which purports to set the public pulse a-tingle with the theory that no poor American girl is safe from the Italian white slavers. Not a bit more ridiculous, not a bit less justifiable (from a " reform " viewpoint), than such a theme as that of the play " Today," arguing that it is not uncustomary for American wives whose husbands are unable to purchase for them the gee-gaws they cherish, to indulge in countless assignations in order to gain the treasures. This latter play was lifted bodily out of the East Side, that shilling haunt of theatric sensationalism, to shock the uptown spine at two dollars the spine. And in the instance of " The Fight," we discover the arbitrary introduction of a bawdy house scene into a play which, in its two original versions, was found to be without the believedly necessary box-office " punch." The locâle of the play was a small town. The resort in point was situated in the heart of its business dis-

trict.   The woman who conducted the establishment
"lured" a young girl of the town into the house.
Her leading patron was the town's most prominent
personage, a Senator.   The whole to-do occurred in
broad day-light!

What we must quickly come to, however, is that
the paying theatre public likes this sort of trumped-
up sensationalism.   The fact that "The Fight"
showed a very marked decline in revenue immediately the authorities had censored the scene in
point out of the play, together with the fact that
the box-office discloses a consistently heavy income
in such cases where the so-called sensational qualities
have not suffered the censor's scalpel-stroke to the
same damaging degree, seems to prove this.   Therefore, as the American public — or, at least, the
New York public (which, contradict if you will, still
does exercise the most profound influence on the
American drama, because the American drama is
in the hands of the New York theatrical managers
who, in turn, are in the hands of the New York
public), patronizes liberally this species of "realism," we must be convinced that such "realism"
must exert a tempting and malignant influence on the
pens of our stage scriveners.

Briefly to reiterate, the situation is this: the public that patronizes our theatres most regularly and
thus keeps our theatres going, is a public given to
a fat admiration for spurious "realism," an admiration that is reckoned with and gratified by our

fat playwrights almost unanimously and by our fat theatrical managers in fat part. For honest realism, the American theatre would seem on its record to have small use. For the presentation of the unvarnished fact, for the presentation of realism untainted by the star-spangled extravaganza of sentimentality and platitude, we, as a theatrical nation, care not a continental. The statistics prove this much to us, however much we may bawl the contrary. Such an American play as " The Only Law," that died a death of ridicule and protest a number of years ago, a play of accurate realism, of the sinister quality of Gorky at bottom, of fact rather than of fancy, is unwelcome to the artistic nostril of the native mob, where such plays as take similarly veined themes and distort and perfume those themes are hailed by the writers for the newspapers and patronized by the readers of the writers for the newspapers as the sort of American drama to be encouraged because (recall the words?) " it deals with the problems of our every-day life." But how does it deal? Better not to deal with our every-day life and seek to create a native drama out of it! For in such tawdry dealing, deliberately falsifying, deliberately selling the truth for pieces of silver, we gain not only no native drama, but we gradually and coincidentally lose the viewpoint and intelligence of our audiences. Granting, of course, for argument, that our audiences have viewpoint and intelligence — which, obviously, they have not.

POLISH *VERSUS* SHINE

DAWDLING at the window of a London club and gazing with bored mien upon the thoroughfare, lounged two English dandiprats — and behind them, upon the long davenport, another. An automobile was resting at the opposite curb. Presently and with a balmy languor, one of the Englishmen at the window adjusted his monocle, stared painstakingly at the car, nonchalantly abstracted the crystal and remarked: "Buick." After a sedative period, the second Englishman, feeling for his monocle, finding it and with equal deliberation inserting it in his eye, permitted his vision to appraise the motor and, having appraised it, withdrew his glass and remarked: "Mércedès." Another cataleptic interlude, rent only by the ticking of the clock upon the distant mantel, and the Englishman upon the davenport arose *adagio* and slowly drew his hat down upon his ears. The first Englishman permitted his eye to lift. "Going?" he inquired. The other nodded. "Cawn't stand this blarsted wrangling," he returned.

Wherewith, a notion of Alfred Sutro's comedy "The Two Virtues." Well-mannered as a valet,

unruffled as a poke collar and exciting as a girl
with nose-glasses, the piece is at once typical of the
stereotyped species of London sugar-pill which provides the Englishman with his evening's excuse for
dressing and the American manager with his yearly
excuse for mistaking a drawing-room set for a polite
comedy. The play was an immitigable failure
when presented overseas by George Alexander in the
St. James's Theatre. But, since the piece contained
in its cast a character with a title, a tea-pot and tray
of muffins, a line in which the hero says to a lady,
after he has that-will-do'd the butler: " Forgive
my correcting Baylis before you, but I am very for-
getful," a couple of disparaging allusions to money,
a reference to a Prince, a Count and an F.R.S., a
sniffish statement by one of the lady characters that
one of the other lady characters is of *bourgeois* or-
igin, a charge by one of the men characters that one
of the other men characters has acted " like a green-
grocer " and similar component parts of what, on
Broadway, is known as " classy stuff "— to say nothing of the substitution of the word *pension* for board-
ing-house — it was not altogether surprising that the
piece should be forthwith snapped up by an American manager to enchant the native hoddy-doddies.

It has been claimed for the play that one of its
merits lies in the circumstance that the author has
not apologized sentimentally for his lady with a
past, that he has permitted her rather to brave out
her transgressions with a pretty unconcern. But

where a greater sentimentality than in this very
Sutro thing? The unsentimental writer is he who
allows his heroine to apologize for her sins. The
sentimental fellow, on the other hand, ever will
realize that by keeping his heroine from apologizing
he will invest her with his audiences' melting sympathy, the sympathy always accorded an accused
character who shuts up. Again, though true enough,
Sutro's Mrs. Guildford does not explain away her
temptation in the usual terms of low lights, soft
Chopin and scent of lilacs on the night air, she cannot resist the not untypical Sutro impulse to
allude to herself somewhat pathetically and wistfully
as a bit of seaweed. " Do you ever go to the sea-
side? " she asks of the hero, nose-napkin ready.
" Then you may remember having seen — a bit of
seaweed — thrown up on the beach? Well, that's
me. Just a bit of — stranded — seaweed. But —
though it's far away from the sea — and will never
get back there — the sea standing for Society and
the hall-marked woman," *et cetera.* . . . You recognize the melody.

The two virtues of which Mr. Sutro composes are
our old comrades, chastity and charity. And the
philosophy which Mr. Sutro visits upon them is our
old bed-fellow, Is-there-only-one-virtue-in-woman-
One - that - is - paramount - and - its - name - is - chas-
tity-I-thought-there-was-another-called-charity. It is
staggering news that the play distils. Nor of the
other éclair juices of the theatre is there an undue

drought. Thus, along about nine-forty-five, we find
the heroine cinderellaing " I was brought up in the
country, with a nurse — I was an only child — and
no one seemed particularly to want me." And along
about nine-forty-six, " I don't think my father dis-
liked me, but he died very soon and my mother was
by way of being very young and very fashionable,
and I was a nuisance to her." And along about nine-
forty-seven, " So I made friends with an old cobbler
— a lame old cobbler — and I used to sit on the
floor, sucking my thumb, in a queer barn-sort of
place where he worked — I could get to it through
our garden — and he'd tell me stories, etc., etc."
And at nine-forty-seven-and-a-half, the hero *dolo-
roso:* " You — were — a — lonely — child —
Freda."

What a transpontine buncombe rests upon the
world! The mere presence in such an overseas
dramatic manuscript of the phrase " I dare say " in
place of the American " you bettcha," of the word
" fortnight " for the American " coupla weeks," of
" really " in place of " quit your kidding," is sufficient to confuse and englamour and ravish the eye-
ball of the native producer. And probably rightly
and reasonably. But mere polish does not make a
play. Nor does a tasty selection of language. The
difficulty — to speak from the left teeth — with the
American, as opposed to the British, playwright is
not so much that he lacks the Briton's polish, polite
grammatical sense and word skill as that he lacks the

Briton's knowledge of the right times and places wherein to use them. In plays by American writers, accordingly, the heroes generally act and talk like butlers while the butlers act and talk like the kind of butlers Charles Klein used to make.

Nevertheless, it remains that the best sample of good British comedy on the New York stage at the moment of writing is an American comedy. To wit, Mr. Langdon Mitchell's "The New York Idea." The revival of this modish embroidery of wit accents once again the integrity of the contention that it is unreasonable and futile for us to expect polite comedies from the droll bar-brothers of Broadway: that it takes a gentleman to write a gentleman's play just as certainly as it takes a gentleman to fox hunt, read Max Beerbohm or drink light wines. Some things, one must be born for. And nine-tenths of our American rabble-writers were assuredly not born to the estate of smart satiric composition. Sitting before "The New York Idea," one never forgets that one is in the presence of a writing fellow possessed of the Pullman attitude — of a fellow who, as a youngster, had a governess, went to a private school and looked, at his university, with amused tolerance upon such out-of-place louts as were working their way through college by waiting on table and the like — of a fellow who, as a man, belongs to smart clubs but of course never enters them, does not feel it necessary to return the bow of any person who chooses to bow to

him, would never dream of eating liver and does
not wear hole-proof hose. Of one, in short, who
has the instincts of a well-bred, educated, well-poised
and altogether possible companion.

It takes such a soul to write a piece like " The
New York Idea." Public school boys do not grow
up to be the authors of satiric drawing-room comedy.
It being drawing-room comedy alone with which we
are here concerned — not other moulds of drama.
Who but a man who back at home knew the difference
between filets de truite grillès à la Jeanne d'Arc and
filets de truite grillès à la Sévigné could have written
a " Gay Lord Quex "? Who but one able to insult
ladies with charm and skill, an " Anatol "? Chic
satire is born in a man, it isn't made. It is born in
him just as clean fingernails, a preference for the
most secluded table in a restaurant, an aversion to
the sound of such words as " wart," a dislike for
talking over the telephone and a taste for thin women
are born in him.

An interesting element concerned with the revival
of this saucy specimen of theatrical composition
is the performance in it by Miss Grace George of
the rôle of Cynthia Karslake, originally divulged by
Mrs. Fiske. Interesting, I say, because, though
from a strictly critical point of view Miss George's
interpretation is inferior to Mrs. Fiske's, it is none-
theless a much better interpretation. Mrs. Fiske
played the part accurately, reasonably, logically.
She knew she was playing artificial satiric comedy

and so played from first to last in the artificial satiric
comedy spirit.   And as a consequence of this sound
and appropriate interpretation of the rôle, became
exceedingly monotonous and tiresome ere the second of the four acts was done.   Miss George, on
the other hand, plays the part inaccurately, unreason-
ably, illogically.   She forgets she is playing artificial satiric comedy and so plays it with small regard
for the correct artificial satiric comedy spirit.   Instead, she injects periodically into her delineation of
the rôle a perfectly inappropriate and erroneous
sentiment and serious dramatic note.   And, though
thus from a technical standpoint she presents an in-
correct interpretation, she yet contrives, by the false
variety which she gives her labours, to hold the attention of her audience where Mrs. Fiske lost it.   Does
this not once more clearly exhibit how inutile it is
to regard acting as a thing seriously to be criticized?
If Mrs. Fiske's performance was technically admirable and if Miss George's performance is technically full of holes and if Miss George's performance
is therefore vastly the better of the two so far as
the staging of the Langdon Mitchell manuscript is
concerned — where was Montrose Moses when the
lights went out?   Acting has only one reason-to-be
and that, obviously, is to be effective upon a theatrical audience.   One cannot stay at home and read
acting as one can stay at home and read plays.   Acting is mere trickery, like playing " The Rosary " on
a resined string attached to an empty baking-powder

can, or making the ace of hearts jump out of the deck, or writing such paradoxical, though perfectly sound, arguments as this.   Acting is good acting in proportion to its effectiveness and it is not infrequently effective in proportion to its departure from the best critical standards for appraising it.   Acting is good acting in proportion to its effect upon the average audience just as a play is a good play in proportion to its lack of effect upon the average audience.   Miss George's is a wrongly conceived and hence brilliant performance.   And, while we are at it, let's be entirely honest.   Good performance or no good performance, you and I would anyway — either in or out of our professional capacity — as much prefer to watch Miss George's Cynthia Karslake to Mrs. Fiske's as we would Peggy Rush's to that of Sarah Bernhardt.

THE CUT RATE MIND AND THE
PREMIUM SEAT

JUST as one dislikes instinctively the sort of person whose essay to be genial and popular is overly assiduous, so does the mob audience similarly fail to be impressed by the sort of play whose effort to stroke its fur is too transparent. Like many another, I admit to having believed, and often written, the contrary. But more lately the conclusion has been harvested that in order to achieve a signal box-office prosperity a play of the genre designated as popular must indulge itself in an *escamoterie* somewhat more suave and cagey.

A play, for example, like Mr. Lee Wilson Dodd's " Pals First," to no small degree loses its audience by virtue of its unremitting effort to please that audience. One has from it a constant impression of the manuscript leaning over the footlights, fervently shaking hands with the audience, affectionately calling the audience " old man " and giving it Masonic slaps on the back. And while a casual deduction from the popular, or mob, plays might seem to indicate that this is a fruit-bearing tactic, a closer scrutiny discloses to the situation a rather different countenance.

The long line at a box-office window means less a

play that is pleasing an audience than an audience that is pleasing a play. When a playwriter with the box-office as his sole aim addresses himself to the composition of a dollar-distilling stage exhibit, his first thought is not that church bells ringing on Christmas Eve and bringing repentance to a wayward youth will arouse the nobler impulses of his audience, but that his audience is so given through habit to remitting its familiarity with the situation that the church bells will constitute as fetching a box-office springle as ever. A mob play is successful to the degree that its audience is charitable in forgiving its banalities. The success of such a piece as " Turn to the Right " is certainly not founded on the circumstance that its plot concerns the mediæval lifting of a mortgage off the old farm so much as on the circumstance that its audiences are pleased to overlook that squashy wheeze because of the humours with which the authors have refreshed it.

The play designed for the wholesale consumption of the horde is written not from the stage to the audience, but from the audience to the stage. It must not please its audience so much as its audience must please it. Winchell Smith, one of the authors of " Turn to the Right," and one of the shrewdest of native box-office mesmerists, recently pointed this most acutely while touching on the case of Hermann Bahr's " The Master." This estimable play, argued Smith, pleased its audiences, but did not make money. Had he written the play, said Smith, he

would have made of it a stunning box-office success
by having a woman rush out on the stage at one
point in the traffic, slobber around on the floor at
the great surgeon's feet and beseech him with loud
wails and whifflings to save her little child's life.

This may sound very silly, but the truth remains
that Smith is a clever man and unquestionably knows
what he is talking about. And where Bahr, an
artist, wrote a play that merely pleased its audience
and so lost money, Smith, a business man, would have
written an audience that pleased its play and so
probably made a shapely fortune. For certainly the
so-called sympathetic situation described by Smith
as constituting the necessary injection of box-office
strychnine does not belong in the play — Smith
plainly granted as much: it belongs in the audience.
The situation indeed is less a situation than it *is* an
audience. Originally a thing of the stage, it has in
one form or another rolled down the years like a
snowball — growing, growing — and has become a
thing of the auditorium, a veritable part of the popular theatregoing crowd. This traditional situation
and all its many traditional fellows have been trans-
muted, through endless and ceaseless repetitions, into
so many component parts of the popular theatre audience. And it is thus that the popular playwright of
to-day must compose less a play than an audience.

For years, an audience has been accustomed upon
seating itself to slide its hats into the wire holders
under its seats. Mr. Ames' Little Theatre has been

open now some four years, and its audiences have
come to know perfectly well there are no such holders
beneath its seats, yet every night one may see the
auditorium force of habit still vainly essaying to adjust its hats in the holders that aren't there. The
group of persons who go to make up a theatre audience have become, by virtue of protracted theatrical
attendance, less a group of persons than a group of
habits, of traditions, of *situations*. What goes to
our popular theatres to-day is therefore not so much
a group of persons as a group of stereotyped dramatic situations disposed to behold themselves in
process of reminiscence by a group of professional
actors. The auditoriums of our popular playhouses
no longer contain human beings, but instead so many
codicils to the will, eleventh-hour acquisitions of the
proxies, redemptions through the purity of country
maidens, rapes by drunken German corporals, and
unmaskings of the Duke.

But just as in all reminiscence there is small
pleasure for the man looking backward save he
adorn the past with wistful little fibberies as unction
to his vanity, and just as his pleasurable glow would
promptly melt away were the fair lady of his memories suddenly to burst in upon his reflective solitude
and amiably establish that his wistful little self-fib-
beries were not fibberies at all, but rather forgotten
facts — just so, and in probably equally evasive paradox, must the play in these circumstances not flatter
the audience, but must rather the audience flatter it-

self.   And flatter itself by fooling itself.   The audience must pretend: it must read into the old stage situations elements that are not, and doubtless were
never, there.   It must pretend, with a charitable
warmth, that for the time being it is not familiar with
the Cinderella story . . . the inevitable arrival of
the Ninth Cavalry at the stockade in the nick of
time . . . the you-don't-mean — oh-my-poor-brave-
little-woman impending baby that is destined to re-
unite the hero and heroine . . . the ultimate reveal-
ment of the smug hypocrisy of the deacon. . . .

The more or less prevalent notion that an audience
at a popular play is interested in the solution of the
plot of the play is surely a ridiculous one.   What the
audience is interested in is not what will happen but
what won't happen.   One will quickly grant, for example, that no civilized audience under the broad
heavens expects for an instant that the leading lady
in " Mr. Wu " or " The Conquerors " or " Tosca "
or any such play will be ravished on the stage by the
villain before its very eyes.   Why, then, is the audience interested?   It is interested, simply enough, because a theatre audience is interested ever more in
the preventive of an act than in the consummation of
that act.   It is not the hero's triumph over obstacles
that intrigues the mob — the mob knows the hero
will triumph when it buys its tickets — it is the obstacles themselves.   The popular play, in short, is that
play which most adroitly employs the greatest number of semi-colons in its narration of an old story.

What suspensive interest might attach to such a mob play as " The Man Who Came Back " is de-leted from the play before the curtain's rise by the title. What suspensive interest might attach to such a mob specimen as " Experience " is deleted from the play immediately the audience looks first at its pro-gram and detects that the final scene is laid in the same sweet duchy as the prologue. To argue, there-fore, that the large commercial prosperity of these plays is due considerably to an interest in the solution of their stories is akin to a belief that one is less amused at the spectacle of a fat gentleman falling on the slippery pavement than in watching him get up again.

To make the audience please the popular play it is necessary for the popular playwright to dramatize not the audience's best impulses and emotions, as claimed by the professors, but the audience's worst impulses and emotions. That play which capital-izes, approves and justifies most effectively the evil side of a mob audience's moral nature is the play that makes the fortune for its sponsors. " Alias Jimmy Valentine," " Officer 666," and " Turn to the Right " capitalized and countenanced the mob audi-ence's more or less repressed impulse to break the eighth commandment and steal . . . " Madame X " and " On Trial," like certain of the Sardou plays, the audience's periodic impulse to break the sixth and kill . . . " Marie-Odile," " Romance " and " The Lily," to break the seventh and commit charming and forgivable adulteries . . . " The Unchastened Woman," the ninth . . . " Mary Jane's Pa," the fifth . . . " The Great Lover " the covetous tenth — and " Kismet " (a rare combination of the first-rate and popular play), the whole lot from one to ten. . . .

A popular audience, like an old bachelor or a young girl, likes to be told, not that it is good, but that it is bad. And the audience, figuratively speaking, likes to tell it back again to the play. And so it comes about that the history of the popular, or mob, play is — with of course the usual reservations — a catalogue, not as is generally maintained, of virtuous loves and holy preachments and scowlings on sin so much as one of crooks, seducers, swindlers and liars.

The popular play — the play manufactured to make money — as we have come in the last fifteen years to know it, must not punish sin : it must condone it, or approve it, or forgive it. Your popular stage hero who is a swindler is not sent to jail (as he was in old days when he was the villain), but instead is rewarded at eleven o'clock with the hand of a rich and personable country lass and the sight of an il-luminated trolley car running along the back drop. Your professional seducer (the one-time odious Jem Dalton, but now the bewitching Jean Paurel) no longer expiates his sins in the cold moonlit waters beneath the Brooklyn Bridge. To-day as the final curtain descends on him to loud hand-clapping, he is planning still another assignation with a mobile married lady. And your popular stage hero, the thief. Fifteen years ago, eleven o'clock saw him halted by the gendarmes at the left upper entrance just as he was about to make his escape, and packed off, heavily braceleted, to Sing Sing. To-day, he makes a speech that causes all the ladies out front to sniffle, is wistfully shaken by the hand by the young woman whom he has robbed, and leaves gracefully by the French window for a life of ease and luxury in the Riviera.

Had Jimmy Valentine been sent back to prison at the end of the play, would the play have succeeded? The character was quite as guilty of crime at that time as in the beginning of the play; but the astute Mr. Armstrong knew his popular audience too well to commit so unforgivable a *faux pas*. Would "Cheating Cheaters" have been the popular success it is had its thief hero been sentenced to prison instead of to matrimony with the pretty leading lady? Consider the morals and ethics of that prodigious success "Within the Law." Reflect on the morals and ethics of "Wallingford"— of eight out of every ten of the great popular successes of late years.

In the matter of the reminiscence upon the stage of the stereotyped situations that, metaphorically, go to constitute the popular theatre audience, it is essential to box-office affluence, as has already been pointed out, that these situations be not too literally repeated. The audience resents a too faithful plagiarism of itself. Just as a writer is wrathful over a

direct plagiarism of his work but subtly and not in-
considerably flattered over a mere imitation of it, so
will an audience be displeased at a direct transcrip-
tion of its favourite situations and, contrariwise,
greatly pleased at an imitative treatment. " Sis
Hopkins," brought into New York to-day with Miss
Rose Melville, would doubtless be a dismal failure.
But when Miss Laurette Taylor brings it back to
town and calls it " Peg O' My Heart " it achieves an
almost stupefying popular triumph.

I have observed that a popular audience resents a
too palpable stroking of its fur.   Though it may not
at first glance so appear, it is yet probably true that
the success of the plays written by Mr. William
Hodge is due to the tactful hocus-pocus which that
gentleman visits upon them.   For all that a lot of
impudent boys like myself have in the past written to
the contrary, one knows perfectly well that the average American is by no means so inconceivably vulgar
a buck as he is represented to be in the person of the
Hodge heroes.   Mr. Hodge is unquestionably aware
of the fact himself and, by so exaggerating the vul-
garities of the average American (which is to say
the popular audience), he wins his audiences' golden
hosannahs through the simple stratagem of leading
them in this essentially sly and oblique manner to believe that they are above the average.   He permits
each native son in his audience to compare himself
with an English nobleman — and to the native son's
large advantage — by the left-handed trick of hiring

a thirty-five-dollar-a-week actor to play the nobleman, permitting the actor to go the limit in dressing
the part the way the actor thinks it ought to be
dressed and so making the nobleman appear to the
unsuspecting and subtly larded native son approximately as regal as a shoe.

Mr. Hodge, further, buys twenty-dollar evening
gowns for his chic society belles and so with a shrewd
left hand similarly flatters his fatuous patrons among
the female proletariat. The fellow, say what you
will, is clever. He understands the palate of the
publikum. He knows that the popular play cannot
afford directly to flatter the mob. George M.
Cohan tried the trick in his " Miracle Man " and
came a cropper. George Broadhurst tried it with
" What Money Can't Buy " and came a cropper as
well. Study George Cohan's successes and you will
find that they insult the mob, flout it, make sport of
its vaunted shrewdness and acumen. " Wallingford," " Baldpate," " Hit-the-Trail-Holliday " and
on down the list.

And so, a play such as " Pals First," by virtue of
its continuous prostration before the popular audience's optimisms and benevolences and self-delusions,
can never achieve great popular success. It is a
mere morality of Magnanimity, Chivalry, Honour,
Loyalty, Faith, Virtue, Altruism, Self-Immolation
and Handshaking told in terms of a so-called crook
play. It is a " Pollyanna " without a John Pendle-
ton. It is the Lord's Prayer rewritten by Orison

Swett Marden to be interpreted by the required num-
ber of Mary Pickfords in trousers —" Abendstern "
on a dozen ukeleles — the poetry of Cale Young
Rice recited in unison by the sophomore class at
Wellesley — Eleanor Hallowell Abbott shopping in
Page and Shaw's. . . .

MISTS OF DELUSION

I

THE chancellors of the miniature Punch and Judy Theatre wrought wisely when they temporarily gave over the thirsty pulpit of their masque mosque to melodrama. For, contrary to the so prevalent hocus-pocus, melodrama may achieve its best effect not in large playhouses like the Drury Lane or the Manhattan Opera House, but in very small ones like the Bandbox, the Little Theatre and this very Punch and Judy. Properly and with conviction to exercise its power over a theatre audience, melodrama should be so produced that it at no time impresses its spectators as anything other than a hollow compound of noise and pasteboard. That is, melodrama in the generally accepted meaning of the word. Any suspicion of realism forthwith deletes that particular portion of the melodrama of persuasion and credibility. Max Maurey, director of the Grand Guignol, is doubtless the most consistently proficient and successful producer of melodrama in the world and he produces his melodramas (even such as " S. O. S.," " Toward the Light," " The Submarine " and others which require comparatively elaborate scenic devices and trickeries) in a theatre not so large as even the Punch and Judy.

The explanation of the theory is simple. The producer who presents his melodrama in a big theatre does so under the impression that the further an audience is removed from the stage trappings and traffic the less flawful and more real these trappings and traffic will seem to it. And the producer is, in this, correct; but, being correct, he yet bamboozles himself. For his audience is thus placed in the, in this instance, theatrically less desirable mood of imagining and believing in the realism of the proceedings than in the more prosperous mood of detecting, from a closer look, the holes in the ocean waves and the shirt-sleeved and perspiring O'Brien pushing the 18,000-ton papier-maché battleship across the backdrop and so being made safely appreciative of the entire artificiality of the drama it is beholding. That the stuff of melodrama is purely artificial, an audience must be made constantly to feel. Just as an audience will laugh heartily at the spectacle of Fields poking his finger in Weber's eye so long as it knows Weber's eye isn't being hurt and just as the same audience would, as Fields himself has observed, stop laughing immediately if it believed the pain were actual, so will an audience be pleasurably thrilled by a melodrama just so long as it feels the whole thing is merely a show, and so will the audience cease to be pleasurably thrilled and become lost to the producer the moment it feels a too great sense of illusion and reality in the proceedings. Certainly, most successful melodramas have owed their prosperity to their clearly patent ar-tificiality. The audience naturally knew that the thrilling time-clock infernal machine of " The Fatal Card " could not possibly be loaded and go off on the stage because, if it were and did, it would blow up with it the first half dozen rows of the audience. The audience naturally knew that the great cannon of " The Cherry Pickers " couldn't possibly go off while the hero was strapped to its mouth, because, if it did, it would spatter the hero all over the ladies' dresses out front. Maurey lets you see closely the trap-door covered with brown cloth representing the pit of quicksand, the obvious waxness of the hand under which the villain holds the lighted candle. And Maurey's task is admittedly a simpler one than were he a caterer to the baby-blue sensibilities of us Americans.

The two prime requisites of a successful melodrama are, therefore, (1) that it shall lack complete conviction and (2) that it shall make its audience feel itself pro tem in the place of the melodrama's stage producer. The ingenuity of a melodrama's production is of infinitely more interest to an audience than the melodrama itself. Else why the lure of the mechanical " big scene "? Was it the story or plausibility of " The Whip " that interested audiences or was it the toy trickery of the moving train? Did not Lincoln Carter make all his money out of mechanical automobile races and stereopticon forest

fires? Is it the plot of " The Sporting Duchess " or
is it the horse race that is remembered? Is it " The
White Heather " or the balloon? " The Span of
Life " or the three acrobats who formed the human
bridge?

This being the case, why should not melodrama be
more successful in a small theatre wherein an audience is made privy to its tricks? Is Ching Ling Foo
less amusing than Kellar because he shows you how
the tricks are done? A melodrama audience is an
audience in a youngster frame of mind. It wants
to see what's inside the doll.

II

Just as melodrama is to be best viewed in a small
show-bourse, so is a play by Shaw best critically to
be viewed in a large one. For, whereas every
man who doesn't wear coloured socks is already
thoroughly familiar with Shaw's plays and therefore sees no reason why he should go to the theatre
and be misled into imagining from garbled interpretations that they aren't so good as he knows they
are, it follows that the real sport of an acted Shaw
play is not the play but the audience of more or
less gaping and startled yahoos in attendance thereupon. And, obviously, the larger the audience the
greater the sport. A Shaw audience, in New York
at least, is a lovely berry. To go slumming amongst
such a droll people, to give surreptitious ear to its
deductions and corollaries, is a *brochette* of treats.

And such a brochette was again and lately provided in the presentation, upon the lighted gibbosity at the Playhouse, of " Major Barbara."

Inasmuch as Shaw wrote this piece some twelve years ago and inasmuch as it deals, as you know, with the question of war munitions and the ethics appertaining thereto, the audience in attendance upon the induction was audible in its astonishment over Shaw's remarkable prevision, over his anticipation, as it were, of current conditions and events. There was or is, of course, no prevision whatever — but rather post-vision; for Shaw conditioned his remarks on the controversies that had grown out of the British troubles in South Africa.

A second treat was to be enjoyed in the usual Shaw audience's usual whiffling over the imperfections and minus marks of the Shaw dramatic technique. It is a peculiarity of Shaw's theatrical audiences that when they are confessedly most engrossed by his plays they are coincidentally most emphatic in their argument that his technique is faulty. Thus, though the good folk are ten times more interested and entertained by a Shaw play with its lack of what they call technique than they are interested in and entertained by a Horace Annesley Vachell play with its oodles of technique, they are still obediently convinced that Shaw's technique, because it doesn't follow certain more or less occult rules, is the less proper and efficient of the two. Will this *suprême* of technique walla-walla never be done with? As H. L.

Mencken has nicely observed " The drama is a facile
and easy art form (despite all the gabble about
' technique ' that one hears from jitney dramatists
who couldn't write a decent triolet to save their
hides), and so it is natural that it should occasionally
appeal to great artists, particularly in their moments
of fatigue and indolence."   If dramatic technique is,
forsooth, the difficult thing some professors would
have us believe, why is it that so many numskulls
succeed at it?   Why are many of the plays technically perfect the product of writers without a single
idea, a trace of imagination, an ounce of character
sense or a whit of fancy?   Why, in another direction, is it then that so many beginners achieve it with
apparently astonishing ease and auspiciousness the
very first time they tackle it?   Jean Webster, a
writer of magazine stories for young girls, did
" Daddy Longlegs " at her first try.   Catherine
Chisholm Cushing followed up her " Real Thing "
with " Kitty MacKay " and " Jerry."   Thompson
Buchanan dropped newspaper work and wrote the
adroit and equally successful " Woman's Way."   A.
E. Thomas left the *Sun* and turned out the deft
" Her Husband's Wife."   Young Reizenstein left
a lawyer's office and delivered " On Trial."   Marcin
quit the *Press* and negotiated " The House of
Glass."   Robert McLaughlin was a stock company
manager and turned out " The Eternal Magdalene."
The list is without end.   Whatever the plays therein
may not be from a critical point of view, they are

full of the "technique" beloved of the whiskered classes. Charles K. Hoyt was a press-agent. His first bout with Technique was eminently successful. So was James Forbes', also a press-agent. Henry Arthur Jones was a travelling salesman. He quit telling naughty stories in the smoking-car and achieved Technique at the first crack. Charles Rann Kennedy was an actor and his first try at Technique was "The Servant in the House." Thus the situation! And Shaw, Wedekind, Andreyev, Synge, Dunsany, Tchekov, *et al,* still have the pesky thing to master!

Treat *le troisième.* The notion, favourite always of Shaw's audience of critics, that Shaw's plays are deficient in the visualizing of this or that episode, in permitting an audience to see this or that thing rather — as is the case — than having the characters merely talk about its being, or having been, done. Voila! There, by the same hook, go Schiller's "Maid of Orleans," Shakespeare's "Macbeth" and eight out of ten of the world's best plays. To visualize everything in a play is to compose merely a cheap melodrama. The drama of ideas is the drama of the ear. The eye is the little brother of Kiralfy and Belasco. Sardou, the Charles M. Schwab of cheap melodrama, craftily and not unsuccessfully sought to give a loftier tone to his compositions and so assure himself of some literary standing by inventing the action of his plays and — as Shaw himself has expressed it — then carefully

246 Mr. George Jean Nathan Presents

keeping it out of sight in the wings and having it announced by letters and telegrams.

" Major Barbara," as already amply appreciated, is a mixture of Nietzsche and " The Belle of New York," done after the formula of Aristophanes, Beaumarchais and Will Cressy, and, while one of the least important of Shaw's satiric compositions, is still better than the most important of any native dramatist I can summon to mind. The play's enactment by the Playhouse repertory company was a valuable argument against the theory that a permanent group of modern actors may possess a sufficient flexibility to interpret with skill such diverse moulds of drama as a repertory company is called upon to present.

III

Several years ago they produced in the Longacre Theatre a play hight " Are You a Crook? " At the dress rehearsal, they saw that the incidents of the piece were so utterly ridiculous that not even a Broadway audience would accept them as they were intended. At the last moment, accordingly, it was decided to put in an addendum wherein the whole of the enacted play was disclosed to the spectators to have been merely a rehearsal for a motion picture. The play failed.

Several months ago they produced in the Cort Theatre, a play hight " Pay Day." At one of the rehearsals, they saw that the incidents of the piece

were so utterly ridiculous that not even a Broadway
audience would accept them as they were intended.
At the last moment, accordingly, it was decided to
put in an addendum wherein the whole of the enacted
play was disclosed to the spectators to have been
merely a reading rehearsal of a motion picture.
The play failed.

Why the plays failed, Heaven and Mr. Louis V.
De Foe alone know! Worse plays have made a
fortune. But we may be privileged at least to make
a few critical guesses. Both plays were denominated satires; satires, that is, on the moving picture
melodramas. And both plays, i.e., both plays within
the plays, were in themselves no better than the
plays they sought to satirize. Patently enough, a
bad play or general type of bad play may not be
satirized with an equally bad play. The satire must
be a better play, a deftier instance of writing, than
the original. Satire, the edelweiss of literature, is
the most aloof of all the writing forms. It is, obviously enough, not to be confused with mere burlesque.

To illustrate the general point. George Cohan's
travesty of " The Great Lover " in the Cohan Revue,
wherein following the leading protagonist's loss of
voice as he is about to go out upon the stage of the
Metropolitan Opera House, the young rival in taunt-
ing the hero also loses his voice, is good burlesque.
But it is not satire. Satire, as has been said, must
not merely lightly ridicule the original, it must actu-

ally be of finer fabric than the original. Thus, were
Mr. Cohan to attempt to satirize " The Great
Lover " in place of simply burlesquing that play, he
would have to work out some such idea as having the
tenor who has lost his voice go out upon the Metropolitan Opera House stage and achieve a bigger artistic success with the American public and critics
than ever before!

Such a melodrama as " Pay Day " is intrinsically
not a whit more ridiculous than such melodramas as
" The House of Glass," which it closely resembles
and which was taken seriously on Broadway for six
months.   Having for its basis the venerable ancient
of the innocent girl accused of crime, convicted and
subsequently hounded by the vindictive gendarmes,
it has sought to make itself up-to-date merely by
adding a revenge on the part of its persecuted
heroine that was practised in quite the same manner
six years ago in a yellow-back called " Lady Jim of
Curzon Street " and, several years before that, in a
pocket-edition melodrama at the Guignol.   Thus, in
short, the melodrama is not a satire on either the
Broadway melodrama or the cinema melodrama.
It *is* a Broadway melodrama; it *is* a cinema melodrama.

To summarize.   A bad play may not be made into
a success arbitrarily by giving it a so-called surprise
tag.   Such a tag, or curtain, offends the audience.
The audience will like the bad play if it is left alone
— and the play will so in all probability prove very

successful — but it is adding insult to injury to spoil the audience's pleasure by *telling* it the play it likes and has been enjoying is a bad one.

IV

One of Mr. David Belasco's sterling contributions to American dramatic art and letters is a play entilted "The Heart of Wetona," by Mr. George Scarborough, a work dealing with the life, customs and ethical and moral code of the American Indian of to-day and reflecting that life, code, *et cetera,* with the same searching fidelity, vraisemblance and pertinacity that marked the treatment of the subject by Messrs. Pixley and Luders in the Indian chorus number of "The Burgomaster."

Set forth not as a mere tin-pot melodrama for reuben revenue only — which in all honesty it is — but, more seriously and elegantly, as " a new American play," the presentation affords us a not unexcellent instance of and insight into the strapping essences of the Belasco dramaturgy. As originally conceived and written by Mr. Scarborough — and so promulgated in Atlantic City under the title " The Girl "— the play, which treated of a young woman's seduction and the attitude of her father toward the entertainment, had as its characters a set of Puritanic Anglo-Saxons. The piece in this form appearing evidently to Mr. Belasco to lack the gauds and pretty enamels necessary to captivate the Broadway audience, Mr. Belasco, altering the theme not at all,

simply shifted the locâle to an Indian reservation,
took off the characters' Kuppenheimers and Dunlaps
and by sticking feather-dusters on their heads, smearing their Anglo-Saxon faces with Hess' No. 17 war
paint and decorating the walls of the Anglo-Saxon
house with a Frederic Remington colour supplement
and a couple of Navajo blankets of the sort bought
through the Pullman window from the squaw venders
at the railroad station at Albuquerque, achieved —
presto! —" a new American play dealing with the
modern American Indian."

So much for the play as an exhibition deserving
serious or respectful consideration. As a cap-pistol
melodrama, it probably serves its purpose more
prettily, having as its leading elements all the philosophic and mechanical jewelry of the ten-twenty
classics. The villain — a low fellow — wears rid-
ing boots and smokes cigarettes. When dared by
the contemptuous hero to " take that revolver and
shoot me, if you're a man! " the villain, foreseeing
the absurdity and consequences of such an act, naturally issues the hero a laugh, whereupon the hero,
who wears a bandana draped at his throat, scorns
him for the coward he is — to the rapturous applause of the clients. The innocent Indian heroine who has been unwittingly seduced (she
believed she was merely picking wild flowers in the
moonlight, so she tells us sophomoric cynics) is a
" poor little flower " to the hero, who " has travelled
in the far places and knows a good woman when he

sees one." And the little one's cruel Indian father
tells her (in a grunting patois that is a cross between
a stomach-ache and a doctor's prescription) that
" she is no better than a woman of the streets." It
is all here!

The play is produced with all Mr. Belasco's char-
acteristic attention to detail and inattentior. to gen-
erality. Although the lights click on and off with the
customary precision, the Indians look as if they had
just come from the Swiss Hand Laundry. And
though the door opening at the back of the stage in
the second act reveals a completely furnished bedroom lighted by a costly pink lamp, both the tribal
house and the room in the house of the Indian agent
are as dustless and spotless as to furniture and walls
as a residence on the Avenue. Obviously, however,
the production came in for the usual Belasco lard
blast on the part of a number of my colleagues. As
a matter of record, the play is staged not one-half
so well as was the Shuberts' " Hobson's Choice "
(B. Iden Payne) or the Corey-Williams' " Erstwhile
Susan " (Harrison Grey Fiske) or " The Melody of
Youth " (Brandon Tynan) or " Treasure Island "
(Hopkins and Emery) — and not one-fiftieth so well
as this same Mr. Belasco's own staging of " The
Boomerang."

Of the actors, Mr. William Courtleigh yells
at the top of his voice, makes faces like
Frank Daniels and believes he is so depicting
a Comanche chief. Mr. John Miltern, generally a

likeable performer, has, in his portrayal of the hero, joined the Listerine school of acting and gargles his rôle. With his exaggerated voice shadings, his arpeggios from *piano* to *forte,* the gentleman gives one the impression of having swallowed a ukelele. Mr. Lowell Sherman would be a better actor if he refrained from indicating doubt, nervous alarm and deep cogitation each and all by turning himself sideways and slowly brushing his hand across his lips.

V

The score of " The Road to Mandalay," a lucidly poor musical comedy, is yet to the analytical fellow an interesting laboratory specimen. The work of a Mr. Oreste Vessella, a musician the prime years of whose life have been spent in a brave effort to drown out with a good brass pier band the noise of the waves and gum chewers of Atlantic City, it is remarkable in that there are included in its manufacture in variable degree portions of the thirty-two compositions which mark the grand total of the scholarship of the average American music lover. Whether or not the thing was done deliberately by way of satire by this Mr. Vessella — a belief somewhat difficult to conjure up — whether that gentleman thought thus to guarantee the applauding ear of the mob or whether, on the other hand, the whole thing was sheer accident, is not given the stranger to record. Yet the fact remains that, fortuitously or otherwise, the score of this piece is as clever a

satire of the native musical taste, as good a lampoon
of the Broadway musical education, as one may page
in the recesses of memory.

In the score, as I have said, one discovers the
presence of samples — some of the samples of liberal
size indeed — of the thirty-two compositions which,
by and large, compromise the musical tutelage of
the average local.   The which thirty-two are as
follows:

1. " The Rosary."
2. Tosti's " Good-bye."
3. " Hearts and Flowers."
4. Schubert's " Serenade."
5. Mendelssohn's " Spring Song."
6. Dvořák's " Humoréske " (Op. 101, No. 7).
7. Michaelis' " Turkish Patrol."
8. { Mendelssohn's " Wedding March."
     { Chopin's " Funeral March."
9. Handel's " Largo."
10. Mascagni's Intermezzo from " Cavalleria
     Rusticana."
11. The Merry Widow Waltz.
12. " Narcissus."
13. The clog dance.
14. Strauss' " Blue Danube."
15. " Asthore."
16. Rubinstein's " Melody in F."
17. The " Donna é Mobile " from " Rigoletto."
18. " The Night of Love " from " The Tales of
     Hoffman."

19. The " Evening Star " from " Tannhäuser."
20. " I Dreamt I Dwelt in Marble Halls " from " The Bohemian Girl."
21. The Toreador Song from " Carmen."
22. Sullivan's " The Lost Chord."
23. " Rocked in the Cradle of the Deep."
24. " La Paloma."
25. Schumann's " Träumerei."
26. " Believe Me If All Those Endearing Young Charms."
27. " Drink to Me Only With Thine Eyes."
28. " Old Black Joe."
29. " Ach Du Lieber Augustin."
30. Badarczevska's " The Maiden's Prayer."
31. The Sextette from " Lucia."
32. The Hoochee-Coochee.

Aside from this ingenious musical spoofing of the mob palate, the entertainment harks back to the music show days of Pauline Hall, Nella Bergen, Zelma Rawlston, Della Fox, Marie Jansen, Ruth Peebles, Madge Lessing, Mabel Carrier, Paula Edwards, Mabelle Gilman, Eleanor Mayo, Frankie Raymond, Jeanette Lowrie, the days of John T. Kelly and Francis Wilson, Seabrooke and Jerome Sykes, the days of " Panjandrum " and " Tobasco," " The Oolah," " The Grand Mogul " and " The Begum," the days when the leading comedian still bore such nomenclature as the Szetzetze of Szutzutzu or something of the sort.

VI

It would appear from the writings of our theatrical reviewers that the Shakespeare tercentenary was celebrated not, as one might have suspected, in paying homage to Shakespeare so much as in paying homage to the Messrs. Urban, Harker and other scene painters. Three quarters of the various journalistic reviews treating with Mr. Hackett's presentations of " Macbeth " and " The Merry Wives " in the Criterion were devoted to veneration of the beauty of Urban's cheese-cloths and canvasses and one reluctant (and prescriptive) quarter to allowing that, after all, Shakespeare's lines were still " rich in word music," *et cetera.* And Mr. Herbert Beerbohm Tree's exhibition of " Henry VIII " in the New Amsterdam was made the commemorative occasion for rapturous fealty to the fellow who designed the scenery for the banqueting hall in Wolsey's palace and the hall in Blackfriars and the added jubilee occasion for congratulating Mr. Tree on having cut down Shakespeare's original five-act text to the very limit.

The wistful humour of this tercentenary business as it was conducted in our neighbourhood cannot but appeal to those real lovers of Shakespeare who, tolerantly and not without amusement, were content to watch the pother from the sidelines. Excepting the respectful and intelligent performances of Shakespeare in the York and the Irving Place Theatres —

the exhibition of " The Taming of the Shrew " in the
latter playhouse, text uncut, stage demeanour unal-
tered, atmosphere politely and rigidly retained, was
the one actual Shakespearean representation vouchsafed New York — excepting, as I say, the dignified
productions in these theatres, the Shakespeare anniversary was marked in celebration with a fuddled
hypocrisy, much fine talking and not a little gushing
ignorance.   Were George Washington's birthday to
be celebrated by complimenting Mr. Hepner for
having designed a more lovely wig than that worn
by Mr. Washington, the procedure were not a whit
less genial than the business of celebrating the
Shakespearean anniversary by complimenting Mr.
Norman Wilkinson for having designed a more
lovely scenic investiture than that which originally
adorned the Globe Theatre.   Certainly when, from
a presentation of " King Henry VIII," such lines as
" And those about her from her shall read the perfect ways of honour, and by these claim their great-
ness, not by blood," are deleted on the ground that
the uninterrupted text were too long to hold an
audience in a modern theatre, and in their place yet
substituted a twenty-minute curtain speech by the
main actor detailing the source and number of con-
gratulatory telegrams and cablegrams the main
actor has received from his fellow actors, certainly
then does the whole enterprise become somewhat —
well, let us say, droll.   If Shakespeare is to be cut
— and that he may to theatrical advantage be cut is

not to be disputed — let him be cut for this reason
and to this prosperity. But let not Shakespeare be
cut merely to gratify the incompetence of scene
shifters and the star gentleman's desire to inform us
American yokels that he is actually a warm friend
to the great Mr. Asquith!

VII

Just as in Mr. Herman Sheffauer's belated,
credulous and soporific play " The Bargain," Miss
Dorothy Donnelly's idea of interpreting the rôle of
a Jewess was to act without a corset, so it would seem
in the Goddard-Dickey anthology, " Miss Information," to be Miss Elsie Janis' idea of versatility that
versatility consists merely in doing a whole lot of perfectly irrelevant things. Just why jumping in and
out of half a dozen costumes, achieving a somersault,
singing a song and giving an imitation of Miss Ethel
Barrymore should be regarded as marks of virtuosity
and versatility, I am somewhat unable to compre-
hend. I, for example, am believed by some persons
(about whom I have written nice things) to be a
dramatic critic. Now, if, during the reviewing of a
play, I were suddenly to jump out of my seat and do
a split in the aisle and while in this gay posture give
an imitation of Miss Dorothy Gish, would it indicate
that I was versatile or would it indicate simply that I
was a plain idiot? A dramatic critic is a dramatic
critic (at least cases have been known) ; a plumber
is a plumber; a beer-wagon driver is a beer-wagon

driver. And a music-hall mimic is a music-hall
mimic. One doesn't regard the plumber as a
greater plumber if he can also drive a beer-wagon
or the beer-wagon driver as a greater beer-wagon
driver if he knows how to perform upon the bath-
room. Nor do I quite see why one should regard a
music-hall mimic as something greater than a music-
hall mimic because in addition to her talent for good
mimicry she possesses a talent for bad somersaulting.
The truth about Elsie Janis is that she is a clever
little vaudeville woman with an unquestioned knack
for imitating the mannerisms of her fellow snifflers,
face-makers and gesture-chefs, and that beyond this
she owns nothing of genuine versatility. What
they otherwise call versatility in impersonation in
Miss Janis is actually merely a faculty for changing
costumes with rapidity. This confusion of versatility with costumes being a not uncommon practice
of the reviewing mind. Miss Janis, true, can sing
a bit and dance a bit, besides mimic; but she can
neither sing nor dance so well as young women who
have specialized in singing or dancing, or both.
The Elsie Janis versatility hallucination is, in short,
a triumph of press-agent over newspaper reviewer's
waste-basket.

VIII

A poor play that is habitually threatening to be
good, and never remains anything but poor, is the
best estimate of Mr. Louis K. Anspacher's latest

grand doings, "The Unchastened Woman." But, though poor the play is, it yet contains one very' nearly brilliant instance of character drawing in the person of its central female and at least one interesting and not unsubtle flash in the instance of her young woman companion. So clear and quick are these two appraisals that they have caused a sufficient confusion in several quarters to bring the play itself to be regarded as a composition of consequence. Still, this is a not unfamiliar occurrence. So saturated is the community with the sweetened syrups of the theatre, its senses so benumbed by the theatre's amber vapourings, that, suddenly confronted with an unsentimental play, however bad, it forthwith believes that play to be a good play. The thing is a simple, and obvious, study in sudden contrasts. After a series of " Peg O' My Hearts " and " Kitty Mackays ". and such like honey breweries, the public is quite as certain to overestimate an antithetical and equally inconsequent piece of sourball dramaturgy like " Hindle Wakes " as it is to admire the acting of Mr. William Gillette merely because that gentleman speaks his lines in soft and tranquil tones when all the other actors in the company are made to deliver theirs *fortississimo, furiosamente*. It is the nature of the unsophisticated ever to be deluded, entranced, roped in by contrasts. Why, otherwise, does a man whose first wife was a brunette, always, when he marries a second time, succumb to a blonde ? And vice versa ? Why, otherwise, was " Ruther-

ford and Son " acclaimed a noteworthy play?   And
why, otherwise, do persons with homes and home-
cooking now and again relish a bad meal in a restaurant?   The Anspacher masque is, in short, the
college boy's notion of a strong play.

The character which the author has manœuvred
with so considerable an adroitness is a sort of light
comedy reincarnation of the première hussy out of
Bernstein's " Secret," a sort of tame vampire.   The
type is a familiar one — the married salamander,
the lady who is willing to play football, but without
goal posts.   The story in which the playwright has
placed this personage is a commonplace potpourri
of young artist lover, indulgent husband and 11 p. m.
worm-turn.

IX

" The Mark of the Beast " is a sex play by two
American ladies, the Mesdames Georgia Earle and
Fanny Cannon, and hence twice as silly as if it had
been written by but one.   Like nine out of ten such
domestic compositions, it commits the familiar mistake of viewing women as a problem instead of as an
amusement.   The play is so solemnly serious that
the authors would seem to have a fortune in store
for them if they will wait until the war is over, trans-
late it word for word and produce it in Paris as a
farce.   Consider the meat.   A man's wife goes
bacheloring.   The man finds her out.   He, ada-
mant to her tears, determines at once to divorce her.

Her counsel, a learned judge, seeks out the husband and, by the exercise of the celebrated "you neg-·lected her for your business and a woman must have love" theorem, succeeds in persuading him to relent. This no sooner accomplished than the judge learns that his own wife has also been bacheloring and — oh my God how could she where is that revolver I'll kill the scoundrel! But Husband I now into the breach. The baby-collar, blue-eyed philosophy once again to the fore, and Husband II, like Husband I before him, falls. A profoundly impressive spectacle for all girls under eleven and over forty, and for all persons who use the double negative, believe it is unlucky to walk under a ladder, admire pianos with mandolin attachments, believe that fifteen drops of camphor in half a glass of water will prevent colds or think that kissing a girl in the ear is immoral. The stellar rôle in this trump was occupied by Mr. George Nash, one of the school of actors who, when the butler brings in a visitor's card, meditatively flicks it three times against his thumb before bidding the servant show the caller in.

CURTAIN-RAISERS AND HAIR-RAISERS

SPEAKING broadly of the current theatre, a one-act play may be defined as a play which is only one-third as tiresome as a three-act play. That is, of course, a one-act play not written to serve its purpose as a curtain-raiser in the London theatres. For, as every one knows, such a one-act play is designed with what would seem to be a deliberate purposefulness to be three times as tiresome as the long play which follows it.[1]

If one enters a London playhouse in time for the curtain-raiser (something that no gentleman does), one is as generally certain to witness a witless exhibition as one is generally certain, upon picking up an American newspaper, to encounter a piece concerning a romance between two lowly souls which came out of the finding, in the pocket of a suit of overalls, of a random note that had been placed there by the sweatshop girl who made the garment. Or as one is generally certain, after mentally enveloping a newly met and beautiful morsel with the romantic fumes of a fragrant fancy, with the imaginative perfumes of the kingdom of Micomicon and

---

[1] Thus, in comparison, causing the long play to appear somewhat less tedious than it actually is.

the dreams of Alnaschar, to hear an abrupt rape of one's reverie in the baggage's inevitable allusion to her " pet corn." Let us approach, for example, the curtain-raiser called " A Dear Little Wife," by Gerald Dunn, one evidently so popular that it has been called on to lift the curtain at more than one London theatre.

We have here what is known as a " Japanese play." Mr. Dunn's brain-child follows the established ritual of the " Japanese play " as closely as all American military plays follow the especial ritual laid down in their case. (Did you, for instance, ever see one of these military plays in whose second act " the enemy " was not announced 'mid wild alarms to be just on the point of crossing something — bridge, river or what not?) Thus, we have Fuji on the backdrop, a Sugihara San doing the usual arranging thing with the flowers and singing to herself the meantime (" How lovely they are, these flowers," muses the little Sugihara; " how I love them! "), the usual " O Takejiro, be honourably pleased to enter " form of speech, and all the additional usual ingredients of such a play.

For example, the goldfish business, as follows:

SUGIHARA SAN.   There are these flowers to be arranged, and the goldfish are waiting for me to feed them —

TAKEJIRO.   Oh, happy goldfish!   How I wish I were one of them!

SUGIHARA SAN.   No, I do not think you would like it, lying all day in the water underneath the lilies.

TAKEJIRO.   Yes, Sugihara San, if I might look at you!

For example, the moon business, as follows:

TAKEJIRO.   Oh, Sugihara, you are very cruel. I sing to you "My Lady Moon," and you *are* just like the moon — just as beautiful and radiant, but just as cold and far away.

SUGIHARA SAN.   And you, Takejiro, are like the children crying in the night because they cannot call the moon out of the sky to come and play with them! How can the moon, for all she loves them, leave her sky?

For example, the cherry blossom business, with the usual John Luther Long Japanese orchestration, as follows:

TAKEJIRO.   I could never be angry with you, Sugihara. I would make your life like the blossoming of the cherry trees for happiness; and we would sit by the sea where the pines sway like girls in the dance, or wander under the high woods and listen to the water leaping down the rocks; and the fireflies would be our lanterns, and the birds our flute players, as they called to one another in the darkness, "Sugihara, O Sugihara San!"

In addition to these many novelties, Mr. Dunn has conceived the dramatic innovation of having one character narrate, in the form of fable, to another and unsuspecting character events that have actually happened.   Lest you forget the formula, observe:

"Listen and hear the story of a clever woman. Oh, yes; she was very clever, much cleverer than Sugihara, and she had a husband — no, not at all like you, Hagiyama! — who was full of fancies and jealousies and not at all a nice kind of husband, because he suspected that his wife was unfaithful.   Et cetera."

But let us not tarry longer in Shaftsbury Avenue with Gerald and his Sugihara. On to the Vaude-ville and to "The Rest Cure" of Miss Gertrude Jennings. Miss Jennings would appear to be a prolific mother in the matter of these curtain-raisers. A round of the London theatres discovers her as a pit-masseuse of alarming fructification. In addition to "The Rest Cure," her "Acid Drops" has teased the asbestos at the Royalty, her "Between the Soup and the Savoury" has been done at the Playhouse and her "Pros and Cons" has similarly been invoked to beguile the Two-and-Sixpences. If these pieces are ever done in America, our critics will say of Miss Jennings that she "assuredly possesses the knack of the theatre." This, alas, is true. Miss Jennings has evidently been an omnivorous student of "manuals of playmaking," the Manual Movement being distinctly observable in the bulk of her work. She "builds up laughs," "mixes comedy with a tear," and so on, with so zealous an obedience to book rules and injunctions that her characters are resolved into the conventional artificial puppets born of such a dramatic education.

I am scarcely one of the profound dolts who loudly debates for "living," "real," "flesh and blood" characters in the drama, being aware that if a playwright has anything genuinely interesting, or even merely diverting, to say, he is at whole liberty to put that something into the mouths of the stock sawdust dolls of the stage — since as proportionately few

living, real, flesh and blood persons ever have anything worth while to say, it follows that a careless
employment of too " real " play characters by the
dramatist must succeed in lending to his work a
marked air of spuriousness and artificiality.   Wilde
realized this yesterday as Molnar, Shaw, *et al.* realize it to-day.   On the other hand, however, when
along come play-makers like Miss Jennings, who
have little more in their mouths than a tongue and
some teeth and a couple of tonsils, it follows that,
having nothing interesting to articulate, they needs
must place that lack of something interesting in the
mouths of " living " characters, characters taken out
of life, if they would have their plays seem not
spurious and not artificial, but real.   Or at least
partly or vaguely suggestive of life.

Given the title " The Rest Cure," apprised
that the scene is " a bedroom in a nursing home "
and that the piece is a comedy, it should be a matter
for your left hand to deduce the materials of
the play.   Certainly.   Man, worn down by over-
work, goes to nursing home for quiet and recupera-
tion, and is so disturbed by noises, nurses and nuisances of the establishment that he makes escape
back to comparative peace of his home with deep-
breathed pleasure.   Ward and Vokes *redivivi!*
Hearken to Miss Jennings' way of " laughs ":

MURIEL.   Yes, nurse.   [*Going reluctantly to the door.*]
That there gent in No. 5 hollers at me somethin' awful.
He says if I come into the room again he'll wring my neck.

ALICE. I can't help *his* troubles. The grate must be done.

Again:

CLARENCE. My bed squeaks disgracefully. When I didn't jump at the sound of motorbuses, I flinched at the squeaking of the bed.

NURSE. How very strange. Our beds have always been considered quite noiseless.

Laughter is further provoked by Miss Jennings through the employment of a scuttle of coal which (see bus.) "*Muriel pours on fire with a deafening crash. Clarence gives prolonged scream*"; of a large portmanteau which (see bus.) "*man carries in and throws on floor with a bang*"; and of wild jumpings in and out of bed on the part of the central actor, already familiar to us Americans as a standard element in our native dramatic humour.

In "Acid Drops," the scene of which is a workhouse ward for women, and the action of which concerns, so far as I can make out, nothing beyond killing time until the long play of the evening is ready, the recommended "tear that should be mixed with comedy" takes the form of one of the usual "sweet old women, optimistic and smiling in the face of pain and adversity." Ah me, how many the time we have attended the dear old nuisances and given ear to their sweet prattle — and laughed at them where we shouldn't! In "Acid Drops," the old girl's name is Mrs. Gilbert who "do hopes I

live till Sunday " but (*smiling*) " I'm not afeard to
go, my dears, I'm not afeard to go ! " But the real
tear, the salt drop maître d'hôtel, is yet to come.
The old girl, as many a character like her on the
stage in days gone by, begins " recollectin'." The
Mose Tobani cue. The Maison Blanc cue.

Thus, Mrs. Gilbert: " I mind the days when I
was a maid as clear as yesterday. In Kent it were
— nigh to Benenden. . . . I mind one day in May
month when Jim spoke to me first. ' You're my
little lass now, ain't you? ' he sez, and I sez, ' Yes,
Jim.' There was a wonnerful blue sky that day,
I mind, and a great singin' of birds, and the blossoms
was somethin' fine. There's not many can remember as fur as that, my dear, nor see the apple orchard
as plain as I can now. The Lord's been wonnerful
good to me (Mrs. Gilbert, remember, is in the workhouse) and He'll be the same to you, my dear."

But wait, the saline solution of which I have made
mention has not yet been coaxed into flow. Are you
ready? Then—

Mrs. Gilbert. I've been turnin' over just a few things
in my mind as I've bin lyin' here; I've been thinkin' over
my life's doings, and 'ow wonnerful blessed I've bin. Them
that's young and 'asty don't always know the joyfulness of
life. When I was a girl I 'ad Jim, but I didn't 'ardly realize, not till I lost him. We never got married, Jim and
me. We was courtin' in the spring, same as I told you —
then came the fruit season. We was picking the cherries,
Jim and me, and we fell out, and I spoke 'arshly to him.
Jim was alwuz quick to take hurt. " Then it's good-bye,"

he sez to me at last. "You'll never see me no more," he sez, and off he goes down the long road that led to Cran-·brook. I wouldn't call after 'im, my dear, for I was 'ard of 'eart those days, but I climbed up to my little bedroom winder that I could see the road from, hopin' he'd come back.

FLORA. And did he?

MRS. GILBERT. No, dearie. He never come back again —never. I looked down that long road many a day, but 'twas all in vain. It giv me a sort of feelin' even now to think of it, tho' Jim's been dead and gone many a long year. I married in my time, and my man turned out proper enough; but somehow I'm thinkin' it'll be Jim that'll meet me when I've crossed the other side. "You're my little lass now," he'll say, and I'll say, "Yes, Jim." [*Pause.*] I've often wished when I 'ear of young folks falling out that they could 'ear tell of those many times I climbed up to my little winder, for, thinks I, they'd never want to do the like. There, there, my dear, you're crying.

Let us pause to dry an eye.

"Between the Soup and the Savoury" begins rather entertainingly with a scene in the kitchen of a moderately smart English house during the service of dinner, but quickly remembers it is a London curtain-raiser and corrects itself. The "tear in the comedy" here assumes the shape of a plain drab of a slavey who longs vainly to be loved, who is taunted by her servant associates and who, unable longer to endure their gibes, steals the love letters belonging to the daughter of the house and passes them off as her own.

But time presses and we must leave Miss Ger-

trude and her Mrs. Gilbert and her Clarence and
her slavey with Gerald and his Sugihara — and proceed to Wilfred T. Coleby's " The Silver Lining,"
which introduces the play at the Haymarket.   This
Mr. Coleby, you will recall, was Edward Knoblauch's collaborator in " The Headmaster."   Now,
although it is an uncomforting and profitless duty
for a critic to speak ill and find fault to the extent
which I have in the present chapter — for any critic
may sneak out for himself a name for " fairness,"
" broadness," " sympathy," " impartiality " and all
the other intrinsically absurd things of which the
public in its critical ignorance speaks, by the simple
trick of arbitrarily sprinkling his adverse appraisals
with pinches of magnanimous allowance and charitable amiability — I am in the sad plight of finding
myself at the moment so ridiculously upright that
I cannot persuade myself into deceiving you, by the
use of the above trick, to rate me higher in your
critical estimation than, after reading this chapter,
you will.

Mr. Coleby's piece is a jog trot with ennui; a
war of words; a Derby day in which a cluster of
more or less obvious characterizations race against
somnolence.   The obtruding fable is of a grasping
old woman who blackmails a clergyman out of several pounds and, through paving the way for the
institution of a similar stratagem, contrives to match
up her daughter with a wealthy young man.   The
piece is of perfectly patent fabrication; the comedy

of the mid-Charles T. Dazey period; the situations static. The acting of the play is, like the acting of every curtain-raiser visible in London at the time of writing, worse than merely mediocre.

At the Strand and at Wyndham's, the curtain is hoisted by two bands of minstrels calling themselves, respectively, "The Entertainers" and "The Quaints," who make noises with their mouths to the effect that the moon in June is in tune with a spoon, who engage in protracted dialogue as to what street is Watt Street and who, when the electrician throws on the purple lights, put their heads together and conclude with a *sotto voce* barber shop on a "Slumberland" number.

And now we are once again on our annual pilgrimage to the Rue Chaptal and to the Guignol of Max Maurey. A clever soul, this Max, probably the most fertile prestidigitator of the stage amongst us. Time and again I have sat before his tiny *bühne* and marvelled at the fellow's placid cunning in the suggestion of effects which the plays bade him create for us out in the auditorium. I have seen him suggest with what was almost a shuddering realism the collision of a giant liner of the seas with an iceberg. And this through the humorously unintricate device of suddenly halting a stagehand in the wings who, up to the moment of the "collision," had with periodic regularity been pounding on the floor with a padded mallet to suggest the throb of the steamship's engines. I have

seen him send the spine into a chill by suggest-
ing the supernatural through the simple trick of
causing the door of an empty chamber to be slowly
and " mysteriously " pulled ajar by an invisible black
thread.   I have seen him suggest the dead cold of a
winter night by making a slyly taken puff at a cigarette
in exhalation appear to be frosted breath.   An innocent and somewhat boyish business, all this, true;
yet one which, taken in the total of the two hundred
and seventy-three plays produced at the Guignol to
the present time, amounts to a mastery of the cyclo-
pedia of theatrical effect, a virtuosity in the surface
aspects of the acted drama.

But Maurey has other talents than these.   In
addition to his abilities as a writer of amiable, if
quite inconsequent, small pieces for his playhouse,
he is a director of peculiar intelligence and acumen.
In the matter of actors, Maurey, instead of hiring
inefficient clowns and posturers at exaggerated wage,
has gathered about him a company of able per-
formers who work in well oiled accord and to electric
result.   Some actors and some actresses are born
stars, others achieve stardom — and others know a
broker.   None of this crew for Max.   No stars for
him.   Merely capable actors.   Look down his list
— Ratineau and Viguier and Brizard, Mercelle
Barry and Delville and the rest of them — and note
the difference.

" Mirette a Ses Raisons," or " Mirette Has Her

Reasons," to illustrate the Guignol style of farce, is a typical Parisian tidbit by Romain Coolus, of the sort known to visiting American school-teachers as " spicy." The trouble with this particular little piece is in the circumstance that the entire plot lies in one line, and that once that particular line is spoken, nothing remains to the play. Mirette, though domiciled in the quarters of her chief lover, Fred, is in the habit of liaisoning clandestinely with Fred's friend, Albert. Fred discovers what has been going on and — then the line. Mirette sweetly confides to him that she is terribly superstitious, that she already has had a dozen lovers, and that if her dear Fred had remained the thirteenth it would have been awfully unlucky, so, *mon cher zigue,* she took on Albert in order that misfortune might not befall her loved one. And of course Fred, as any true lover would, begs her forgive him for his rude doubts as to her virtue. The outline of the piece has a more entrancing air than the play in actual movement. Whatever his play's deficiencies, it must be admitted, however, that Coolus has devised a more ingenious defence for adultery than did two of the stellar pioneers in that direction of dramatic theme, Marsten (" The Dutch Courtezan," 1605) and George Lillo (" The Merchant of London," 1731).

Here, the kind of play that in England and America would be dubbed immoral. Your An-

glo-Saxon regards as immoral any play in which
a loose woman does not account for the fact of her
unchastity in one of four specific ways:

1. That she " was very young and innocent and
knew nothing of the world and believed him."

2. That she " had trusted him (he was so kind
to her) and had believed him when he told her their
marriage was legal."

3. That " he had taken her by the hand and
promised to marry her immediately the divorce was
granted."

4. That " she didn't know, she didn't know what
she was doing — it's all like a terrible dream —
and then — one day, one day word came to her that
he, that he had been — lost at sea."

Your Anglo-Saxon refuses to admit to himself
that any condition of affairs other than these may
explain a lady's dereliction or derelictions from the
path of continence and, as a consequence, pretends
to a seizure of shock when visited with a theme
which dares suggest that a lady's appetite for *car-
dons à la Savoyarde* and for sex may be generically
of quite the same normal, matter of fact and undramatic nature. In addition to this point of view,
there is, patently, another reason for the Anglo-
Saxon attitude toward French farce of the class typi-
fied by the Coolus piece. The oft repeated epigram of Walpole to the effect that life is a comedy
to the man who thinks and a tragedy to the man
who feels is here in good point: for, in personal

matters of sex, your Anglo-Saxon feels where your
Frenchman thinks. Your Anglo-Saxon is a very
sentimental fellow when it comes to a view of sex.
(Hence his relative unattractiveness to women as
compared with your Frenchman.)

This comparative difference in personal attitude on the part of the Anglo-Saxon and the Gaul
easily explains away a portion of the theatrical side
of the sex thing. But still another relevant theatrical phase of the question obtrudes, a phase that has
been approached by one who is probably the sharpest
of British dramatic critics created since Shaw and
Walkley, Mr. John Palmer of the *Saturday Review*.
Observes he:

"'Either,' says the Frenchman, 'I will think
about life and write a comedy; or I will feel about
life and write a tragedy. But,' the Frenchman in-
sists, 'I will not do these things simultaneously.'
. . . The Englishman's difficulty is precisely the
reverse. He point blank refuses to be departmen-
tal."

Mr. Palmer has further analyzed the situation
in this fashion:

"If sex be not comically treated in the fashion
of Gargantua's birth, we are driven next to the
modern way of the Palais Royal. We have only
to understand why seventeenth century England and
modern France have perfectly succeeded in this particular comic vein to realize why English authors
to-day (Mr. Palmer might truthfully include Ameri-

can authors) invariably fail.   The comedy of sex
in this kind rests, roughly, upon an assumption which
no good modern Englishman writing for the modern
English theatre dare honestly and without veiling
accept — the assumption that men and women are
polygamous by nature and monogamous by necessity.   If this assumption is to be taken as a joke
and lead to laughter, we must clearly avoid anything in the way of emotion or romance.   The
comic treatment of sex in social comedy must be
passionless.   In a comedy of sex there must be no
sex feeling. . . . Breaches of the seventh commandment are only funny so long as they are never serious.   This may sound like a pleonasm; but it is
rarely realized by English authors who write the
modern comedy of sex."

In part, reasonable words, but Mr. Palmer,
like the authors with whom he here deals, is an
Englishman; and must we not bear in mind the
possibility that an English critic may unconsciously
suffer from native traces of the same Anglo-
Saxonism which he lays against those other
Englishmen he criticizes?   It would seem to me,
who am no Englishman, that the idea that breaches
of No. 7 are only humorous so long as they are
never serious is too characteristically British — and,
hence, largely preposterous.   Can it be that my admirable colleague has never seen or read the
excellent Continental pieces in which breaches
of the species in point are at once serious and

genuinely funny? Happy comedies of sex, like Schmidt's, for example, in which there *is* sex feeling? Happy comedies and farcical comedies like those of Schnitzler, in which there *is* emotion and romance? Is it possible that the good Palmer is, *au fond,* something of a sentimentalist and blue stocking?

THE CASE OF MR. WINTHROP AMES

MR. HENRY MILLER once said that the trouble with the business he was in was that it was too theatrical. One sometimes feels that the trouble with the business Mr. Winthrop Ames is in is that it isn't theatrical enough. There is a something to the efforts of the latter — a slight aloofness, an undue reticence, mayhap — that one feels handicaps in a measure the theatre he cicerones. A talented, educated fellow and one pleasant to behold in a play world peopled, as is the present day play world, so largely by ex-sidewalk-solicitors for the Newsboys' Home, Ames brings to his work a sense of discrimination, a sense of beauty and ideals, at once charming and timeful. And as for the contention one hears now and again from serious clowns that he is impracticable, it may be dismissed with the statement that the difficulty with the theatre at the present time is that there are already altogether too many practical producers in it. As a writer for a better theatre, give me any day a so-called impracticable man like Ames above a hundred practical Moroscos. But what one wishes Mr. Ames had more of is that direct bluntness, that saucy fire, which injects into even the best of acted plays a better and a warmer glow.

278

When I sit in Mr. Ames' Little Theatre, I am, by the very feel in the air, charmed as I am charmed in the home of a congenial host — and when I am not pleased with what Mr. Ames presents me I feel somehow the same distaste for finding fault, however deserved, that I feel upon arising from a friend's dinner table (though in such cases no one has ever accused my manners getting the better of my feelings) — yet I often in that lovely little playhouse feel like whistling or giving my nose a lusty blow or doing something disgraceful by way of injecting into the surroundings an air of greater excitement and camaraderie. I am quite certain, knowing Mr. Ames as I do, that he would be the last man in the world to object to my doing such a thing — he would, indeed, probably like me to do it — but I am equally certain, knowing the gentleman as I do, that he would be the last man in the world to ask me to do such a thing. Yet I wish he would. It would, I feel sure, help the both of us.

Aside from the merits of the play, " Hush," by Miss Violet Pearn, with which Mr. Ames reopened his theatre for a recent season (personally I was not at all beguiled by it for it seemed to me to lack the satiric wit absolutely essential to the telling of a tale of a young pseudo-radical who seeks vainly to shock people), one could not help believing that a more bourgeois showmanship would have better projected into the auditorium the materials in the manuscript. Mr. Ames staged the play carefully and attractively and, in the main, cast it efficiently, but one missed in its exhibition and manœuvring the nearness and warmth that one must feel in the playhouse. The Little Theatre stage was probably not more than twenty-five feet from my seat on the aisle in J, but it seemed a full quarter of a mile away. I could see plainly; I could hear clearly; but I couldn't feel at all. In the great spaces of the late New Theatre Mr. Ames once made two manuscripts glow — "The Piper" of Josephine Preston Peabody and the "Strife" of John Galsworthy — two of the very finest instances of staging the modern theatre has known. The paradox of the very vastly less great spaces of the Little Theatre and the corresponding diminution of the sense of warm propinquity, I leave for explanation to some critic more penetrating than I.

The notion, incidentally, that the New Theatre failed because its auditorium was too big is the merest gabble. The auditoriums of the famous theatres of thirty years and more ago — the particular theatres, that is, from which have come down to us the best traditions of our stage — were in several cases as hulky as the auditorium of the New Theatre. The notion that the New Theatre failed, further, because the plays presented there were poor plays is equally sorry. Look over the list of productions made in that theatre and compare them, in any way you choose, with the list of productions made in a corresponding period of time in any other theatre in

America. Ames probably did as well with the New
Theatre as any man one can summon to mind could
have done with it. The New Theatre failed, very
simply and very uncritically, for the same reason
that the Ritz hotels have succeeded. It was too
democratic and not sufficiently exclusive. It made a
good start and then slipped. For, after its first
month and with high prosperity staring it in the face,
it began with diligent gusto to inform the yokelry
that it did not have to put on evening dress to get in.
And the yokelry, thus persuaded that any mere hooli-
gan might attend, remained sniffishly away. Had
the New Theatre let it be felt that no person un-
adorned with a boiled shirt could enter, it would have
been quite as impossible to get a seat at its box-office
as it was to get a table in the Savoy supper room in
London during the American travelling season.

Such is the republican essence.

A CLINICAL REPORT

AMONG all the many three or four act plays produced in New York in the course of thirty recent typical evenings selected for clinical investigation, there was revealed but one of sufficient mettle to interest the non-theatregoing, which is to say the drama-loving, person. With this single exception, the presentations were so-called uplifting, or depressing, comedies like " The Road to Happiness," which guggle such mellow drops of wisdom as " A smiling face cures lumbago "; so-called farces like " See My Lawyer " in which the *mot* " This is a wedding, not a funeral " vies for chuckle precedence with the business of the gentleman who, being handed an expensive cigar, places it in his pocket and continues smoking his own frowzy stogie; to say nothing of so-called dramas like " Common Clay " in which the author, seized with a revolutionary spirit, contends that poor people have a much less pleasant time in this world than rich people and — say what you will against him — proves it.

The exception to this vesuviation of mediocrity was from the hand of Frederick Ballard and bears the name " Young America." Crude as it is and sketchy, and though in small degree departing the

obvious, the play was yet the most refreshing thing
of its month: a play which vouchsafed a few emotions to its audience instead of reserving them entirely for the actors; a play with a nary a corset-
heave, nary an "Oh, my God!", nary a fist-bang
upon library table, nary a single rôle that could be
played by Mr. John Mason. Rather, a simple,
happy-go-lucky, artless, thoroughly nice little affair,
treading over the familiar ground of Mark Twain's
"Huck Finn" and "Tom Sawyer" and Tarkington's "Penrod," over the ground of Judge Shute's
"Real Boys" and the celebrated Peck Classic; an
homely little play of respectable sentiment, honest
laughter and quick observation; a vaudeville of human nature humanly presented in the place of a
keith-and-proctoring of the usual sniffle-sonata performed by a cast of star nose-blowers.

There is little enough, in the Broadway sense,
to the piece. It is merely a biography of tick-tack-
ing upon windows, pulling front door bells, stealing
things out of the neighbours' yards, stretching wires
across sidewalks to trip up stately pedestrians and
such like inconsequentialities — all bound 'round the
love of a boy for a mutt of a dog. It is a play
even without the held to be all vital "love interest,"
love interest, that is to say, of the Broadway gender,
which means the interest which an audience is re-
quested to manifest over the spectacle of Mr. Robert
Edeson expressing his overpowering passion for the
leading lady by approaching her with both hands

in the pockets of his dinner jacket and making a
wistful *moué*. It is a play without a single scene,
alas, in which the stellar pantaloon refers to a gentleman's whiskers as alfalfa or in which, when the
composer Wagner is mentioned, a character mistakes him for the shortstop on the Pittsburgh base-
ball team.   But, in spite of these flaws, Mr. Ballard's effort (doubtless ministered to in passing by
George M. Cohan) is so completely unforced an
effort, so like a simple and unimportant story told
simply and casually, that it leaves one merry and
grateful.

Many of the comedy episodes of the piece call
for especial mention, as for example, the cross-examination by the judge of the juvenile court of a
small coloured boy with the latter's fat, hot, black
mother guarding her little angel from the rear; as
for example, the deft bringing of the action to a
solution through the wild manœuvring of the entire cast to bring back to life a dog that has been
run down by an automobile; as for example, the
scene wherein three married couples, close friends,
are suddenly projected into a violent and devastating
quarrel over absolutely nothing.   But of particular
pleasure was the performance in this play of a lad
rejoicing in the nabob patronymic of Benny Sweeney,
a youngster who, so goes the tale, was captured in
a cigar factory and impressed into thespian service.
Loth as I am to encourage such depredations and
blighting of young men's careers, I cannot resist the

temptation to compliment young Mr. Sweeney as an actor — though in so doing I probably become a further factor in his *dégringolade*.

A second exception to the prevailing panorama of ennui — but an exception for a reason quite other than that attaching to " Young America " and so in itself a thing entirely apart from this general process of appraisal — was Mr. Cohan's own play, " Hit-the-Trail Holliday." On the night of the first presentation of this piece, Mr. Cohan, in response to a deafening pounding of palms, stepped out upon the stage from the wings, bowed, signalled for silence and did not say: " You — poor — boobs, so you've fallen for the old bunk once again and fallen as hard as ever, have you? — even if you don't know it! " This doubtless is what was in the keen Mr. Cohan's mind, even though what he actually said was little else than a pseudo-bashful and surprised thank-you. For, in this latest play of his, Mr. Cohan has composed a bravura piece of the ballyhoo order; a piece made up, from first to last, of all the ancient stuff which he himself has frequently pointed out is " sure-fire " with the native Messrs. Snooks, Tony Lumpkins and their fellow bogtrotters. As an example of theatrical challenge to the individual known as *l'homme sur la rue*, Mr. Cohan's exhibit marks a real feat. And it succinctly demonstrates once again that he knows the American public as probably no other theatrician of the day knows that fowl.

" Hit-the-Trail Holliday " is " Broadway Jones."
" Broadway Jones " was " Get-Rich-Quick Wallingford."   " Get-Rich-Quick Wallingford " was " The
Fortune Hunter."   " The Fortune Hunter " was
" Quincy Adams Sawyer."   And " Quincy Adams
Sawyer " was " Hit-the-Trail Holliday."   The only
difference is that, though the mortgage is lifted by
the hero of " Hit-the-Trail Holliday " just as it was
by the hero of " Quincy Adams Sawyer," the hero of
" Hit-the-Trail Holliday " lifts it off an hotel instead
of a farm house.   And the only other difference is
that, where in " Broadway Jones " the hero was a
Broadway rounder who reformed both himself and
a country town, in the latest Cohan piece he is a
Broadway bartender who reforms both himself and
a country town.

Consider these sure-fire ingredients out of which
Mr. Cohan has fashioned the play:

1. The landlord villain who bulldozes his poor
tenant, who speaks in a loud, gruff voice, who wears
a heavy gold watch-chain and who, turning at the
door, tells the poor tenant that if he doesn't do
soandso by to-morrow he'll have to suffer the consequences.

2. The noble hero with curly hair and a blue suit
who turns to the poor tenant, says " Will you leave
this matter to me?   Thank you," steps nose to nose
with the villain and tells him to go to hell.

3. The villain's equally villainous son who bulldozes the poor tenant and the poor heroine, who

speaks in a loud, gruff voice, who wears fancy clothes and who sneers at the hero, who, in turn, blithely laughs his contempt for the son, snaps his fingers under the latter's nostril, refers to him jocularly as "the merry little cut-up," and so arouses the son's ire to the fighting point.

4. The villain's son who, being thereupon urged by his father to strike the hero, says "Hm, I wouldn't soil my hands on such a person!"

5. The line about listening to a character eat soup.

6. The joke about the wife who talks her husband to death.

7. The joke about marriage.

8. The other joke about marriage.

9. The kindly, sweet-natured, impoverished old minister and his kindly, sweet-natured daughter.

10. The Star Spangled Banner.

11. The rundown business enterprise which the hero, by up-to-date methods, builds into an enormously prosperous organization in two days.

12. Talk about hundreds of thousands of dollars.

13. Talk about millions of dollars.

14. The hero who coolly faces the gang of disgruntled, threatening labourers, conciliates them and wins them over to his side.

15. The speech of the hero to the crowd beneath the window.

16. The fat coloured maid who persistently mispronounces the hero's name.

17. The whistling office boy.

18. The comic policeman.

19. The reiteration of the command to *sit down*.

20. The triumph of virtue over villainy.

These, but a few illustrations, yet sufficing to serve as a criterion. All Mr. Cohan has done to beguile the great unwashed is to sketch, in his hero, a superficial parallel to Billy Sunday. And the great unwashed, as always, has, as Mr. Cohan accurately knew it would, swallowed its favourite bait hook, line, sinker and row-boat.

The series of deliberately unfriendly acts and an epilogue called " Common Clay," I have already briefly alluded to. This, the handiwork of a Mr. Cleves Kinkead, who, appraising himself from his curtain speech on the opening night of his trump, is the sort of author who believes that a playwright owes everything to the actors. Mr. Kinkead is a graduate member of the legislature of a middle-western State, an alumnus of playwriting under Professor Baker of Harvard College, a winner with this play of the Bostonian Craig grand prix, and, as such and probably in view of which, the most promising candidate for the authorship of dramas for servant girls that Broadway has seen in some time. Aside from one well-written slice of dialogue in which the central figure of the play describes the dingy emptiness of her life preceding the epoch of her defloration, his work is a mere commonplace and shabby reflex of Coppée's " Guilty Man," descending at times to the limit of precisely that species of

sweetened concubinage which so irresistibly capti-
vates the fancies of upstairs maids, butlers, footmen·
and the average Broadway theatregoer.

The tale is of a poor girl violated by the gaudy
son of the household in which she is employed, of
the attempt on the part of the young man's father
to shelter him from responsibility for the act and
the concomitant scandal, of the girl's discovery that
she is the illegitimate offspring of a man high in
public affairs, of the latter's "atonement," of the
girl's decision henceforth to abandon the sex motif
and lead a pure and moral life and of her recon-
sidering this decision and becoming an opera singer.
Such the prize-winning tooth of our conterraneous
drama; such the confections sponsored by the master
of the drama in America's leading university. How
now about this Professor Baker, he who has been
press-agented so copiously and, shall we not say,
persuasively? Consider his producers and their
products, not in their later years when his influence
upon them may or may not have been dissipated, as
in the cases of Sheldon and Ballard, but fresh from
his class-room. In all honesty, has this touted
professor done one thing, soever small, to improve
the American drama? I doubt it. True, he has
taught numerous young fellows the facile trick of
building shows, but has he taught them how to write
plays? A different thing this latter, and vastly.
Has one single dramatic effort containing an ounce
of philosophy, an ounce of sober theme, a dash of

cultured wit or a trace of smart observation and penetration come directly from his lecture chamber? Have his products not been rather the products of the cheap showshop mind? What the use of teaching young men how to write plays if the young men have no plays to write? You can't be a conductor unless you've got a street-car.

" The Road to Happiness " is a play whose scenes are laid in the country, whose plot concerns the parentage of an illegitimate baby and whose characters are a congregation of ignoramuses — a play, to wit, which is dubbed " optimistic " and " wholesome." In a word, it is the kind of thing in which the main actor in the rôle of one of God's noblemen stands under the old chestnut tree in a suit of overalls for a couple of hours and, with eyes half closed as if meditating upon the exquisite beauty of the sentiments contained therein, exudes such benevolent gumdrops as " What difference does it make who has all the money as long as everybody's happy? Cheerfulness is better than money. You might lose your money, but you can keep on bein' cheerful if you only keep up hope."

The play, on the whole, amounts to nothing but a monologue of mush. From 8:15 to 11 the heroic figure of the traffic is busy taking under his wing the girl who has been driven forth into the night by the cruel stepfather —" she shall come home with *me!* " defiantly proclaims our hero —; holding his crippled old white-haired mother's hand and telling her she will surely get well if she only has faith; petting a dog, patting a horse and dispensing such noble, if occult, texts as " Laughter on the lips makes sunshine in the heart." From first to last a laboriously aimed and fired battery of dum-dum platitudes and wall mottoes; an antique of the " God Bless Our Home " school of drama.

The piece has not a single justification, of whatever sort. Unlike the plays of James A. Herne, upon the pattern of which it presumably has been built, this play confounds chin whiskers and gingham aprons with types of rural character. As a consequence, its personages are approximately as authentic and relevant as the indeciduous country constable of musical comedy with his badge pinned upon his stomach. It is, in short, an unintentional — and very good — burlesque. Staged by Willie Collier, acted by George Bickel and played in the farce tempo, it would unquestionably be quite entertaining.

Of " Rosalind," J. M. Barrie's one-act play, there is little I can think of to say. The piece leaves no particular impression other than a feeling that its author has in this instance Fletcherized a marshmallow. The central notion of the bonbon, to wit, that it is utterly impossible for a popular actress to leave the stage, however she may long to, because her public will not permit her, is, to say the least, somewhat bizarre. And the extravagant sentimental treatment which Barrie has visited upon this notion tends only to make it slightly more quizzical.

The speech of the middle-aged actress to her young lover, in which the actress, moist of eye, indulges in the stereotyped lament over what-is-fame-after-all-when - one - compares - it - with - what - might - have been - kiddies - tugging - at - my - apron - strings - and a - little - home - by - the - sea - and - contentment misses coaxing a disrespectful snicker only by virtue of the dramatist's polished writing of it.   And so, too, does this hold in the instance of several of the related recitals and episodes.

AUDIENCES, ACTING AND SOME
OTHER FARCES

IT is frequently recommended by the more droll
among our dramatic reviewers that audiences,
in order to enjoy this or that Broadway play,
ought, before they enter the theatre, check their
brains in the coat-room. Say what you will against
the idea, you must yet admit its thorough practica-
bility. There would still be lots of room left for the
coats.

I allude, of course, to New York audiences, and
more particularly to New York first-night audiences:
those gaudy and ribald compounds of kept women,
Mosaic men-about-town, overdressed, chattering, og-
ling actors out of jobs, ladies' underwear impresarios
and such like metropolitan provosts of the drama.
The stratagem of the Messrs. Shubert in suddenly
opening Mr. Harold Brighouse's comedy "Hobson's Choice" in the Princess Theatre at a matinée,
while the fancy girls were still snoozing, the crescent-
nosed men-about-town busy matching linings in East
Houston Street and the out-of-work grimaciers just
going to bed, not only accounts for the intelligent
audition permitted that play but also, doubtless, for
what consequent success it deservedly achieved.

In all my years of New York critical service, I have
not seen so respectable and so satisfying an audience
as the one in point.   Even some of the regular dramatic critics were absent.   Mr. Brighouse's piece is
so uniformly engaging a composition that it would
not have stood much of a chance with a New York
first-night audience.   In the first place, it is a play
of character acted by expert character actors in place
of a play of Russ Whytals in white wigs acted by
Russ Whytals in white wigs.   In the second place, it
is a play in which the heroine, called by the manuscript to wear severely plain frocks throughout the
presentation, does not waddle out in a bogus epilogue
written by Lucile to regale and bewitch the numskulls.   And in the third place, its risqué third act
climax might offend the first-night kept ladies.

This climax, with its accompanying saucy line of
dialogue (probably the most Rabelaisian spoken into
an audience's ear from the American pantaloon platform) is an integral part of a comedy of Lancashire
in the early '80's, a comedy of brusque manners and
motives told with fluency yet admirable artistic re-
straint.   Its materials in themselves commonplace
enough and suffering dramatically from somewhat
undue expansion, the play is given the dew of vitality by the humorous and unromantic twinkle of its
creator's eye, past which gay orb the ancient materials are made to goose-step.   Thus, to the old
theme of the ugly duckling who achieves a mate and
sets herself to develop him from the dull lout he is

into a man of tang and position, there is brought a
salt and sparkle that make the dish highly toothful.
This Brighouse, verily, had done a good job.   And
his play is an object lesson to all local yammerers
who, when the ancient countenance of their dramatic
compositions is criticized, yowl that there are only
so many situations after all and that everything depends upon the way the playwright looks at them.
The object lesson is this: Brighouse has taken
a dilapidated idea and has looked at it through
the eyes of Brighouse.   Nine out of ten American show-makers, taking the same moss-eared idea,
would have looked at it through the eyes of Madeleine Lucette Ryley.   Or, worse still, through their
own.

Another frayed idea handled with rare skill is
made visible in Mr. Avery Hopwood's farce " Fair
and Warmer."   Founding his composition upon a
theme familiar to the vaudevilles, the theme to wit
of the two mismated couples and of the straight-laced
husband of couple number one and the straight-laced
wife of couple number two getting together, kicking
up their heels and astounding their now made jeal-
ous respective mates, Hopwood has exercised a so
considerable ingenuity and a so robust sense of humour that his farce makes of the stomach of its every
auditor a La Belle Fatima.   The thing, in a word,
is one continuous hooch-cooch of the intestines.   The
piece belongs to the school of farce designated as
" suggestive," which is to say, it deals with subjects

that are discussed, when at all, only by young girls
— and then only in public.

But Hopwood's suggestiveness is gorgeously forth-
right and indelicate.   His not the mincing suggestiveness of the old maid playwright, nor on the other
hand the unhumorous dirt of the hack Broadway
whortleberry.   His rather the touch of a Sacha.
Guitry, a Rip and Bousquet, a Max Maurey, a Lothar Schmidt, a Romain Coolus.   He indulges in no
timid equivoque, no falsetto synonym.   His bedroom
is a bedroom, not a boudoir.   His intruder into the
bedroom takes another and more plausible form than
that of the usual stage burglar.   One of the indeed
unjust criticisms which has been visited upon Mr.
Hopwood by the precisians of the daily press concerns itself with complimenting him upon his device
of letting the audience know beforehand that everything, despite its naughty air, is perfectly innocent.
Mr. Hopwood, in the preparation of his play, assuredly had no such intention of easing any potential
auditorium shock.   And he should not be made to
suffer such silly and groundless praise.   He is altogether too much a scholar of the world not to have
known, and knowing to have appreciated, the doubled
risqué force and greater suggestiveness of a *mot*
which precedes the fact over a *mot* which follows the
fact.   The night before is ever infinitely more suggestive than the morning after.   To argue that the
naughtiness is less naughty because there is nothing
back of it, because it is founded on innocence, as in

the present instance have some of the local blue-
noses, is to argue that " Resurrection " is a more
risqué play than " Have You Anything to Declare? "
And to argue further that the naughtiness of the dialogue is made less naughty by the Hopwood device of
casting the leading figure in the person of a baby-
eyed ingénue is to argue that a young cutie reading
" Droll Stories " aloud is a less disquieting spectacle
than a hag of twenty-five engaged in the same business.

This Hopwood is a farce composer of the first
native order. He has a quick eye to the crazy-quilt
of sex humours and a keen vision to the foibles of the
cosmopolite. If he maintains his French frankness
and abjures the puritanical Anglo-Saxon pettinesses
that in time seem to assail the writers for our American stage, he is headed for high farce estate.

Another excellent farce — albeit promulgated as
serious drama — is Mr. Robert McLaughlin's " The
Eternal Magdalene," a kind of *gelée* of " The Servant in the House," " The Passing of the Third Floor
Back," " Mrs. Warren's Profession " and Primrose
and Dockstader's Minstrels. The play is so unmis-
takably draggletailed that it calls for little criticism.
To say simply that an egg is bad is sufficient. And
assuredly a satisfying enough characterization. It is
fruitless to go into the reasons for the egg's badness:
to discuss the egg's parentage, its Wassermann reac-
tion, its childhood, college career and amours. And
yet so superior in its badness is the stage work men-

tioned that, by this very excess of virtuosity, a brief eye to its anatomy may not be without tonic result.

In a story which Mr. Charles Belmont Davis wrote for one of the magazines, appeared the following remarks (addressed by a man to a woman who has been hoisting sweet sex mush in his direction): " Miss Leslie, when I was much younger I saw a good deal of women — good and bad — all kinds. . . . I have known the kind of women who owned their carriages and their sealskin coats and who hung diamond necklaces and such junk around their throats. And I have known the lowest class — poor devils who worked in dance-halls and back-room saloons and such like. But I found that both kinds — all kinds — had generally one trait in common, and it usually broke out in the sordid, early-morning hours when the talk had become personal and maudlin. The lie they told, and pretty much all of them told the same lie, was to excuse their present social position. They claimed they were what they were because . . ."

Mr. McLaughlin's play indicates that Mr. Mc-Laughlin has succumbed to the girls' early morning sob sonata, the-story-of-my-life nocturne, the Yale - and - Princeton - flags - on - the - wall intermezzo. His play is the play every sophomore, after a week-end visit to New York, plans sometime to write. In brief, a defence of the slipped sister. But Mr. McLaughlin's defence is, strictly speaking, less Mr. McLaughlin's than the slipped sister's own.

Which is to say, a sort of boozy crying onto the egg sandwich when the all-night restaurant orchestra in-vades Ethelbert Nevin. The play is cheaply conceived and cheaply written. It is full of loud speeches and baby spotlights. In the first act the author, when a smug clergyman has recourse to the Bible in announcing his stand against prostitution, hotly retorts, "Whenever a man has a particularly weak argument, he tries to bolster it up with quotations from the Scriptures." And thenceforth, for the balance of the evening, the author proceeds to do that very thing, backing up each of his feeble pronunciamentos with a Sunday-school motto and winding up his shindig with the calliope tooting "Let him who is without sin" to the full of its steam.

Imagine the Magdalene in the place of the character of Manson in "The Servant in the House"; imagine then "The Servant in the House" written by a peculiarly bad imitator of Mr. George M. Cohan; and imagine, then, the whole thing before going into rehearsal sweetened up by Marjorie Benton Cooke, and you have a clear notion of the evening's aspect. Miss Julia Arthur returned in this piece to the stage after an absence of some fourteen years. The lady, despite her long rest, still reveals herself to be of the school of acting which believes that the dramatic content of a speech may be made the more impressive by spilling into it quarts of punctuation. Mr. Emmett Corrigan, in the leading male rôle, as Guillaume L'Hiver once put it, dis-

plays all the attributes of a poker save its occasional
warmth.   The balance of the histrionic congregation
lends the two central figures appropriately bad support.

Let us pursue the pertinent subject of contemporaneous native mummer art a trifle further.   Where,
for instance, more bizarre spectacles than in the persons of the young male actors of home manufacture
currently cavorting behind the metropolitan incandescent troughs?   The young native ladies, as a general thing, are a measurably lovelier and more proficient set — though still quite as conspicuously deficient in the matter of good taste in dress as are their
young male associates.   The average young American actor dresses himself up after the recipé of the
affluent American negro.   And the young ladies, four
out of five of the sweet dears, bead and garter themselves like the cocottes of the Théâtre Marigny.

And what do they know of the histrionic art?
From a studious contemplation of the young fellows'
antics on the stage of the hour, I gather that if one
were suddenly to take away from them their cigarette cases, and the 'kerchiefs from the pockets of
their dinner jackets, they would be unable to act at
all.   A cigarette case and a 'kerchief are first aids
to the young American actor.   Such a pickle-herring
plays his part after this fashion: " I beg your par-
don — all of you!   (*Takes out 'kerchief and mops
brow.*)   That woman (*takes out cigarette case*) is.
Olympe Taverny!   (*Opens case and extracts ciga-*

rette.) Forgive me, father, for having dishon-
oured the name you bear (*closes case and knocks*
bottom of cigarette seven or eight times upon it),
for having allowed that woman to impose on me
(*throws cigarette violently into the fire-place*), for
having polluted this pure house (*opens case and*
takes out another cigarette) by her presence!"
(*Lights cigarette, puffs, takes out 'kerchief again*
and wipes off brow, face, nose, ears and neck.)

The young ladies, on the other hand, at least
many of them — though as I have observed they
compose in the aggregate a vastly more able junta
than their longer-haired colleagues — would be unable to continue with their performing were some
scamp to take them out of a rainy night and permit
them to catch the rheumatism in their right legs.
A young American actress' right leg is used less
for standing purposes than for purposes of curling
up, when seated, under the nether physiology in
order to denote a coy and irresponsible girlishness.
Many of these little dears are also of the opinion
that the best manner in which to point the emphatic
portions of a speech is to rise at such times upon
the toes.   The recital of dramatic dialogue by these
young persons accordingly takes on the appearance
of a Swoboda lesson.

Compared with the posturings and legerdemain
indulged in by the young male mimes, however, these
feminine faults seem trivial enough — and few and
far between. For every young actor lady who has,

for example, sought to register affection by fixing
the juvenile's tie, think of the young American troubadours one has envisaged whose notion of the beau,
the swell, has chiefly consisted in not pulling up the
trousers when sitting down.   For every mademoi-
selle who has, for example, registered annoyance
by stamping her foot, turning her back and smell-
ing the roses, recall the native young buffoons whose
idea of drawing-room *savoir faire* is keeping the
hands out of the pockets.   And for every young
sweetmeat whose words ending in " s " sound like
so many peanut machines and for every one who is
given to expressing emotion mainly by a sudden con-
traction and distension of her Little Mary, consider
the young American Jack Puddings whose notion of
delineating the rôle of a fine gentleman is buying
a dress shirt like Sir George Alexander's.

STUPIDITY AS A FINE ART

(*Valedictory*)

THE stupidity of the native professional stage has attained to a splendour so grand and unmistakable that one opens one's mouth in dazzled awe before the very majesty of the thing. It is stupidity not of a mean and lowly order, but stupidity brought to its highest point of perfection, stupidity so full-blown and fascinating as to betoken something akin almost to genius.

It takes brains to be so stupid as this — brains, imagination and courage. For the popular notion that any idiot can achieve such drivellings as are current in our theatres is, of course, absurd. The thing calls for experience, for training, for technique. It took a genius like Brahms to negotiate a composition so violinistically stupid that it could move a Joachim to ribald mirth. It took a genius like Hauptmann to achieve the empurpled stupidities of "The Bow of Odysseus." Little men and little minds may bore the yokelry in little ways, but it is given only to men of superlative talent to produce in the cognoscenti the true *aesthetik* of a supreme and soul-satisfying dumps. When a George V. Hobart writes a "Moonlight Mary," an audience merely shuts up and goes to sleep. But when a Shakespeare writes a " Henry VIII," the world sits up on its haunches enchanted and besparkled by its *ennuis,* and chatters and chronicles about the phenomenon years on without end and makes of its boredom a proscenium and literary *cause célèbre.*

And so, lightly to pass over the contemporaneous inanity of the local stage and become flippant in its presence is to be at once maudlin and unjust. Great stupidity is vastly more noteworthy, more epoch-making, than mere great brilliance. The indiscretions of Napoleon, not the discretions of Blücher, turned the tide at Waterloo and changed the history of the world. The thick stupidity of the dairymaids at Berkeley, more than the vivid intelligence of Edward Jenner, was responsible for the giving to the world of medicine of vaccination. It was the dark stupidity of the actors who first did Ibsen in the Anglo-Saxon countries (certainly not the luminosity of Ibsen's scripts) that helped these communities misunderstand the dramatist sufficiently to guarantee him a measure of popular life in the English-speaking theatre and so assist that theatre, thus left-handedly, to its betterment.

The stupidity of our professional theatre at the present time, with but little qualification, is of an excellence so signal and arresting that it is certain to re-awaken the latent interest in the playhouse. By virtue of its very astounding magnitude it is certain to attract again to the theatre such erstwhile rebels as, exasperated by merely mediocre plays and merely mediocre mummering, until now have remained steadfastly away. This intelligent element in the community must assuredly be tempted by the current complete idiocies that strut our stages, just as one's curiosity and interest are more deeply piqued in watching the imbecile actions of the inmates of an insane asylum than (as with merely mediocre plays) in watching the comparatively sane actions of the inmates of an Old Soldiers' Home.

Undiluted stupidity is ever a more interesting spectacle than diluted sapience, for the same reason that a girl of sixteen is more interesting than a woman of twenty-seven. One is new, refreshing, artless, naïve almost to the point of lovableness; the other is like trying to sit through a Belasco play for a second time. An ignorant negro is certainly more amusing than an educated negro. A drum corps sounds better than a café trio of mandolin, piano and flute. A novel on life in the harem written by an old maid living in Brooklyn is louder amusement than one written by some Turkish Harold Bell Wright. And just so must the supreme stupidities of the theatre entertain our better element of theatregoers where the diluted stupidities have failed. . . . Bismarck tossed aside Marcus Aurelius to read " Die Familie Buchholz."

As a specimen of the noteworthy nonesuchs that have been exhibited lately at two dollars the head upon the municipal platforms, let us first engage

" The Flame," by Mr. Richard Walton Tully, and study precisely what happens during the course of the evening.

The scene of this opus is laid somewhere in Central America. When the curtain goes up, we discern a maiden hight Maya, whose face and arms are smeared with brown paint and who, by way of being in character, talks like a Dolly Sister. Maya, it appears, is the jilted lady-love of Geronimo Zabina, a revolutionist who has been educated in an American university and who, accordingly, wears a fancy hat-band. Geronimo Zabina presently loves Pamela Cabot, a blonde beauty who has come down on a yacht with an American multi-millionaire desirous of bringing peace to the stewing land. But the Cabot imperiously rejects the proposal of Geronimo Zabina and Geronimo Zabina, with a sour snicker that promises some sardouing in the near future, makes sneeringly off. The Cabot has meantime set eye on one Wayne Putnam, a young Americano in glistening puttees, whom she has not seen in years and, following the advice of Maya, who lives in a deep well consecrated to the sun god, decides to run afoul of her society mother's wish and go off to the mountains with the young gringo as his wife. This ends the first act.

The second act brings news that the Cabot is soon to have a baby and Maya, appearing mysteriously in a pale green light, implores the young wife to have the baby even if Cabot, *mère,* urges to the

contrary. Putnam's life is now threatened by a
voodoo doctor in the employ of Geronimo Zabina,
but he is prevented from smoking the poisoned tobacco which has been set out for him by the sudden
extinguishing of the lights in his house. During
the period of darkness he departs, revolver in hand,
and a negro servant named Jefferson Clay surreptitiously partakes of the tobacco and meets with
instant death. Don Benito Garvanza, a second
revolutionist, approaches now and, upon Putnam's
reappearance, demands the money he has set aside
to pay off his workmen. Then, this catastrophe
over, Geronimo Zabina again sneaks upon the scene,
casts a spell upon Maya, who has been hiding behind
a chair, and makes off with the erstwhile Cabot.
Screaming, he drags the fair one by night to "the
green jungle of the Goat Without Any Horns"
(so is it described upon the programme) and pre-
pares there to Dumas-fils her. A great storm suddenly comes up, however, and Geromino Zabina tot-
ters off, leaving the fair one lying on the floor.

The last act reveals Putnam and his bride (who
was saved from the storm by the irrepressible Maya)
once again in Geromino's toils. Geronimo offers
the lovely one her husband's life if she will but
surrender her proud body to him. But this the
lady declines to do and the villain orders that both
be shot by his henchmen. "I will give you five
minutes' grace to say your good-byes," snaps the
cur, turning on his heel. The Cabot discovers now

that the old padre, Fernando, who these many years
has been in charge of the local tabernacle, is none
other than her own long lost father. Geronimo,
also learning this, has Fernando hauled off-stage and
whopped. Putnam and his bride are resigned to
die. When — appears the ever timely Maya up
from the bottom of the well! " I will save you,"
cries Maya. And, while the villainous Geronimo
Zabina's back is turned, she leads the young folks
down into the well to safety and presents them with
a baby which she found in the green jungle.

This stunning, if somewhat subtle, *conte* is inter-
spersed in the telling with several presumably atmos-
pheric dances on the part of ladies in opalescent
chemises and drawers, dances of the familiar species
which put one in mind of a stout woman attempting
to wriggle herself into a small-size corset; opportune sightings in the harbour of an American battleship on the several occasions when the bandits have
the hero at bay; and much pounding on tom-toms.

A second specimen: " The Man Who Came
Back," by Mr. Jules Eckert Goodman out of a fifteen-
cent periodical parable. At eight-thirty, an actor
playing a New York millionaire bids his dissolute
son not again to darken the portals of his mansion
until such a time as he has proved his worth. At
nine-thirty, the dissolute son is carrying on with a
chanteuse in a San Francisco cabaret. He suggests
that she become his mistress, but the lady shrinks
from him in righteous wrath —" So! It was *that*

you meant when you made love to me and led me
to believe you respected me and desired to make me
your wife!"— and, agents of the dissolute young
man's father heaving at this juncture upon the platform, the young man is shanghaied and put aboard
a steamer bound for China. There, in an opium
dive, an half-hour later we find him. And, too, in
a dark corner, the *chanteuse*. They come face to
face. "You!" Then thus the lady: "Yes, *I!*
I was determined to get even with you. Look at
me! I've smoked opium and soaked myself in
strong liquor and sunk to the lowest depths of degra-
dation. I've become the most notorious, most depraved white woman in all of China. But — there
is *one* thing I have kept, *one* thing that I have never
defiled!" The young man grasps the edge of the
table. "And that is —?"

"My *virtue!*" booms the angel.

The young man, recalling Samuel French's Select
List of Plays, now grabs the remarkable one pas-
sionately to him, proposes that they get married
and fight it out side by side, and — fifteen minutes
later — we glimpse the couple in their home in
Honolulu. Comes news that the young man's
father is dying, that the young man must make his
choice between going to the bedside or remaining
with his wife. The latter overhears and, recalling
"David Garrick," pretends she has resumed the
opium habit in order to disgust her beloved and
drive him from her. . . . And so on until the con-

310 Mr. George Jean Nathan Presents

ventional eleven o'clock lancers with every one bow-
ing low to every one else.

A third, and finally illustrative, specimen:
"Somebody's Luggage," by the Messrs. Mark
Swan and F. J. Randall, disclosing Mr. James T.
Powers in the fat part. Mr. Powers belongs to
the now distant theatrical day when any actor was
regarded as a comedian if he appeared on the stage
wearing one red sock and one green sock. His
methods are uniformly suggestive of the musical-
comedy era when the grand entrance of the stellar
comique was brought about by having the entire
chorus line up facing L 3 and singing "Hail, Hail,
To the Shah," and then having the stellar *comique*
come on from R 1. Mr. Powers' comedic technique consists in extracting laughter not from his
lines, but from movements of his bottom accompanying the lines. The farce in which the gentleman appears has to do with the epic of mixed-
up baggage and consequent mixing up of identities.
The humour relies almost entirely upon simulated
sea-sickness and intoxication, a whiskey flask fastened to the trouser pocket with a chain, sudden
collisions with persons walking backward, detachable
cuffs, and a top hat that falls down over Mr. Powers'
eyes.

THE END